God as Communion

God as Communion

John Zizioulas, Elizabeth Johnson,
and the Retrieval of the Symbol of the Triune God

Patricia A. Fox

A Michael Glazier Book
THE LITURGICAL PRESS
Collegeville, Minnesota

www.litpress.org

A Michael Glazier Book published by The Liturgical Press.

Cover design by David Manahan, O.S.B.

Passages from the documents of the Second Vatican Council are taken from *Vatican Council II: A Completely Revised Translation in Inclusive Language*, edited by Austin Flannery, O.P., and published by Dominican Publications, Dublin, and Costello Publishing Company, Northport, New York, 1996.

1   2   3   4   5   6   7   8   9

Library of Congress Cataloging-in-Publication Data

Fox, Patricia, 1943–
    God as communion : John Zizioulas, Elizabeth Johnson, and the retrieval of the symbol of the Triune God / Patricia Fox.
        p.   cm.
    "A Michael Glazier book."
    Includes bibliographical references and index.
    ISBN 0-8146-5082-1 (alk. paper)
    1. Trinity. 2. Zizioulas, Jean, 1931—Contributions in doctrine of the Trinity. 3. Johnson, Elizabeth A., 1941—Contributions in doctrine of the Trinity. I. Title.

BT111.3 .F69   2001
231'.044—dc21

00-049561

Contents

Preface

This book is based on the premise that symbols of God exercise enormous power within the lives of human beings and that they are significant for the well-being of all creation. It is a contribution toward the retrieval of the symbol of God that is at the center of the Christian tradition: God as Trinity, God as communion.

My awareness of the practical significance of the doctrine of God arose out of specific experiences of pastoral leadership within the Roman Catholic archdiocese of Adelaide in South Australia.[1] At that time I came to understand experientially that whether consciously or not, the symbol of God functions in people's lives to shape their understandings of Church and world. During that same period I became increasingly aware of the damaging effects of sexism in every dimension of life. The impetus to focus on the symbol of God as Trinity arises, therefore, from two different but related motivations. One has to do with the recognition that symbols used for God function to obscure as well as reveal the divine presence. In either case, the symbol of God exercises very significant power in shaping social and political realities as well as personal lives. The other motivation springs from the conviction that if Christianity is to be redemptive—be a source of liberation—for the peoples of this planet in this new millennium, the destructive power of sexism inherent in Christian theology and praxis must be addressed and transformed at its very roots.

---

[1] In 1986 Archbishop Leonard Faulkner established a Diocesan Pastoral Team to work with him in the leadership of the Roman Catholic Archdiocese of Adelaide. This team was to consist of a vicar general, a lay person, and a member of a religious order. There was a commitment to work in a collaborative and inclusive way that would model the vision of the archdiocese articulated as a Community for the World. I served a five-year term as a member of the first team. This form of prophetic pastoral leadership continues within this local Church in 2000.

My purpose in this book is to contribute to the ongoing work of retrieval of this ancient symbol, whose power has remained largely dor-
mant for so many centuries, especially within the Western Christian
tradition. The urgency of contemporary questions of meaning that
have surfaced at this time encourages such a work of retrieval. They
prompt a return to the origins of the symbol's formulation, to the period before the divide between Christian East and West, to the Hellenistic world of the first centuries of Christianity. The twentieth century
witnessed a return of theological scholarship to its sources, and much
of the vibrancy of recent Trinitarian theology springs from this move.
The Trinitarian theologies of Greek Orthodox John Zizioulas and
Roman Catholic feminist theologian Elizabeth Johnson provide significant examples of this movement in theology. Both these theologians
draw from early sources of the doctrine, and, from very different perspectives, they both seek to engage these sources with the critical questions of our times.

Zizioulas focuses on the first centuries of Christian development in
order to address the roots of the concept of "person" both in the original
formulation of the doctrine of the Trinity and as it now surfaces within
contemporary existential and theological questions. He draws specifically from the patristic period to ground contemporary critical discussions of Church and world within a framework of Trinitarian theology.
Elizabeth Johnson returns to biblical and doctrinal sources through the
perspectives afforded by her training in classical Catholic theology that
has been profoundly shaped by medieval scholar Thomas Aquinas. Her
work is specifically focused through the lens of women's experience
and the methods of feminist theology. Thus Johnson simultaneously
brings into play a second element necessary for this work of retrieval of
the triune God: she addresses the inherent sexism of Christian sources.

These two theologians, with their return to the sources of Christianity and their engagement with contemporary issues, make powerful individual contributions toward a retrieval of the doctrine of the
triune God. However, I believe that when their respective contributions
are brought into dialogue with each other, they become even more significant. Such an interchange yields further benefit toward the enormous challenge facing theology today—that of reclaiming the triune
symbol at the center of Christian life and mission in the world. I also
want to suggest that contemporary scientific and philosophical understandings of the interrelatedness of all created entities create a contemporary climate within which the Mystery of God as Trinity can be
received in ways that have literally not been possible before in the history of Christianity.

In these pages I examine the Trinitarian theology of John Zizioulas and Elizabeth Johnson's feminist exploration of the Mystery of the triune God and then pursue a mutually critical correlation of key elements within the Trinitarian theologies of both. I conclude by offering my own contribution toward a constructive Trinitarian theology within the context of a contemporary awareness of the interconnectedness of all creation.

Several people were instrumental in enabling me to pursue this study, but it would not have been possible to begin without the encouragement of Christine Keain, then leader of the Congregation of the Sisters of Mercy, Adelaide. Throughout the work this community of sisters has provided me with loving support in literally countless ways. I am particularly grateful for Rosemary Day's constant kindness.

Locating the body of John Zizioulas's work has required a lot of ingenuity. I am very grateful to those who have assisted in this task: Paul McPartlan provided me with a number of articles and unpublished manuscripts. Janette Gray tracked down articles at Cambridge. Patricia Pak Poy found others at the WCC library in Geneva. Sheila O'Dea searched libraries in Toronto. Aristotle Papaniliolaou sent others from the University of Chicago. Deirdre Jordan helped me to track down Dr. Zizioulas himself. Her connection with the Ecumenical Patriarch Bartholomew led to an invitation for me to participate in a summer seminar in Turkey in 1997 at which the Metropolitan was a keynote speaker. Archbishop Leonard Faulkner assisted with funds for the journey, and Deacon Tarasios was a kind host. This opportunity to meet the Metropolitan and to imbibe Orthodox culture firsthand provided me with invaluable learning.

I was also very fortunate to be able to participate in a summer school in 1995 at the University of Notre Dame Indiana, where Dr. Elizabeth Johnson taught a course in feminist theology. Opportunities to speak with her personally then, and later during her visit to Australia in 1997 and since, have been very helpful. I have been greatly encouraged by her personal interest and support in my research.

Kate Conley and Christine Burke read each chapter as it was written and interacted with the material. This has provided an important grounding for this work, and I am very grateful for their friendship and challenge. Several people very kindly read some form of the finished manuscript and assisted with corrections and comments: James McEvoy, Deirdre Jordan, Bob Wilkinson, Joan Gaskell, Margaret Press, and Mary Britt. Special thanks are due to Denis Edwards and Catherine Hilkert, O.P. From these good friends I have learned valuable lessons in doing theology.

Finally, I want to acknowledge my family. It was among them that I first glimpsed what "difference in communion" can mean. And it is here that the journey of this research on the triune God has led me again. It is to Jack, Suse, John, Noreen, and Brian that I dedicate this work.

Pentecost Sunday 2000

CHAPTER 1

A Symbol Whose Time Has Come

To be in the image of God is to be in community. It is not simply a man or a woman who can reflect God, but it is a community in relationship.[1]

Ultimately, bringing women's experience into the conversation that is theology is about walking in the dark, the unexplored worlds in which we have lived, but not fully because they have not borne their proper names. . . . As it is a prophet's journey so also is it a mystic's way because we must risk the many new faces of our God when we tell the truth of ourselves as best we can.[2]

The very act of crossing over a boundary opens up new possibilities. Within the Western world there is a sense abroad that the period of the new millennium invites a new consciousness. It provides a moment for stepping beyond the brink. Primordial questions about the meaning of life, the existence of God, and the future of the planet and of the universe have surfaced and are being focused in new ways.

In order to harness the opportunity offered by this momentum, the Christian Churches prepared in a variety of ways for what has been called "The Great Jubilee of the Year 2000." In the three years prior to

[1] Elizabeth Dominguez, "A Continuing Challenge for Women's Ministry," in *In God's Image* (August 1983) 7. Quoted in Ursula King, ed., *Feminist Theology from the Third World: A Reader* (London: SPCK, 1994) 253.

[2] Ann O'Hara Graff, ed., *In the Embrace of God: Feminist Approaches to Theological Anthropology* (Maryknoll, New York: Orbis Books, 1995) 84–85.

this commemoration of the birth of Christ, the Vatican encouraged members of the Roman Catholic Church to prepare for the year of jubilee by focusing on the symbol of God that is at the heart of the Christian tradition—God as Trinity. This book takes up that challenge. In these pages I propose that the Trinity is a symbol whose time has come. Movements that have been shaping life and theological reflection in the last decades of the twentieth century have enabled this ancient Christian symbol to become accessible in ways that have not existed before. In this work I seek to show that, in these times, Christians are invited into a more complete reception of the revelation of God as Trinity.

The Christian creeds, formulated by the end of the fourth century, confessed that the God revealed by Jesus the Christ is one God, of three co-equal, co-eternal persons. Contemporary scholarship suggests that very soon after the doctrine was formulated, theological discourse began to separate the triune God of salvation history from the trinity of persons within God.[3] By the medieval period in both Latin and Byzantine theology, the doctrine of the Trinity was understood to refer to the inner life of God, God in Godself, with little reference to God's deeds in history. This has meant that for a millennium and a half, the doctrine of the Trinity has largely been restricted to consideration of the immanent Trinity. By this century Karl Rahner could make his oft-quoted remark that one could dispense with the doctrine of the Trinity and the major part of religious literature would remain virtually unchanged.[4]

Thus, despite the fact that Christianity has preserved a living tradition of belief in the triune God through its liturgy and spirituality, a powerful monotheistic image of God as an omnipotent, omniscient male monarch has shaped both popular devotion and the discourse of Christian Churches into the modern era. It is only within the last decades that a significant alternative direction has emerged within theology. There has been a movement toward a retrieval of the Holy Mystery of the triune God, who was foreshadowed in the Scriptures, claimed in Christian doctrine, and constantly confessed in public worship through the ages.

The two very different contributions to Trinitarian theology that I examine in this book have been shaped by the different existential realities of the lives of these two theologians. One comes from the essen-

---

[3] See Catherine Mowry LaCugna, *God for Us: The Trinity and Christian Life* (New York: HarperSanFrancisco, 1991), for one description of this process and its consequences. For a critical appraisal of LaCugna's thesis, see Duncan Reid, "The Defeat of the Trinitarian Theology: An Alternative View," *Pacifica* 9 (1996) 289–300.

[4] Karl Rahner, *The Trinity*, trans. Joseph Donceel (New York: Herder and Herder, 1970) 11.

tially male world of Greek Orthodox ecclesial culture and Western academia, from the creative, synthetic mind of a theologian-ecumenist become cleric, at work at the center of the Christian tradition. John Zizioulas is a leading contemporary theologian and spokesman for the Eastern Orthodox Church. Formerly professor of systematic theology at the University of Glasgow, he is Metropolitan of the ancient see of Pergamon and member of the Ecumenical Patriarchate of Constantinople. The second contribution comes from a member of a religious congregation of women who has been deeply formed by the classical Roman Catholic tradition and "converted . . . to the feminist paradigm in theology and in life."[5] As such, with many of her sister theologians she has experienced herself as a "resident alien"[6] within a male world of Church and academy. Elizabeth Johnson, C.S.J., is presently Distinguished Professor of Theology at Fordham University, New York City. A lucid and creative theologian of "the first world," Johnson has deliberately set out to include in her theology voices from the oppressed of the oppressed—women living in the "third world."[7]

In this chapter I will begin the journey into the respective works of these two theologians by giving an overview of how their Trinitarian theologies fit within the context of their work. Then, with a view to establishing further the structure for this work of retrieval, I will identify three main topics or strands within their theologies of the triune God. These will provide the basis for the chapters in Part One on Zizioulas and Part Two on Johnson that follow.

The Theological Vision of John Zizioulas: "Being as Communion"

John Zizioulas's theological education began in the universities of Thessalonika and Athens (1950–1954).[8] In the next academic year

[5] Elizabeth Johnson, "Review Symposium: Author's Response," *Horizons* 20 (1993) 339.

[6] See Elisabeth Schüssler Fiorenza, *But She Said: Feminist Practices of Biblical Interpretation* (Boston: Beacon Press, 1992) 170.

[7] I have used quotation marks with the terms "first world" and "third world" to acknowledge that this is a construct of Western speech and as such is value-laden language of "the first world."

[8] See Gaëtan Baillargeon, *Perspectives orthodoxes sur l'Eglise-communion: L'oeuvre de Jean Zizioulas* (Montréal: Editions Paulines, 1989) 27. In the section that follows I rely significantly on Baillargeon's work for biographical details on Zizioulas. Baillargeon notes that his information was principally obtained from discussions with Zizioulas himself as other sources of written biographical information are rare. I also draw from Paul McPartlan, *The Eucharist Makes the Church: Henri de Lubac and*

(1954–1955), Zizioulas spent a semester of formation for graduate students at the ecumenical Institute of Bossey near Geneva. This was his first contact with the West and his first serious engagement with an issue that has shaped his life—the question of ecumenism. Thanks to a scholarship awarded by Conseil Oecumenique des Eglises (C.O.E.), Zizioulas left for the United States in 1955 to undertake a Masters course at Harvard that would lead to doctoral studies. Among his teachers were Georges Florovsky in patristics and Paul Tillich in philosophy. After fulfilling his obligatory two years of military service, he returned to Harvard on a scholarship for a further three years. Gaëtan Baillargeon records that "during these years he pursued two areas of research simultaneously: one in view of a thesis at Harvard on the christology of Maximus the Confessor, under the direction of Georges Florovsky, and the other for the University of Athens on the unity of the Church in the bishop and the Eucharist during the first three centuries, under the direction of A. G. Williams, professor of Church history at Harvard."[9]

It is significant to note that Zizioulas's time in the United States enabled him to engage with leading Russian Orthodox theologians of the diaspora. Georges Florovsky, who had exercised a decisive influence in securing Orthodox participation in the World Council of Churches in 1950, was passionate in his commitment to both patristic theology and ecumenism.[10] Florovsky became a mentor as well as a research supervisor for Zizioulas. Both were committed to working toward a neopatristic synthesis that could provide the basis for union between West and East, and both understood that a return to patristic sources is a return to a theology rooted in the worship of the ecclesial community.[11] During this same time Zizioulas was invited to teach courses at St. Vladimir's, the Russian Orthodox seminary in New York, and there he met Jean Meyendorff and Alexander Schmemann, both formerly from Saint-Serge in Paris and disciples of Nicolas Afanasiev.[12]

In 1964 John Zizioulas returned to the University of Athens and in 1965 became assistant professor of Church history. In 1966 he successfully defended his doctoral thesis in Athens.[13] By this time Zizioulas

---

John Zizioulas Dialogue (Edinburgh: T&T Clark, 1993), and from other details that sometimes accompany Zizioulas's published works.

[9] Baillargeon, *Perspectives orthodoxes*, 29.

[10] See McPartlan, *The Eucharist Makes the Church*, 130.

[11] See ibid., 127, 130. See also Zizioulas, *Being as Communion*, 26.

[12] See Baillargeon, *Perspectives orthodoxes*, 30.

[13] Zizioulas's thesis was first published in Greek in Athens in 1965. In 1993 the first French edition was published and then republished a year later. See Métropolite

had already been a member of work groups on "Eucharist" and on the "Development of Conciliar Structures" for the Faith and Order Commission of the World Council of Churches.[14] Such was the quality and originality of his work that he was soon after co-opted onto the permanent membership of the Commission in Geneva. As Baillargeaon observes, the two and a half years that he spent in Geneva provided strong grounding for the young ecumenist: "His contacts with the Protestants, the Catholics, and even the pre-Chalcedonian Churches, without neglecting the connections with the different Orthodox Churches, would open him to an understanding of the different traditions."[15] At the same time he became a spokesperson for his own tradition, and this served to ground him further in its theological roots. Zizioulas left Geneva in the autumn of 1970 to take up a teaching post in patristic theology at the University of Edinburgh. From there he moved to Glasgow in 1973 to become professor of systematic theology. During these years Zizioulas's theological interests and ecumenical involvements led to the publication of numerous journal articles and studies in various periodicals. Some of the articles appear in the French volume *L'Etre Ecclésial,*[16] and in 1985 these same articles, with important additions, were included in *Being as Communion: Studies in Personhood and the Church.*[17] This has become his best known work in English. In 1975 Zizioulas became a delegate of the Ecumenical Patriarchate on the central committee of the WCC and the Faith and Order Commission.[18] He remained in Glasgow until he was "called from the laity" to ordination at Pentecost in 1986 as Metropolitan of Pergamon and to become a member of the Ecumenical Patriarchate based in Istanbul, Turkey.

Zizioulas has taught theology at the University of Thessaloniki and held visiting professorships at the Universities of Geneva, London, and the Gregorian. He was a founding member in 1979 of the International Joint Commission for Theological Dialogue with the Roman Catholic Church and is also co-chairman of the international Anglican-Orthodox

---

Jean de Pergame, *L'Eucharistie, l'évêque et l'église durant les trois premiers siècles,* trans. Jean-Louis Parlierne. (Paris: Theophanie, Desclee de Brouwer, 1994).

[14] Hereafter referred to as WCC.

[15] Baillargeon, *Perspectives orthodoxes,* 43.

[16] Jean Zizioulas, *L'Etre Ecclésial* (Paris: Labor et Fides, 1981).

[17] John D. Zizioulas, *Being as Communion: Studies in Personhood and the Church* (New York: St. Vladimir's Seminary Press, 1993).

[18] For a very detailed account of Zizioulas's ecumenical activity until he was ordained as Metropolitan of Pergamon on 22 June 1986, see Baillargeon, *Perspectives orthodoxes,* 34–58.

dialogue. Such involvements have meant that Zizioulas has had an on-going engagement with persons of many cultures and that he has been constantly drawn into an awareness of global perspectives. The challenge and asceticism of ecumenical dialogue, always seeking what he calls "the sacred cause of the restoration of church unity,"[19] have in many ways provided the forge for the firing and hammering out of Zizioulas's theological system.

In the last decade of the century, Zizioulas, in his capacity as Metropolitan of Pergamon, embraced another challenge. His concern for the ecological crisis that is confronting the peoples of the earth has led him to engage the Christian theological tradition with this critical contemporary issue. In January 1989 he gave a series of lectures entitled "Preserving God's Creation" at King's College, London,[20] and from 1994 he acted as director of an annual summer seminar on ecology on the island of Halki (Heybeliada) in the Sea of Marmara near Istanbul. This has been jointly sponsored by the Ecumenical Patriarchate and the World Wide Fund for Nature. His stance on this issue is congruent with his attitude toward ecumenism and the work of the World Council of Churches. He has always insisted that the Orthodox must not restrict their concerns to the doctrinal matters within the Faith and Order Commission but must become involved in the social and political concerns of the council. He has argued that the Orthodox members should commit themselves to "bringing to light the existential implications of their faith and traditional structure."[21]

Roman Catholic scholar Yves Congar has described Zizioulas as "one of the most original and profound theologians of our age."[22] On the occasion of Zizioulas's theology being honored at L'Institut Catholique in Paris in 1987, Hervé Legrand drew attention to the synthetic and organic nature of his work. Legrand quoted one of Zizioulas's methodological reflections from a paper on ordained ministry entitled "Ordination—A Sacrament?" which clearly illustrates this point. In this paper Zizioulas writes:

---

[19] Metropolitan John (Zizioulas) of Pergamon, "The Church as Communion," *St Vladimir's Theological Quarterly* 38 (1994) 3. This is the text of the keynote address given at the World Conference of Faith and Order, August 1993.

[20] See John D. Zizioulas, "Preserving God's Creation: Three Lectures on Theology and Ecology," *King's Theological Review* 12 (1989) 1–5; 41–45; 13 (1990) 1–5.

[21] John D. Zizioulas, "Ortodossia," in *Enciclopedia del Novecento* (Rome: Istituto della Enciclopedia Italiana, 1980) 5:13. Quoted in McPartlan, *The Eucharist Makes the Church*, 130.

[22] Yves Congar, "Bulletin d' ecclésiologie," *Revue des sciences philosophiques et théologiques* 66 (1982) 88.

The main components of the theological perspective . . . could be summarised as follows:

(a) It is impossible to treat the sacraments and ordination as autonomous subjects. Both of them form *aspects* of the one indivisible mystery which is indicated by *Christology.*

(b) Christology itself cannot be treated as an autonomous subject: it is conditioned constantly by *Pneumatology,* and as such it is to be organically related to *Ecclesiology.* This brings *Trinitarian Theology* itself into Ecclesiology.

(c) Ecclesiology in its being related to christology in and through Pneumatology is to be conceived in terms of (i) Eschatology, as an inevitable component of Pneumatology (cf. Acts 2) and (ii) the concrete *community* of the local church as a natural creation of the *communion* of the Holy Spirit.

(d) There is a broader *cosmic* dimension to be recognised in this approach: what happens in the sacraments and in ordination concerns the entire creation and not only humanity.[23]

In this excerpt Trinitarian theology is literally the center point into which all the other major strands of his theological work are woven. Normally the links are not as explicit as this. However, this reference does provide a telling example of the synthetic nature of Zizioulas's work. God, world, and Church are inextricably interconnected, with the triune God shown to be the lodestar that holds the other two in relation. It also signals what is at the heart of Zizioulas's Trinitarian vision: an ontology that understands being as communion.

In 1991 Zizioulas had a paper published under the title "Trinitarian Doctrine Today." It was his contribution to a study commission established by the British Council of Churches to address the issue of the irrelevance of the triune God in the lives of many believers.[24] This article reveals the centrality of Trinitarian doctrine to his whole theological endeavor and describes the essential elements of his overall theological vision. It also identifies what he believes to be the agenda for Trinitarian theology today: God's being, the Church, and the world.[25]

---

[23] Zizioulas, "Ordination—A Sacrament?" *Concilium* 4 (1972) 34. See also Hervé Legrand, "Eloge de Mgr Jean Zizioulas," *Centenaire de la Faculté de Théologie* (Paris: L'Institut Catholique de Paris, 1987) 107.

[24] J. D. Zizioulas, "The Doctrine of God the Trinity Today: Suggestions for an Ecumenical Study," *The Forgotten Trinity* 3: *A Selection of Papers Presented to the BCC Study Commission on Trinitarian Doctrine Today,* ed., Alasdair I. C. Heron (London: British Council of Churches, 1991) 19–32. The British Council of Churches will hereafter be referred to as BCC.

[25] In the same year that the BCC Study Commission Report was published, Zizioulas also published an article entitled "The Being of God and the Being of

The BCC Study Commission on "Trinitarian Doctrine Today" held ten meetings between 1983 and 1988. Its eighteen members, including Zizioulas, were theologians from across the mainline Christian churches,[26] and it becomes evident from the final report of this commission as well as from the study guide[27] and selected published papers that Zizioulas's contribution was significant.[28] The commission adopted the key questions identified by Zizioulas and incorporated much of his integral theological vision into the final report.[29] The significance of these facts for this study is that they point to the credibility of his vision across denominational lines. It demonstrates that Zizioulas's retrieval of the centrality of the doctrine of the triune God from patristics, especially from the work of the Cappadocians, and his placing of this doctrine at the center of his theological vision rang true to this group of fellow Christian theologians in Britain. It was a considered reception, so to speak, because the participants of this study gathered from their respective communities for a period of six years to consider this critical theological issue, which was deemed to have significant pastoral implications for the Church as a whole. They had the time and opportunity to test the credibility of the emerging principles and conclusions with their respective congregations and communities again and again.

Humanity" in the Greek periodical *Synaxis* 37 (1991) 11–36. In this he addresses his Orthodox critics, who in the same journal some years earlier queried the possibility of discussing the meaning of the human person in relation to the dogma of the Trinity. Zizioulas was specifically responding to John Panagopoulos, "Ontology or Theology of Person?" *Synaxis* 13/14 (1985) 63–79; 35–47, and Savas Agourides, "Can the Persons of the Holy Trinity Provide the Basis for a Personalist view of Humanity?" *Synaxis* 33 (1990) 67–78. His response spells out with clarity his argument for the necessity of a theological "ontology" in Orthodox thought that is firmly rooted in God's Trinitarian being. It also provides a strong rationale, based on patristic practice, for the necessity of theologians to bring the contemporary questions of each age into dialogue with the dogmas at the center of the Christian faith. Thus in the late eighties, in the period after the publication of his work *Being as Communion*, Zizioulas was drawn to articulate for members of both Eastern and Western traditions expositions of his Trinitarian theology and the reasons why Trinitarian theology holds such significance for the contemporary world.

[26] Church of England, United Reform Church, Baptist, Methodist, Church of Scotland, Society of Friends, Roman Catholic, Orthodox. See Heron, *The Forgotten Trinity*, 196, for a list of membership.

[27] See Alasdair I. C. Heron, ed., *The Forgotten Trinity 2: Study Guide* (London: British Council of Churches, 1991).

[28] In some of the selected papers the references to his work are explicit. See, for example, Heron, *The Forgotten Trinity*, the papers of Gunton, 123, 127–32; Walker, 137; Carras, 159.

[29] See Heron, *The Forgotten Trinity*, iii.

A catch phrase that echoes throughout Zizioulas's work both explicitly and implicitly is that "Trinitarian theology has profound existential consequences."[30] His whole theological enterprise is based on the premise that faith in the Trinity is not about accepting a theoretical proposition about God but about a dynamic relationship that exists between all creation (particularly the human person) and the living God. A person is initiated into an explicit relationship with this triune God who is communion through the Christian ritual of baptism into an ecclesial community. Zizioulas holds that it is through the existential experience of being initiated into the life of an inclusive ecclesial community that the profound existential consequences of this doctrine can begin to be glimpsed.[31]

He agrees, however, with many theologians this century that the doctrine of the Trinity has become irrelevant to the lives of most Christians.[32] Moreover, he observes that many theologians themselves fail to articulate the practical significance of the distinction of persons in the Trinity and thus compound the problem for believers. He points out that in much theological work, the distinctiveness of the three persons is overshadowed by the unity of the Godhead. Likewise, he notes that many writings in spirituality do not encourage the Christian to relate to the three distinct persons.[33] In fact, Zizioulas observes that "the Trinity is irrelevant" in such writings. According to many spiritual books on Christian spirituality, one can be a "spiritual" Christian without even having thought about it.[34]

Reflection on this current situation of belief and practice within an ecumenical context prompts Zizioulas to spell out a constructive agenda for the study of Trinitarian theology in the contemporary world. To do this, he focuses on three topics that for him "emerge as critical for theological reflection." He lists these as: (1) "the question of God's being in relation to the world"; (2) "the problem of God's being in himself";[35] and (3) "the place of Trinitarian theology in Ecclesiology."[36] Zizioulas

---

[30] Zizioulas, "The Doctrine of God the Trinity Today," 19.

[31] See Zizioulas, *Being as Communion*, 16–17, where he describes the pastoral origins of the formulation of the doctrine.

[32] See, for example, Zizioulas, "The Doctrine of God the Trinity Today," 19–21, where he refers specifically to the work of Barth, Rahner, and Lossky.

[33] For an example of an exception to this, see Christopher Kiesling, "On Relating to the Persons of the Trinity," *Theological Studies* 47 (1986) 599–616.

[34] Zizioulas, "The Doctrine of God the Trinity Today," 21.

[35] Zizioulas consistently uses masculine pronouns when referring to God and "man" to refer to humanity. I desist from drawing attention to this fact, since the implications of this usage will be fully addressed in Parts One and Two of this book.

[36] Zizioulas, "The Doctrine of God the Trinity Today," 22–23.

argues in his paper to the BCC that these three areas "constitute the most important ground of the problematic which is emerging as the crucial one for our time." He suggests, moreover, that Trinitarian theology has much to contribute to humanity's quest for "personhood, freedom, community and the world's survival" and that it is the task of Christian theology to "uncover and show all this."[37]

The motivation for this book has been prompted by very similar concerns and convictions as those spelled out by Zizioulas. In Part One the three interconnected areas of Trinitarian theology that Zizioulas identified as needing research provide the basic agenda for the exploration of his understanding of the symbol of the Trinity. Chapter 2 will address the issue of God in Godself essentially by focusing on *the concept of person within Trinitarian theology.* Chapter 3 will explore the question of God's *being in relation to the world,* and Chapter 4 will examine *the shaping of ecclesiology by Trinitarian theology* and, in turn, what the lived communion of believers reveals about the Mystery of God as Holy Trinity.

Elizabeth Johnson's Feminist Vision of the Trinity: "She Who Is"

Elizabeth A. Johnson, C.S.J., is a Sister of St. Joseph from Brentwood, New York. She received her B.S. from Brentwood College, New York, an M.A. from Manhattan College, New York, and a Ph.D. in theology from the Catholic University of America in 1981. She was one of the first women to earn a doctorate in theology from that university. She was invited to join the faculty as an assistant professor of theology. After ten years of teaching and after attaining tenure, she returned to New York to the theology department at Fordham University. She now holds the position of Distinguished Professor of Theology at the same university.

Elizabeth Johnson's work toward a retrieval of the doctrine of God began in one sense with her doctoral thesis, entitled: "Analogy/Doxology and Their Connection with Christology in the Thought of Wolfhart Pannenberg."[38] Her work on Pannenberg's christology and on his use of analogical speech provided the specific ground for her interest in

---

[37] Ibid., 29.

[38] See articles published from this thesis: Elizabeth Johnson, "The Right Way to Speak About God? Pannenberg on Analogy," *Theological Studies* 43 (1982) 673–92; "The Ongoing Christology of Wolfhart Pannenberg," *Horizons* 9/2 (1982) 237–50; "Resurrection and Reality in the Thought of Wolfhart Pannenberg," *Heythrop Journal* 24 (1983) 1–18.

and inquiry into a concern for "speaking rightly about God." Her first book, published in 1990 and entitled *Consider Jesus: Waves of Renewal in Christology*,[39] provided a further foundation for her 1992 publication on Trinitarian theology, *SHE WHO IS: The Mystery of God in Feminist Theological Discourse*, a book that has won many awards.[40] Johnson's *Friends of God and Prophets*, published in 1998, is a feminist theological reading of the communion of saints.[41]

Johnson's theological vision has been shaped both by her formation as a theologian in the Roman Catholic tradition and by her commitment as a teacher and academic to the feminist cause of promoting the full humanity of women. Her entry into religious life in the community of the Sisters of St. Joseph in New York coincided with the liberating winds of change that swept through Roman Catholicism with the Second Vatican Council. Excitement and hope were tangibly present in that period of seismic transformations. Doors and windows of every kind were flung open. Theological research was revitalized. A long overdue engagement of the Catholic Church with the contemporary world occurred. The Church formally acknowledged that the "joys and hopes, the grief and anguish of the people of our time, especially of those who are poor or afflicted, are the joys and hopes, the grief and anguish of the followers of Christ as well" (*Gaudium et Spes* 1). Roman Catholic historian Eamon Duffy has appealed to a verse from the poet Wordsworth to try to communicate the feel of that historic period of change for many within the Church: "Bliss it was in that dawn to be alive, but to be young was very heaven."[42] Elizabeth Johnson was young at this time.

This dawn of a new era within Roman Catholicism coincided with massive societal shifts within Western democracies, particularly in areas of human rights and civil liberties. The war in Vietnam, for example, led to a radical questioning of authorities who continued to seek a solution to international conflicts through military supremacy.

---

[39] Elizabeth Johnson, *Consider Jesus: Waves of Renewal in Christology* (New York: Crossroad, 1990).

[40] These include the Grawemeyer Award for Best Book in Religious Studies, 1992; Featured Selection of Catholic Book Club, September 1992; Featured Selection of Clergy Book Service, September 1992; Crossroad Women's Studies Award, 1992; Catholic Press Association Book Award, Academic Books, 1993; *Choice:* Outstanding Academic Books in Religion, 1994.

[41] Elizabeth A. Johnson, *Friends of God and Prophets: A Feminist Theological Reading of the Communion of Saints* (New York: Continuum, 1998).

[42] Wordsworth was remembering the revolutionary 1790s when he wrote these words. See Eamon Duffy's book review of *History of Vatican II*, vol. 1, in *The Tablet* (1996) 1704.

As a young religious woman, Elizabeth Johnson, like many of her generation, was caught up in these questions and movements and was profoundly encouraged by the hope engendered by documents such as *Gaudium et Spes*.[43] Johnson was also drawn into the mandate given to all religious congregations of men and women to return to the dynamic of their founding charisms. She was thus initiated into an awareness of the transformation of institutions that can occur when charisms and traditions are brought into dialogue with contemporary manifestations of the Spirit, who is always at work to renew and transform. She witnessed the creative energy that is released when living traditions, freed from debilitating accretions, are engaged with current realities.

As a doctoral student at the Catholic University of America in the late seventies, Johnson was further challenged by the issues that were surfacing through an emerging feminist theology and through discussions with other women also being trained in theology.[44] Later, as a writer and teacher in theology herself, Johnson was able to draw from the authoritative teaching of the council to point to the need for the eradication of the blight of sexism, which she had come to recognize as demeaning for men as well as women in Church and society. In *Consider Jesus: Waves of Renewal in Christology*, Johnson refers directly to The Pastoral Constitution on the Church in the Modern World of Vatican II:

> Any kind of social or cultural discrimination in basic personal rights on the grounds of sex, race, color, social conditions, language or religion, must be curbed and eradicated as incompatible with God's design. It is deeply to be deplored that these basic personal rights are not yet being respected everywhere, as is the case with women who are denied the chance freely to choose a husband, or a state of life, or to have access to the same educational and cultural benefits as are available to men.[45]

Thus it was early in her work as a theologian that Johnson began to address this major contemporary issue of justice for women. In this instance she commented that "what is called for is transformation of the self and of social systems that support exploitative relations, the relations between men and women key among them."[46] However, it was

[43] I draw here from a personal conversation with Dr. Johnson.

[44] Women studying theology at Catholic University of America at that time formed a group called W.I.T.—Women In Theology. This group continued to meet for several years, and for Johnson and other women theologians participating, it became an important place to test and clarify their understandings of emerging feminist theologies.

[45] *Gaudium et Spes*, no. 29. See Johnson, *Consider Jesus*, 102–3.

[46] Johnson, *Consider Jesus*, 103.

soon to become clear to her that it was particularly justice for women suffering from the multiple oppressions of classism, racism, sexism, and poverty that needed to become the touchstone of her work as a Christian feminist theologian.

In *SHE WHO IS*, Johnson testifies that her stance as "a white middle-class, educated and hence privileged citizen of a wealthy North American country" became modified by travels in the Middle East and Asia and as the result of teaching in Africa and Central America. She specifies that it was particularly the months of teaching in South Africa that honed for her "the feminist theological paradigm into liberation contours." In this time she grappled with "the meaning and praxis of faith in situations of massive suffering due to injustice, poverty and violence."[47] That encounter also set her theology within a global context. It was out of the forge of such experiences that Johnson came to situate her own stance among the diverse strands of feminist theology "within the liberation stream of Catholic Christian feminist theology." She claimed that for her:

> the goal of feminist religious discourse pivots in its fullness around the flourishing of poor women of color in violent situations. . . . Only when the poorest, black, raped, and brutalized women in a South African township—the epitome of victims of sexism, racism and classism, and at the same time startling examples of women's resiliency, courage, love and dignity—when such women with their dependent children and their sisters around the world may live peacefully in the enjoyment of their human dignity, only then will feminist theology arrive at its goal.[48]

The liberation of poor women thus became her touchstone as a Christian feminist theologian. In claiming this position, Johnson notes that her appeal to women's experience has been a source rarely considered in the history of theology. Acknowledging, with many other feminist theologians, the difficulties in specifying precisely what comprises women's experience,[49] she set out in her work to pursue the three interrelated

[47] Elizabeth Johnson, *SHE WHO IS: The Mystery of God in Feminist Theological Discourse* (New York: Crossroad, 1992) 11.

[48] Ibid.

[49] For a discussion of this issue, see the chapter by Pamela Dickey Young, "Women's Experience as Source and Norm of Theology," in *Feminist Theology/Christian Theology: In Search of a Method* (Minneapolis: Fortress Press, 1990) 49–69. For a mainstream critique of generalizing experience, see Sheila Greeve Davaney, "The Limits of Appeal to Women's Experience," in *Shaping New Vision: Gender and Values in American Culture*, ed. Clarissa Atkinson, Constance Buchanan, and Margaret Miles

tasks that have become the basic methodology of feminist theology: (1) critical analysis of inherited oppression; (2) the search for alternative wisdom and suppressed history; (3) the work of constructive new interpretations of the tradition in tandem with the experience of women's lives.[50]

This method, beginning with critical reflection on existential realities and directed toward transforming action, led Johnson on a theological trajectory that ensured that she would later need to confront another major form of contemporary global injustice with all its horrifying power for destruction of life—the ecological crisis. Her concern for justice for women and the poor of the world inexorably led her to see that "the preferential option for the poor must now include vulnerable, voiceless, non-human species and the natural world itself, all of which are kin to humankind."[51] Johnson came to see that sexism has an ecological face.[52] In 1993 she explicitly addressed this issue in her Madeleva Lecture in Spirituality, sponsored by St. Mary's College, Notre Dame. It was entitled "Women, Earth and Creator Spirit" and was published in book form in the same year.[53] In this lecture she explored the interconnecting injustices of the marginalisation of women and of the destruction of the environment, linking them to the neglect of the Holy Spirit.[54]

In 1995 Johnson was elected to the prestigious position of president of the Catholic Theological Association of America (CTSA), and in her

---

(Ann Arbor, Mich.: Produced and distributed by UMI Research Press, 1987). For examples of different perspectives on the category of "women's experience" from diverse cultural experiences, see Jane Kopas, "Beyond Mere Gender: Transforming Theological Anthropology," in *Women and Theology: The Annual Publication of the College Theology Society, 1994*, ed. Mary Ann Hinsdale and Phyllis H. Kaminski (Maryknoll, N.Y.: Orbis Books, 1995) 232. See also articles by Maria Pilar Aquino, Ann O'Hara Graff, and Ada Maria Isasi-Diaz in Graff, *In the Embrace of God*.

[50] See Johnson, *SHE WHO IS*, 29–30.

[51] Elizabeth A. Johnson, "Heaven and Earth Are Filled with Your Glory: Atheism and Ecological Spirituality," in *Finding God in All Things*, ed. Michael Himes and Stephen Pope (New York: Crossroad, 1996) 94.

[52] See Elizabeth A. Johnson, "Turn to the Heavens and the Earth: Retrieval of the Cosmos in Theology," *CTSA Proceedings* 51 (1996) 18.

[53] Elizabeth A. Johnson, *Women, Earth and Creator Spirit* (New York: Paulist Press, 1993).

[54] Dr. Johnson, in conversation, noted that her interest in the link between ecology and feminism evolved from being a science major and then a science teacher and "always interested in the world and how it works." The invitation to give the Madeleva lecture became the catalyst that brought her ecological and feminist concerns together.

1996 presidential address she offered a challenge to the gathered assembly of colleagues:

> I am going to try and persuade you of the following thesis: as theologians of the twenty-first century, we need to complete our recent anthropological turns by turning to the entire interconnected community of life and the network of life-systems in which the human race is embedded, all of which has its own intrinsic value before God. In a word, we need to convert our intelligence to the heavens and the earth.[55]

She argued that nature is one of the three main pillars of theology, with God and humanity, and that it is crucial for theologians to reclaim the cosmos as a theme in theology so that access to the fullness of theological revelation might be restored.[56] She suggested that "whatever our sub-disciplines, we need to develop theology with a tangible and comprehensive ecological dimension." She further proposed that cosmology should "be a framework within which all theological topics be rethought as well as a substantive partner in theological interpretation."[57] For Johnson, the issue of ecological justice had become inextricably linked with the liberation of women and all the poor of the earth as a touchstone for all theological endeavor.

Johnson's work also benefited from the challenge of ecumenical dialogue. In 1984 she was appointed to be an adviser to the U.S. National Conference of Bishops as consultant theologian and member of the Lutheran-Roman Catholic Dialogue (U.S.A.). Such dialogue is built on the premise that the Spirit of the living God has been at work within all communities of goodwill. The Second Vatican Council sparked a new attitude to world religions, affirming that "the Catholic Church rejects nothing of what is true and holy in these religions. It has a high regard for the manner of life and conduct, the precepts and doctrines, which, although differing in many ways from its own teaching, nevertheless often reflect rays of that truth which enlightens all men and women."[58] Johnson notes that having been formed in such an ethos, she finds herself prepared to trust that, even though classical theology has clearly aided and abetted the exclusion and subordination of women, it too may reflect a ray of "that truth which enlightens all men and women."[59]

[55] Johnson, "Turn to the Heavens and the Earth," 1.

[56] See ibid., 5.

[57] Ibid., 14.

[58] Vatican II, *Nostra Aetate* (Declaration on the Relation of the Church to Non-Christian Religions) no. 2.

[59] Johnson, *SHE WHO IS,* 9. For a description of the processes of this ecumenical dialogue at work, see Elizabeth A. Johnson, C.S.J., "Lutheran/RC Dialogue (USA)

Johnson's concern for the liberation of women, and especially poor women, is intrinsically linked to another primary focus she has as a theologian—the theology of God. The opening sentence of her earliest publication in a theological journal begins with a quotation from Wolfhart Pannenberg: "A crucial, if not the most basic question of all theology is the question about the right way to speak about God."[60] Ten years later she brought her passion for justice for women together with a call for right speech about God. In *SHE WHO IS* Johnson's thesis is that a retrieval of the doctrine of God can serve as a discourse about divine mystery that will further the emancipation of women.[61] The task she set herself in this major work was to probe the inherited discourse of the Christian tradition in order to "accomplish a critical retrieval [of the core religious symbol of God] in the light of women's co-equal humanity."[62] Johnson makes it clear that the scope of her work must be highly selective and that she makes no claim of surveying the whole range of classical positions. She rather expresses the hope that her efforts may be suggestive of other possible critical retrievals of Christian sources.[63]

Three important strands of Johnson's work toward a retrieval of the Trinitarian doctrine are (1) her constructive efforts toward a renaming of the Trinity; (2) her exploration of God's being and the significance of relationality and suffering for the symbol of the Trinitarian God; (3) her reclaiming of the Spirit within Trinitarian theology. These are all central themes in *SHE WHO IS*, but they are foreshadowed in her earlier work. The third of these strands she also develops further in *Women, Earth and Creator Spirit.*

Johnson addresses the issue of the damaging effects of the exclusive centrality of the male image of God and of naming God as male

---

Achieves Statement on The One Mediator, The Saints and Mary," *Ecumenical Trends* 19/7 (1990) 97–101.

[60] Johnson, "The Right Way to Speak About God? Pannenberg on Analogy," 673.

[61] See Johnson, *SHE WHO IS*, 9.

[62] Ibid., 10.

[63] As indeed it has already been. This present book, for example, draws from classical insights of the work of the Cappadocians brought into contemporary Trinitarian discussion by Zizioulas. Catherine Mowry LaCugna is another feminist theologian who has explicitly returned to early Christian sources in her major work of retrieval of the doctrine of the Trinity. See LaCugna, *God for Us*. See also Catherine Mowry LaCugna, "God in Communion with Us: The Trinity," in *Freeing Theology: The Essentials of Theology in Feminist Perspective*, ed. Catherine Mowry LaCugna, (HarperSanFrancisco, 1993) 83–114, and Catherine Mowry LaCugna, "The Trinitarian Mystery of God," in *Systematic Theology: Roman Catholic Perspectives*, ed. Francis Schüssler Fiorenza and John P. Galvin (Minneapolis: Fortress Press, 1991) 149–92.

and female. She initially explored the latter in two articles published in *Theological Studies:* "The Incomprehensibility of God and the Image of God Male and Female" (1984) and "Mary and the Female Face of God" (1989).[64] Johnson is unambiguous in her assessment of the cost of the consistent use of exclusive male imagery for Holy Mystery—it both undermines the human dignity of women and seriously limits thought about, and worship of, God. "The charge, quite simply," she says, "is that of idolatry." The exclusive use of male imagery in naming the persons of the Trinity presents a primary problem when the doctrine is being considered from a feminist perspective. There are at least two male figures, a father and a son, and a third who is usually referred to as *he.* Johnson describes the dilemma thus: "The evocative power of the deeply masculinized symbol of the Trinity points implicitly to an essential divine maleness, inimical to women's being *imago dei* precisely as female."[65] Johnson is therefore clear that an important dimension of the retrieval of the triune God is the task of providing female images that resonate with sound sources within the Christian tradition.

A second strand in Johnson's work of retrieval of Trinitarian theology is her focus on *God's being and the connection between relationality and the suffering God.* She explores the huge shift that has taken place within theology in the light of the growing consciousness of the massive suffering of the world and also by the developments of biblical studies and philosophy. She notes that "large numbers of thoughtful people in the nineteenth and twentieth centuries have rejected the classic idea of the impassible, omnipotent God finding it both intellectually inadequate and religiously repugnant."[66]

A third strand within Johnson's theological vision of the Trinity is her *reclaiming of the importance of the place and the function of the Holy Spirit.* As indicated above, it was her focus on the flourishing of the full humanity of women, of every human person, and of all creation that led her to trace the links between these two situations of massive global injustice and the neglect of the Holy Spirit. She argues that Christian anthropology, the doctrine of creation, and the doctrine of God impinge upon one another and that "all three must be rethought together in a new vision of wholeness."[67]

---

[64] Elizabeth A. Johnson, "The Incomprehensibility of God and the Image of God Male and Female," *Theological Studies* 45 (1984) 441–65; "Mary and the Female Face of God," *Theological Studies* 50 (1989) 500–26.

[65] Johnson, *SHE WHO IS,* 193.

[66] Ibid., 250.

[67] Johnson, *Women, Earth and Creator Spirit,* 3.

With Johnson, I am convinced that any serious retrieval of the symbol of the Trinity cannot properly occur without addressing the issue of the exclusive male imagery that has been used of the triune God for nearly two thousand years. This issue is not some contemporary exercise in political correctness. What is involved is nothing less than the full humanity of women and men and humanity's proper relationship with God. With Johnson, I believe that anything we say of God has to ring true in word and deed in the face of the pain that confronts us in the contemporary world. The issue of suffering and its connection with a relational God needs to be addressed by any serious theology of the triune God today. Finally, to focus on the place of the Spirit in connection with the place of women and the earth is to redress an imbalance and neglect that has occurred within Trinitarian theology. Each of these interconnected areas will be examined through the lens of Johnson's feminist vision in Part Two of this book.

Theological Assumptions and Methodology

The basic method of this contribution to the retrieval of the symbol of the triune God is that of mutually critical correlation set within the context of a feminist liberation theology. I am proposing a correlation between two sets of interpretations of a rereading of the tradition for our times. Both Zizioulas and Johnson return to the sources of Trinitarian doctrine in order to make the "classic event"—the revelation of the God of Jesus Christ—accessible to peoples struggling with global realities at the beginning of the twenty-first century. The different living traditions of East and West, through which these two theologians reread the early sources, need themselves to be brought into a mutually critical correlation if the fullness of the tradition is to be accessed. Because of the limits of both these great Christian traditions, neither one carries within it all the dimensions of this central symbol of Christian faith. If both are brought into conversation and correlation, there is more chance that the revelation of the God of Jesus Christ as a triune God can be retrieved for our times.

I am convinced that if the symbol of God is to be retrieved, the destructive power of sexism inherent in Christian theology and praxis must be addressed at a fundamental level. It is for this reason that I wish to situate the method of mutually critical correlation within the context of feminist liberation theology. By Christian feminist theology I mean a theology that draws both from the Christian tradition and from the overlooked experience of women. In this study I interpret feminist theology to be a critical theology of liberation, a form of faith seeking understanding that is rooted in women's experience and has the goal of transforming inequities. It is not just interested in individuals' equal rights but is profoundly communitarian in emphasis. It is concerned with lifting the oppression of all people and of all creation, and in promoting relationships of equality and mutuality in communion.

A major concern shaping this stance is that from the beginning of Christianity doctrines have been formulated by men alone, and the theological reflection on these doctrines has been done only by men. Half of the human race has for the most part been barred from participating in the human expression of the mysteries of faith. These exist today largely without the benefit of women's contribution to their wisdom and clarity. The texts on the Trinity offered to the Church by the Vatican on the occasion of the new millennium provide but one example of this continuing problem.[68] Similarly, within the wider life and culture of the Church, art, architecture, music, catechisms, and books have also been almost exclusively the work of men. Women have always been the *other* in a male-dominated society. Women have not been subjects within the Church, and that has worked powerfully against the full humanity of women as well as that of men and children.

It is not, therefore, incidental to the overall intent of this work that I have chosen to focus on the theologies of both a woman and a man, and that one is formed within the Eastern Church and the other in the Western. For all the breakthroughs in communication during the last decades over the divides between male and female, and between Eastern and Western traditions within the Church, there are still firm boundaries in place that impede the full creative potential that can be released when the theologies of female as well as male, and of East as well as West, are brought into dynamic communion.

Some would argue that since women's voices have scarcely been heard, feminist theology should only concern itself with the experience of women in dialogue with that which is retrievable from tradition.[69] I believe, however, that a fundamental dimension of feminist theology requires, as theologian M. Shawn Copeland describes it, "a turn, a conversion among all theologians to engage difference in the work toward authentic solidarity in word and deed."[70] The methodology that I will

---

[68] A special theological commission was established by the Vatican to prepare a publication in each of the three years before 2000. These were entitled *Jesus Christ, Word of the Father; The Holy Spirit, Lord and Giver of Life;* and *God, the Father of Mercy.*

[69] See Dickey Young, *Feminist Theology/Christian Theology* for an indication of the spectrum of Christian feminist positions.

[70] M. Shawn Copeland, "Toward a Critical Christian Feminist Theology of Solidarity," in *Women and Theology,* ed. Hinsdale and Kaminski, 11. "Womanist" is a name adopted by North American women theologians of African origin in order to designate a different stance from that of white feminist theologians.

use is based on the premise that one of the strengths of feminist theology is that it can demonstrate what can happen when hitherto impermeable boundaries are crossed and entities that are other are brought into creative communion.[71] This contribution to the retrieval of the symbol of the Trinity brings the work of a contemporary Western feminist theologian into creative dialogue with that of a metropolitan of an Eastern Church.

The patristic revival of this century within both Eastern and Western traditions led one of the great Catholic theologians of the twentieth century, Yves Congar, to observe that the Western tradition without the East is like trying to breathe with only one lung. The Christian Churches have acknowledged in the last decades that they need to draw from the richness of both great traditions if they are to be able to offer the peoples of the world the fullness of the Christian faith.[72] I am arguing that an even more profound distortion within the Christian faith has resulted from the fact that the doctrine of God was formulated and developed within a framework that failed to acknowledge or value the unique and equal humanity of women. As Elizabeth Johnson has stated, the effects of this gross imbalance that has been firmly in place for nearly two thousand years needs to be remedied as a matter of urgency, because of "its complicity in human oppression and its capacity to rob divine reality of goodness and profound mystery."[73]

In the last few decades women's work in theology has begun to address these twin tasks. Expressed positively, the purpose is both to illuminate the mystery of God and to promote the full humanity of all people and the integrity of creation. Both of these factors point to the significance of the contribution that feminist theology is making to the development of doctrine within the living tradition of the Church.[74]

In summary, my purpose is to contribute to the retrieval of the symbol of the triune God, and in so doing to contribute to the full humanity of all persons. I am proposing that the theologies of Zizioulas and Johnson together provide a rich resource for these related tasks. With John Zizioulas, I believe that one of the important tasks of contemporary theology is to work with a view to a synthesis between the two theologies, Eastern and Western. His own attempt is "to offer a contribution to a 'neopatristic synthesis' capable of leading the West

---

[71] For an argument for the need for feminist theology to engage with Orthodoxy, see Celia Dean-Drummond, "Sophia: The Feminine Face of God as a Metaphor for an Ecotheology," *Feminist Theology* 16 (1997) 11.

[72] See, for example, the encyclical letter of Pope John Paul II *Ut Unum Sint* (1995).

[73] Johnson, *SHE WHO IS*, 15.

[74] See Johnson, *Consider Jesus*, 1–3.

and the East nearer to these common roots, in the context of the existential quest of modern man."[75] And with Zizioulas, I want to propose that "Trinitarian theology has profound existential consequences."[76]

With Elizabeth Johnson, I subscribe to the belief that for a faith community, "the symbol of God functions as the primary symbol of the whole religious system, the ultimate point of reference for understanding experience, life and the world."[77] And with Johnson, I acknowledge that the women's movement "has shed a bright light on the pervasive exclusion of women from the realm of public symbol formation and decision-making, and women's consequent, strongly enforced subordination to the imagination and needs of a world designed chiefly by men."[78]

With both these theologians, I am positing that the question of the doctrine of God is central to the whole of theological enterprise and that the doctrine of the Trinity is an eminently practical doctrine for the Church and the world.

Part One of this book examines the Trinitarian theology of John Zizioulas, and Part Two examines Johnson's exploration of the mystery of the Trinitarian God in feminist theological discourse. In these chapters I explore the work of both theologians with the purpose of identifying those elements within their respective works that contribute significantly to the work of retrieval of the symbol of the triune God in these times. In Part Three four chapters will focus on a critical correlation of these two Trinitarian theologies, and then I offer my conclusions in a final chapter entitled "Toward a Constructive Retrieval of the Symbol of the Triune God."

---

[75] Zizioulas, *Being as Communion*, 26.
[76] Zizioulas, "The Doctrine of God the Trinity Today," 19.
[77] Johnson, *SHE WHO IS*, 4.
[78] Ibid.

PART ONE

The Trinitarian Theology of John Zizioulas

CHAPTER 2

The Trinitarian God:
Persons in Communion

*Belief in creation "ex nihilo"—biblical faith—thus encounters
belief in ontology—Greek faith—to give human existence and
thought its most dear and precious good, the concept of person.*[1]

The primary purpose of this chapter is to focus on the centrality of
the concept of person in Zizioulas's Trinitarian theology. I will investigate his ontology of person and begin to explore the implications of
"being" understood as "communion" and of God understood as "persons in communion." In recent decades there has been considerable debate in the West about the legitimacy of retaining the concept of person
within the Trinitarian doctrine. The question centers around whether,
in this era, it is possible to retain a concept of person coined in the theological world of the fourth century, now that the concept itself has ac-
quired many new layers of meaning. Since this concept is so central to
Zizioulas's Trinitarian theology, I will first address this issue.

The Concept of Person and
Contemporary Trinitarian Theology

In this century Protestant theologian Karl Barth and Roman Catholic theologian Karl Rahner have both made major contributions toward

---

[1] John D. Zizioulas, *Being as Communion: Studies in Personhood and the Church*
(New York: St. Vladimir's Seminary Press, 1993) 65.

restoring Trinitarian theology to its central place within Christian theology and belief. However, both acknowledged the problems for contemporary believers that have emerged from the major philosophical developments since the Enlightenment. One particular problem they identified within Trinitarian theology was that person had come to be understood as an individual center of consciousness and freedom. Since person is used to describe the Trinity, there is the danger that the three persons in God can be understood as three centers of consciousness and that this in turn can lead to tritheism.

Barth and Rahner both sought ways of addressing this issue. Barth's way of dealing with the problem was to replace the word altogether. He suggested the alternative formulation of "three modes of being" in God, since this was the equivalent of the ancient Greek formula *tropos hyparxeos*, meaning relation of origin.[2] In a way similar to Barth's, Rahner argued that God is the ultimate self-consciousness and that this absolute subjectivity exists in three distinct ways, that the "one self-communication of the one God occurs in three different manners of given-ness."[3] Rahner did not agree that person should be removed from Trinitarian discourse but rather suggested that the terminology "three distinct manners of subsisting" should be used in conjunction with it so that it "may serve the purpose of overcoming the false opinion [of] what is meant by 'person.'"[4]

There have been numerous criticisms of the proposals of both Barth and Rahner. They are accused by many of modalism (the view that there are three different modes of the one God's operations) and of failing in their respective theologies to give adequate attention to the aspect of reciprocity and relationship in the tradition.[5] Their alternative proposals are also considered entirely unsuitable for preaching and liturgy.[6] But perhaps the most trenchant criticisms center on their focus on a single divine subject and on their narrow interpretation of the modern understanding of person as a center of consciousness. According to Jürgen Moltmann, for example, both theologians identify the divine subject with the unity of God and not with God's plurality. He claims that:

[2] See Karl Barth, *Church Dogmatics* (Edinburgh: T&T Clark, 1975) 1:359.

[3] Rahner, *The Trinity*, trans. Joseph Donceel (New York: Herder and Herder, 1970) 109.

[4] Ibid., 115. See also 26ff.; 42–45; 56ff.; 109–15.

[5] See Josef Ratzinger, *Dogma e Predicazione* (Brescia: Queriniana, 1974) 188. Quoted in John O'Donnell, *The Mystery of the Triune God* (London: Sheed & Ward, 1988) 104–5; see also Catherine Mowry LaCugna, *God for Us: The Trinity and Christian Life* (New York: HarperSanFrancisco, 1991) 254–56.

[6] See Walter Kasper, *The God of Jesus Christ*, trans. Matthew J. O'Connell (New York: Crossroad, 1991) 288.

Barth presents the "doctrine of the Trinity" as Christian monotheism and argues polemically against a "tritheism" which has never existed. That is why he uses a non-Trinitarian concept of the unity of the one God—that is to say, the concept of the identical subject.[7]

Moltmann has a similar criticism of Rahner's position:

Idealistic modalism leads back . . . to the Christian monotheism of "the one unique essence, the singularity of a one single consciousness and of a single liberty of God" who is present in the innermost center of existence "of an individual person."[8]

Moltmann's concern is that this emphasis on the absolute divine subjectivity leads "to a profound alteration in the substance of the Christian doctrine of the Trinity."[9]

On the second issue—the limited interpretation of the modern understanding of person—Walter Kasper's critique of Rahner could also be applied to Barth:

What Rahner describes is in fact not at all the full modern meaning of the person but rather an extreme individualism in which each person is a center of action who possesses himself and is set off over against others. But Fichte and Hegel have already moved beyond such a point of view. Ever since the time of Feuerbach modern personalism, as represented by M. Buber, F. Ebner, F. Rosenzweig and others, has made it entirely clear that person exists only in relation; that the concrete personality exists only as interpersonality, subjectivity only as intersubjectivity.[10]

Despite such strong criticisms of Barth and Rahner, however, the possibility of absorbing the modern concept of person into the doctrine of the Trinity has continued to be a matter of dispute among theologians. Nicholas Lash, for instance, states categorically that "there is no doubt whatsoever, to my mind, but that the arguments for ceasing to speak of persons in Trinitarian theology greatly outweigh those in favour of the term's retention."[11] He continues:

---

[7] Jürgen Moltmann, *The Trinity and the Kingdom of God* (New York: Harper and Row, 1981) 144.

[8] Ibid., 148.

[9] Ibid., 144.

[10] Kasper, *The God of Jesus Christ*, 289. See also LaCugna, *God for Us*, 255.

[11] Nicholas Lash, *Believing Three Ways in One God* (London: SCM Press, 1992) 31.

To say that "God is three persons in one nature" tells us no more about God than would "God is three things in one thing,"or than does "God is three and God is one." Not only does the concept of "person" misleadingly give the impression of telling us something about God which we would not otherwise have known, but the information that it seems to give is false. For us, a person is an individual agent, a conscious center of memory and choice, of action, reflection and decision. But when we say there are, in God, "three persons," we do not mean that God has, as it were, three minds, three memories, three wills.[12]

Like Lash, Elizabeth Johnson refers to Augustine, who contends that the primary reason person has been used is because when speaking of the triune God, "it is necessary to say something when the question arises about what the three are."[13] She notes that the use of the term "person" has recommended itself primarily because it is used by the theological tradition and because Scripture does not contradict it. Johnson does not dispute the importance of personal language about God. She recognizes that it has value because it "points in a unique way to the mysterious depths and freedom of action long associated with the divine."[14] However, Johnson's final assessment of the appropriateness of using the concept of person to speak about the three in God is that it is problematic. She concludes: "Person is perhaps the least inconvenient of labels, but it is highly inadequate, in fact, improper. . . . To say that God is three 'persons' inevitably gives rise to the picture of God as three distinct people with separated consciousnesses who are personally interrelated and somehow one. Tritheism is endemic."[15]

Despite conclusions such as those expressed by Lash and to some extent by Johnson, there seems to be a growing consensus among contemporary theologians regarding the intrinsic value and importance of the retention of the concept of person for an authentic theology of the mystery of God as Trinity. William Hill, for example, argues that "there is no reason whatsoever for supposing that the nuance given to 'person' in contemporary usage is not a development of what *hypostasis* and *substantia* seek to convey."[16] He notes that Bernard Lonergan's interpre-

---

[12] Ibid., 32.

[13] Elizabeth Johnson, *SHE WHO IS: The Mystery of God in Feminist Theological Discourse* (New York: Crossroad, 1992) 203.

[14] Ibid., 55.

[15] Ibid., 203. See also Elizabeth A. Johnson, "Trinity: To Let the Symbol Sing Again," *Theology Today* 34, no. 3 (1997) 304–5.

[16] William Hill, *The Three-Personed God: Trinity as a Mystery of Salvation* (Washington: Catholic University of America Press, 1982) 222.

tation safeguards a single divine consciousness without compromising the assertion that there are three in God who are conscious. He also draws attention to Heribert Mühlen's explication of Richard of St. Victor, which demonstrates how the use of person "transposes the analogy between God and the creature from the static domain of nature to the more dynamic sphere of communication, from individual self-knowledge and self-love to interpersonal exchange."[17] He suggests that the meaning of person "has evolved, thanks to research in both psychology and philosophical anthropology, and now discloses explicitly a world of meaning that previously went unnoticed."[18] Hill is thus arguing that the evolving understandings of person, far from rendering its use improper, are in fact making it more relevant, more expressive of the truth of the mystery of the triune God. He lists the understanding of person as an "extension of consciousness of self and others, its greater emphasis on relationality and its focus on intersubjectivity" as examples of how the contemporary use of person offers certain advantages to Trinitarian theology. For all these reasons, Hill concludes, "the term simply cannot be jettisoned in theological discourse."[19]

Walter Kasper makes an even stronger case for the retention of person in Trinitarian theology. Having observed that the "definition of God as essentially person has the advantage that it is more concrete and alive than the abstract metaphysical definition adopted by the tradition" and that it is also closer to the biblical picture of God, he goes on to claim:

> Person is the highest category we have at our disposal. We can predicate the category in an analogous way. . . . The category of person has three positive values. As a person, God is subject and is utterly and irreplaceably unique. . . . The concept of person precludes any reduction of God to a function. . . . It gives expression to the glory and the holiness of God. . . . When we define God, the reality that determines everything as personal, we are also defining being as a whole as personal. This entails a revolution in the understanding of being. The ultimate and highest reality is not substance but relation. . . . The meaning of being is to be found in self-communicating love.[20]

As will be discussed later in the chapter, it is this "revolution in the understanding of being" and the concept that "the highest reality is not substance but relation" that is central to Zizioulas's work on the ontology of person.

[17] See Hill, *Three-Personed God*, 225–34.
[18] Ibid., 255.
[19] Ibid.
[20] Kasper, *The God of Jesus Christ*, 154–56.

Kasper concedes that it is impossible to accept three consciousnesses in God. He draws from Bernard Lonergan's return to original Scholastic sources and concludes that "in the Trinity we are dealing with three subjects who are reciprocally conscious of each other by reason of the same consciousness which the three subjects 'possess,' each in his own proper way."[21] He further argues that the key to the issue of the viability of retaining the concept of person in Trinitarian discourse is the question of how the human person can be properly understood as the image of the Trinitarian God.[22] With Hill, he believes that it is precisely the modern concept of person that offers an important point of contact for the believer with the doctrine of the Trinity: "The human person exists only in relations of the I-Thou-We kind. Within the horizon of this modern understanding of person, an isolated unipersonal God is inconceivable."[23] Kasper hastens to qualify his strong endorsement for retaining the concept of person in Trinitarian theology by recalling that all personalist categories, as with all speech about God, can be applied only analogically. He acknowledges that human interpersonal relations can give but a glimpse of the interrelationality and interpersonality in God: "the three persons of the Trinity are pure relationality; they are relations in which the nature of God exists in three distinct and non-interchangeable ways."[24]

Anthony Kelly, in his *Trinity of Love*, also focuses on the centrality of love within the corpus of Christian belief and therefore argues with some passion for the consequent importance of the concept of person in Trinitarian discourse:

> The context of person language is that of real or possible love. Love in its most authentic experiences is between persons. To speak the language of love and not use the language of person would be linguistically and psychologically violent. That is why there is some special sensitivity in the retention of this word in Trinitarian theology where what is most loving and what is most personal coincide.[25]

Kelly believes that any erosion of the force of personal language can only deeply disaffect Christian faith, whereas in terms of existential imagination, the love analogy "shows how we human persons are radically 'personalised' by the divine three."[26]

[21] Ibid., 289.
[22] Ibid., 286.
[23] Ibid., 289.
[24] Ibid., 309.
[25] Anthony Kelly, *The Trinity of Love* (Wilmington, Del.: Michael Glazier, 1989) 185.
[26] Ibid., 187.

Catherine LaCugna agrees with Kelly on both of these matters and in her book *God for Us* develops them in some detail. In her analysis of what she calls the "defeat" of the doctrine of the Trinity—the fact that it became essentially irrelevant to Christian believers—she concludes that the primary reason that the doctrine of the Trinity was "defeated" was because Trinitarian discourse was moved from its biblical base in popular religiosity and worship and shifted into the esoteric realms of speculative theology. While retaining "persons" in the theological language of the dogma, de facto it was separated from the personal lives and experience of believers, from the "economy" of their salvation. Revelation of the triune God did not impinge on them personally in any way and therefore faded from the existential imagination of Christian life.

When LaCugna sets out to retrieve the doctrine of the Trinity, she places at the center of her proposal an ontology of relation, a description of what it means to be a person and to exist as persons in communion.[27] However, she too safeguards the analogical use of language for God by cautioning that when "we use the term 'person' of God . . . we are not giving a description of the essence of God as it is in itself, but using a term that points beyond itself to the ineffability of God." She affirms that "the distinction between the economic and immanent Trinity is a way of holding on to the truth that God is personal, that God is free, that God cannot be reduced to human history or human perception." However, she also holds to the assertion that since God is *personal*, "the proper subject matter of the doctrine of the Trinity is the encounter between the divine and human persons in the economy of redemption."[28]

The above discussion indicates that while there is still debate about the issue of the validity of the use of the concept of person in a contemporary Trinitarian theology, there is strong support from some theologians for its continuing relevance.[29] This discussion also helps to situate

[27] See LaCugna, *God for Us*, 243. It should be noted that in developing this point, LaCugna draws significantly upon Zizioulas's work.

[28] Ibid., 304–5.

[29] See also Lawrence B. Porter, "On Keeping 'Persons' in the Trinity: A Linguistic Approach to Trinitarian Thought," *Theological Studies* 41 (1980) 530–48; Denis Edwards, *Jesus the Wisdom of God: An Ecological Theology* (Maryknoll, N.Y.; Orbis Books, 1995); Eberhard Jungel, *God as the Mystery of the World*, trans. Darrell Guder (Grand Rapids, Mich.: Wm. B. Eerdmans, 1983); Christopher Kiesling, "On Relating to the Persons of the Trinity," *Theological Studies* 47 (1986) 599–616; Sallie McFague, *Models of God: Theology for an Ecological, Nuclear Age* (London: SCM Press, 1987); Alan J. Torrance, *Persons in Communion: An Essay on Trinitarian Description and Human Participation* (Edinburgh; T&T Clark, 1996); Thomas F. Torrance, *The Christian Doctrine*

Zizioulas's work within the mainstream of contemporary theological concern and provides a context within which to consider his Trinitarian theology of person.

Origins of a Trinitarian Theology of Person

This section will begin with an investigation of the patristic roots of Zizioulas's concept of person. It will show how the impetus provided by the historical need for a theology of the triune God led to the development of such an ontology of person. It will then explore different dimensions of Zizioulas's ontology of person and begin to trace its connections with his Trinitarian theology and with his whole theological system.

The concept of the person is, according to Zizioulas, humanity's *"most dear and precious good."*[30] This concept, placed as it is at the center of Trinitarian theology, is at the heart of his whole theological system. It is a concept that springs from an ontology of person that has its roots in Greek patristic theology. Zizioulas argues, however, that this concept of person is completely congruent with a twentieth-century understanding of the person as a *relational* category and as such stands in sharp contrast with the individualistic tradition that until recently has been central to Western theology since Boethius.[31]

John Zizioulas situates his theological work within the context of the existential quest of humanity in the modern world with its focus on the question of person and personal identity.[32] It is therefore no accident that the first chapter of his work *Being as Communion* is entitled "Personhood and Being." Nor is it an accident that he begins with the claim that *"historically* as well as *existentially* the concept of person is indissolubly bound up with theology."[33] In fact, because the Trinity is so central to his whole theological system, it could be said that the whole corpus of Zizioulas's work draws the reader inexorably to focus on the significance of a key theological event that took place on the eastern rim of the Mediterranean in the fourth century C.E. It was an event, he

---

of God: One Being Three Persons (Edinburgh: T&T Clark, 1996); Patricia Wilson-Kastner, *Faith, Feminism and the Christ* (Philadelphia: Fortress Press, 1983); Kallistos Ware, "The Human Person as an Icon of the Trinity," *Sobornost* 8, no. 2 (1986) 6–23.

[30] Zizioulas, *Being as Communion*, 65.

[31] John Zizioulas, "Human Capacity and Human Incapacity: A Theological Exploration of Personhood," *Scottish Journal of Theology* (1975) 408n.

[32] See Zizioulas, *Being as Communion*, 26. See also Metropolitan John (Zizioulas) of Pergamon, "To einai tou Theou kai einai tou anthropou," *Synaxis* 37 (1991) 11–36.

[33] Ibid., 27.

argues, in which biblical Christianity and Greek ontology converged within the work of theologically and philosophically trained pastors of Cappadocia to produce a new moment in humanity's understanding of itself: "With a rare creativity worthy of the Greek spirit they gave history the concept of the person."[34]

How, then, did the concept of person develop at that time and place? And why does Zizioulas claim such significance for it? A basic principle of ancient Greek thought was that in the final analysis *being* is *one*, despite the multiplicity of existent things. Therefore, every differentiation was regarded as movement toward *non-being*. Harmony, order, and stability were to be found within the one. Zizioulas focuses on the fact that the place of humanity in this unified *cosmos* of harmony and reason became the theme of Greek theater, and especially of its tragedies. The central drama inevitably enacted in every play was each character's struggle to resist the oppression of the inexorability of this harmonious unity that predetermines her or his fate. The freedom "to become one's own person" was impossible within such a world. Significantly, notes Zizioulas, it is precisely here that the term "person" (*prosōpon*) comes into usage in ancient Greek. It was used to denote the actor's mask. Therefore, before the concept of person had been conceived, the theater became an arena wherein the masked players explored what it was to be a person—"to exist as a free, unique and unrepeatable entity."[35] In the plays the outcome was always tragic; the freedom of the person was always overcome by fate. The message was consistent: a human being does not have the freedom to escape fate and to become a unique self. It was not deemed possible for a human being to *be* in such a way.

Similarly, argues Zizioulas, a consideration of the origin of the ancient Latin word *persona* is suggestive of comparable meanings. In its sociological and later legal use it meant "role." In the Roman state one adopted a *persona*, or role, in one's social or legal relationships in order to achieve particular ends. At that time there was no term that carried the meaning of an individual's essential self or being. As with the Greek *prosōpon*, the Roman use of *persona* illustrated both the affirmation and the denial of the human being's capacity to act in a free and unique manner. That is, the freedom to act out of one's own identity in both societies was, as it were, tasted through the medium of the mask in Greek theater or of *persona* in Roman legal or political life, but it was finally always limited in a human being's life as a whole by the boundaries of the collectively held understandings of a "world" (cosmos

---

[34] Ibid., 35.
[35] Ibid., 33.

or the state), bound by the limits of ontological necessity.[36] Zizioulas thus indicates how these precursory experiences of being a person led to the evolution of these two words within the ancient Greco-Roman world well before those respective societies had arrived at a way of expressing the concept of person.

Many studies that explore the origins of person and personality in Greek and Christian thought reinforce the fact that "the Greek ancients had intuitions about individual personality" and the concept of person.[37] Cornelia de Vogel, a historian of Greek philosophy who traced these "intuitions" from Homer through Herodotos, Pythagoras, Socrates, Plato, Aristotle, Plotinus, and to Cicero through Panaetius of Rhodes, argued in fact that person was "a Greek definition"[38] before Christianity. Here she is in explicit disagreement with the assertion made by the distinguished scholar of medieval philosophy Etienne Gilson and others who hold that classical antiquity had no word for the concept of person.[39] Gilson, however, makes clear his conviction that "because they never denied the reality of the individual, the Greeks opened the way for the Christian recognition of the eminent worth of the person: not only did they not prevent it or even simply retard it, they did a great deal to forward its success."[40] It appears that while most scholars concede that the Greeks promoted a philosophical understanding of many aspects of personhood, they also would agree with the claim that the semantic shift required for the concept of person was only developed within Christianity.[41]

---

[36] Ibid., 33–34.

[37] Gregory Telepneff and Bishop Chrysostomos, "The Transformation of Hellenistic Thought on the Cosmos and Man in the Greek Fathers," *Patristic and Byzantine Review* 9, no. 2–3 (1990) 132. See also Etienne Gilson, *The Spirit of Medieval Philosophy* (New York: Scribners, 1940); Cornelia J. de Vogel, "The Concept of Personality in Greek and Christian Thought," in *Studies in the Philosophy and the History of Philosophy*, ed. John K. Ryan (Washington: The Catholic University Press, 1963) 2:20–60; Gedaliahu G. Stroumsa, "*Caro salutis cardo:* Shaping the Person in Early Christian Thought," *History of Religions* 30 (1990) 25–50. Mary T. Clark, "An Inquiry into Personhood," *Review of Metaphysics* 46 (1992) 3–28.

[38] De Vogel, "The Concept of Personality," 59.

[39] Ibid.

[40] Gilson, *The Spirit of Medieval Philosophy*, 37, quoted in Clark, "Inquiry into Personhood," 10.

[41] See for example, Stroumsa, "Shaping the Person," 27, who quotes Paul Veyne in Peter Brown, *A History of the Private Life*, trans. A. Goldhammer (London: Harvard University Press, 1987) 1:231: "No ancient, not even the poets, is capable of talking about oneself. Nothing is more misleading than the use of 'I' in Graeco-Roman poetry." See also John Rist, "Individuals and Persons," in *Human Value: A*

Russian-born theologian Georges Florovsky (1893–1979), Zizioulas's teacher, traces this development of understandings of human personhood in his writings and illustrates the differences between the Hellenistic philosophers and the early Greek pastor-theologians.[42] For instance, he points to Plato's body-soul dualism and to the fact that Aristotelian anthropology and cosmology do not subscribe to the possibility of life after death. He then demonstrates how the early Christian Greek theologians effected a synthesis by drawing on those elements of those great philosophers' thought that were congruent with Christian experience and theology. He shows, for example, how the Christian thinkers drew from Aristotle's notion of the unity of body and soul and from the concept of the eternal *nous* in Plato.[43] Taking Florovsky's work further, Zizioulas identifies that it is because Greek philosophical thought was unable to endow human individuality with unique permanence that it was unable to arrive at a true ontology of person. Personhood for the Greeks was no more than an adjunct to concrete ontological being.[44] He thus arrives at the conclusion that for the concept of person to be able to be developed, two basic presuppositions are necessary: "(a) a radical change in cosmology that would free the world and man from ontological necessity; and (b) an ontological view of man that would unite the person with the *being* of man, with his permanent and enduring existence, with his genuine and absolute identity."[45]

These presuppositions were simply not present within the ancient Greco-Roman world. Within the primary focus of ontology in Greek thought, being goes on forever, while the particular beings disappear. Ancient Greek thought in all its forms agreed on the fact that "particularity is not ontologically absolute; the many are always ontologically derivative not causative."[46] A personal ontology was therefore impossible. Zizioulas claims, however, that this was not due to a weakness in Greek philosophy but rather is an intrinsic limitation of philosophy itself. He observes that "person as an ontological category cannot be

---

Study in Ancient Philosophical Ethics, Philosophia Antiqua 40 (Leiden: Brill, 1982) 145–63.

[42] Florovsky, "The Patristic Age and Eschatology," in *Collected Works* (Belmont: Nordland, 1975) 4:63–78.

[43] See Telepneff and Chrysostomos, "The Transformation of Hellenistic Thought," 130–31.

[44] Zizioulas, *Being as Communion,* 34.

[45] Ibid., 35.

[46] John Zizioulas, "On Being a Person. Towards an Ontology of Personhood," in *Persons, Divine and Human,* ed. C. Schwöbel and C. Gunton (Edinburgh: T&T Clark, 1991) 36. See also Stroumsa, "Shaping the Person," 32, and Rist, "Individuals and Persons," 152.

extrapolated from experience"[47] and thus argues that philosophy by it-self could never have forged the concept of person.

Biblical thought, however, offered an alternative view of being. As Mary Clark observes: "In the community of Israel the personal 'I' is important. . . . the Hebrews knew that God was not concerned with appearances but with the heart, their metaphor for person."[48] Within a biblical world view, being is caused by *someone*. And the personal causation of all being means that particularity can be understood as causative and not derivative in ontology. Thus biblical thought, when brought in conjunction with Greek thought, was to provide a situation wherein the above conditions required for the development of the concept of the person could be met.

And so in fact it happened. (This is the moment, according to Zizioulas, for the zoom lens and the sound of full orchestra!) It happened through the agency of Greek Christian leaders who were thoroughly steeped in both the worldview of the Bible and in Greek philosophy. And it happened because of dissent and confusion within the communion of the wider life of the Churches about the nature of the God of Jesus Christ. A need arose to formulate statements about God and God's relationship with the world that were congruent with the Christian communal experience of life in the Spirit and with the life, death, and resurrection of Jesus.

At first, concern centered around the oneness and the unity of God and later about the plural manifestation of God in creation, redemption, and in reconciliation. By the middle of the third century, three clearly distinguishable positions had emerged that were inadequate to express the fullness of Christian belief about the God of Jesus Christ. Sabellianism (or modalism) held that there is one God who appears in three different roles according to the three different functions: Creator, Redeemer, and Sanctifier. Tritheism held that there were three Gods instead of one, and subordinationalism recognized a Trinity but made the Son less than the Father and the Spirit less than the Son. Then in the fourth century Arius (d. 336), a priest of Alexandria, carried the tendencies of subordinationalism to an extreme. He taught that Christ was less than God but more than a human being.

It was the consequent struggle to deal with these divergent views and to be able to express essential truths about the God of Jesus Christ that led Christian leaders to develop an ontology of person. That is where Zizioulas claims "a philosophical landmark, a revolution in

---

[47] Zizioulas, "On Being a Person," 37.
[48] Clark, "Inquiry into Personhood," 4.

Greek philosophy" occurred.[49] Because it became clear to the Christian believers that the distinction between God and the world is the distinction between uncreated and created, it also became clear that there is an "*utter* dialectic between God and the world."[50] Moreover, in God, it was argued, it is possible for the particular to be ontologically ultimate because relationship is permanent and unbreakable: the Father, the Son, and the Spirit are always in communion.[51]

Zizioulas argues that this ontology, in fact, came out of the eucharistic experience of the ecclesial communities. The experience of living and worshiping in Christian communities had, he claims, revealed something very important about the God they worshiped. It had revealed that the being of God came to be known through personal relationships and personal love and that "being means life, and life means *communion*."[52] This experience of communion *(koinōnia)* provided an existential reference point for those leaders (bishops) who were working on formulations of the doctrine of the being of God. Zizioulas refers specifically to Athanasius of Alexandria and the Cappadocians, Basil the Great, Gregory Nazianzen, and Gregory of Nyssa. The key question that they had to address was: What does it mean to say that God is Father, Son, and Spirit without ceasing to be *one* God?[53] Biblical Christianity was able to engage with this question because it held that *being*, the existence of the world, was created out of nothing and was therefore a product of freedom. It was not bound by the ontological necessity of Greek philosophy. Moreover, a biblical world picture also held that the basis of this freedom was the being of a God who was *personal.*

By the second half of the fourth century, this theological issue became centered around the need to find the language to express the enduring particularity of the Father, the Son, and the Spirit while honoring the unity of Godself. A formula was required that expressed unity and distinction at the same time. From a very early date those wishing to be baptized into the Christian community were asked to

[49] Zizioulas, *Being as Communion*, 36.

[50] For a discussion of this matter, see J. D. Zizioulas, "The Teaching of the 2nd Ecumenical Council on the Holy Spirit in Historical and Ecumenical Perspective," in *Credo in Spiritum Sanctum*, ed. J. S. Martins (Rome: Libreria Editrice Vaticana, 1983) 1:32.

[51] See Zizioulas, "On Being a Person," 41.

[52] Zizioulas, *Being as Communion*, 16–17.

[53] See J. D. Zizioulas, "The Contribution of Cappadocia to Christian Thought," *Sinasos in Cappadocia*, eds. Frosso Pimenides, Stelios Roãdes (National Trust for Greece: Agra Publications, 1986) 25. Zizioulas refers here to "a whole series of Christian thinkers" including Irenaeus, Clement, Origen, and Athanasius, who addressed this question.

confess faith in the name of God as Father, Son, and Holy Spirit (Matt 25:19). The liturgies and worship of various Christian communities included doxologies "to the Father, through the Son, in the Holy Spirit."[54] Christians were thus initiated into the possibility of establishing personal, salvific relationships with the three in God. The theologian-pastors of Cappadocia therefore needed to search for a way to express in ontological language the enduring collective Christian experience of relating to each of these personal entities within the one God.

Their task was complicated by the position adopted by Sabellius, who taught in Rome in the third century that God was a monad and the Son and the Spirit were both understood as "person," in the sense of "role" or "mask."[55] In order to preclude the Sabellian interpretation, "the Cappadocians started from the assumption that each of the persons of the Trinity was a *full* and *complete* being."[56] At the Council of Nicea in 325 C.E., the words *hypostasis* and *ousia* had been used synonymously in language for God.[57] What the Cappadocian leaders did was to take the word *hypostasis* which meant *concrete* and *full being* and identified it with "person." God as Trinity was therefore to be understood as three *hypostases*, three full beings. Then, to avoid introducing tritheism into God, they suggested that *ousia* should be taken to mean "substance" in the generic sense, and therefore applicable to more than one being.[58] Basil of Caesarea was the first to make a clear distinction between *hypostasis* and *ousia*. Soon after, Gregory Nazianzen identified *hypostasis* with the word *prosōpon*, and Basil's brother, Gregory of Nyssa, reinforced the distinction between *ousia* and *hypostasis* and coined the Trinitarian formula *mia ousia—treis hypostaseis*.[59] The concept of person as an ontological category was thus born.

---

[54] For a discussion of the links between the forms of doxology used and the evolution of trinitarian doctrine, see Zizioulas, "Contribution of Cappadocia," 38, and LaCugna, *God for Us*, 117–23.

[55] Zizioulas, "Contribution of Cappadocia," 26.

[56] Ibid., 27.

[57] There is evidence that even at this time Basil did not understand them as equivalent. See for example *The Nicene and Post-Nicene Fathers*, ed. Philip Schaff and Henry Wace (Grand Rapids, Mich.: Wm. B. Eerdmans, reprint 1979) 5:24.

[58] See LaCugna, *God for Us*, 68, for a further suggestion of interpreting of *ousia* in this context.

[59] See Basil Studer, *Trinity and Incarnation: The Faith of the Early Church* (Collegeville, Minn.: The Liturgical Press, 1993) 142–44. See also Joseph T. Lienhard, "The Cappadocian Settlement," in *The Trinity*, ed. Stephen Davis, Daniel Kendall, S.J., Gerald O'Collins, S.J. (Oxford: Oxford University Press, 1999) 99–109 for a more recent discussion of this formula.

Basil, recognizing the need to safeguard the distinct and ontologically integral existence of each of the persons of the Trinity, determined that the best way to speak of the unity of God was through the notion of *koinōnia*.[60] It was for this reason that he made the controversial move to use a doxology different from the one that prevailed during the early centuries, probably of Alexandrian origin: "Glory be to the Father through *(dia)* the Son in *(en)* the Holy Spirit." He preferred a doxology that he claimed was just as ancient as the first one: "Glory be to the Father with *(syn)* the Son, with *(syn)* the Holy Spirit."[61] Basil argued that the liturgical usage of this doxology, with the three persons placed next to each other without hierarchical distinction, reinforced the understanding that they are equal in honor. He also emphasized the idea that the oneness of God is to be found in the *koinōnia* of the three persons: "So ineffable and so far beyond our understanding are both the communion *(koinōnia)* and the distinctiveness *(dianerisis)* of the divine hypostases."[62]

Zizioulas points to the merit of this "*syn*-doxology," since it faithfully communicates the "co-presence and the co-existence of all three persons at once," and for him it illustrates the value of a theology inspired by the liturgy:

> The safest theology is that which draws not only from the Economy, but also, and perhaps mainly, from the vision of God as He appears in worship. The Cappadocian way of thinking is thus strongly present behind the Eastern preference for a meta-historical or eschatological approach to the mystery of God.[63]

A further critical issue that needed to be addressed during the years between the Council of Nicea (325) and the Council of Constantinople (381) was the question of the source of God's being. The biblical foundation of the Cappadocians' work meant that the identification of the source of God's being was with a person (the Father) rather than with a substance *(ousia)*. "By distinguishing carefully and persistently between the nature of God and God as the Father, they taught that *what causes God to be is the Person of the Father*."[64] The Father out of love freely

---

[60] See Zizioulas, "2nd Ecumenical Council," 35.

[61] See *De Spiritu Santo*, 1, 3f.0; 7, 16, quoted in Zizioulas, "2nd Ecumenical Council," 38.

[62] Zizioulas, "2nd Ecumenical Council," 40. Quoted from Basil's *Epistulae*, 38.

[63] Ibid.

[64] Zizioulas, "Contribution of Cappadocia," 32. For a strong critique of Zizioulas's reading of the personalism of the Cappadocians, see André de Halleux, "Personalisme ou essentialisme trinitaire chez les pères cappadociens? Une mauvaise controverse," *Revue théologique Louvain* 17 (1986) 129–55, 265–92. See also Gaëtan

begets the Son and brings forth the Spirit. Zizioulas stresses what he believes to be "an absolutely crucial point," namely, that "God as person —as the hypostasis of the Father—makes the one divine substance to be that which is the one God."[65] He wants to emphasize that the onto-logical principle of God is a person, that the being of God is identified with a person. The significance of this for Trinitarian theology is that God exists on account of a person, not on account of a substance.

The ground of God's ontological freedom, therefore, lies not in God's nature but in God's personal existence. It is precisely this, argues Zizioulas, that gives human beings the hope of becoming authentic persons. It is the ecstatic character of God, the fact that God's being is identical with an act of communion, that ensures freedom from onto-logical necessity. The Father as a person freely wills communion with the Spirit and the Son. Moreover, Zizioulas points out, it "thus becomes evident that the only exercise of freedom in an ontological manner is *love.* The expression 'God is love' (1 John 4:16) signifies that God 'sub-sists' as Trinity, that he is as person not as substance."[66] In this way love came to be identified with ontological freedom:

> Love is a *relationship,* it is the free coming out of oneself. . . . It is the other and our relationship with him that gives us our identity, our otherness, making us "who we are," i.e., persons; for by being an in-separable part of a relationship that matters ontologically we emerge as *unique* and *irreplaceable* entities. This therefore is what accounts for our being, and being ourselves and not someone else—our personhood.[67]

In language developed to speak about the triune God, *person* was thus conceived not as an adjunct to *being* but being itself, the very *con-stitutive element* of being. "By usurping, as it were, the ontological char-acter of *ousia,* the word *person/hypostasis* became capable of signifying God's being *in an ultimate sense.*"[68] In summary, then, Zizioulas argues

---

Baillargeon, *Perspectives orthodoxes sur l'Eglise-communion: l'oeuvre de Jean Zizioulas* (Montréal: Editions Paulines, 1989) 242–53, who suggests that these two different historical interpretations of the events and emphases following the councils of Nicea and Constantinople may not be so irreconcilable as de Halleux claims. Baillargeon's more nuanced reading of Zizioulas further suggests that the two different perspec-tives espoused (an emphasis on the significance on *person* versus an emphasis on *essence*) in fact represents the classic emphases adopted by the Eastern and Western traditions of Zizioulas and de Halleux respectively.

[65] Zizioulas, *Being as Communion,* 41.

[66] Ibid., 47.

[67] Zizioulas, "Contribution of Cappadocia," 34.

[68] Zizioulas, *Being as Communion,* 88.

that the struggle to find language to communicate the experience of the triune God of love generated a breakthrough in ontology. An entirely new concept was created—the concept of person. In searching to formulate a doctrine of God from the Christian communities' experience, theologians uncovered, in embryo, new understandings about humanity itself.

The Concept of Person for Humanity Today

One of the central convictions expressed in Zizioulas's theology is that understandings of God formulated by the Cappadocians have profound existential implications for humanity today. In order to explore further the basis of his passionate conviction, this section will investigate Zizioulas's elaboration of the ecstatic and hypostatic dimensions of personhood, his presentation of the significance of christology and pneumatology for freedom and personhood, and his understanding of the challenge that the theological concept of person can offer to contemporary expressions of the destructive phenomenon of "fear of the other."

Person as Ecstatic and Hypostatic

In a paper read initially at Oriel College, Oxford, in 1972, entitled "Human Capacity and Human Incapacity: A Theological Exploration of Personhood," Zizioulas explores how being a person is different from being an individual. He argues that in Western thought the historical evolution of a concept of person was derived from a combination of two basic components: *rational individuality* (Boethius) and *psychological experience and consciousness* (Augustine). Person came to be understood as an individual: "a unit endowed with intellectual, psychological and moral qualities centered on the axis of consciousness . . . an *autonomous self* who intends, thinks, decides, acts and produces results."[69] In stark contrast to this understanding of person, Zizioulas wants to reclaim for a contemporary world the patristic concept that developed from within Trinitarian theology. He argues that:

> being a person is basically different from being an individual or "personality" in that the person cannot be conceived in itself as a static identity, but only as it *relates to*. Thus personhood implies the "openness of being," and even more than that, the *ek-stasis* of being, i.e., a movement

[69] Zizioulas, "Human Capacity," 405–6.

toward communion which leads to a transcendence of the boundaries of the "self" and thus to freedom.[70]

This is an extraordinary claim from theology for the meaning and potential of person as a relational category. Zizioulas notes that such a claim is in harmony with other contemporary understandings of person.[71] He asserts that person cannot be understood only as the "ecstasy" of substance, by which he means "a movement toward communion which leads to transcendence of the boundaries of the 'self' and thus to freedom,"[72] but must also be understood as a *hypostasis* of substance, that is, as a particular identity. Thus for him, "*ekstasis* and *hypostasis* represent two basic aspects of Personhood . . . the idea of Person affirms at once that being cannot be 'contained' or 'divided,' and that the mode of its existence, *hypostasis*, is absolutely unique and unrepeatable."[73] Zizioulas emphasizes that theology, unlike philosophy, teaches an ontology that ensures the absolute and unique identity beyond even death. For all created entities death overcomes communion, but in the realm of the uncreated, within the triune God, life and communion coincide.[74] He argues that because life in God is personal—in communion—life is eternal:

> The eternal survival of the person as a unique, unrepeatable and free "hypostasis," as loving and being loved, constitutes the quintessence of salvation . . . this is called "divinisation" *(theosis)*, which means participation not in the nature or substance of God, but in His personal existence.[75]

Here Zizioulas arrives at a key point in his elaboration of the concept of person. He argues that "the goal of salvation is that the personal life which is realised in God should also be realised at the level of per-

---

[70] Ibid., 407–8. Zizioulas notes that the term *ek-stasis* used here is known mainly through the philosophy of Martin Heidegger but that the term was in fact used before him in patristic mystical writings (e.g., Pseudo-Dionysius and Maximus the Confessor).

[71] See Zizioulas, "Human Capacity," 408, where he mentions some representative examples of understandings of the person as a relational category— Martin Buber, *I and Thou*, trans. R. G. Smith (New York: Scribner, 1958); J. Macmurray, *Persons in Relation* (London: Faber and Faber, 1961), and *The Self as Agent* (London: Faber, 1969); W. Pannenberg's article "Person," in *Religion in Geschichte und Gegenwart*, 3rd ed. (Tübingen: J.C.B. Mohr, 1958) 5:230–235.

[72] Zizioulas, "Human Capacity," 408.

[73] Ibid.

[74] See Zizioulas, "The 2nd Ecumenical Council," 53.

[75] Zizioulas, *Being as Communion*, 49–50.

sonal existence." From this he comes to the significant conclusion that "salvation is identified with the realisation of personhood."[76] He is saying that to become fully a person, ecstatically and hypostatically, is to break through the isolating boundaries of individualism into a life of inclusive communion with persons valued for their uniqueness and differences. Coming to complete fullness can only happen in a final way in God *(theōsis)*. Arriving at full personhood in this way, he says, is what it means to be "saved."

Zizioulas claims that this essentially theological understanding of person, besides holding deeply religious meaning, has practical, existential implications for contemporary life. It is difficult to disagree with this claim. Clearly, if it were a universally held truth that becoming fully a person in love and freedom meant a breaking through the narrow boundaries of individualism into a life of valued difference in communion, the world would be a vastly different place from what it is today. Such an understanding of person would radically affect how the peoples of this planet would live together, and indeed how they would together live in relation to all creation. This essentially theological understanding of person as elaborated by Zizioulas from patristic theology, if "received" by contemporary cultures, could hold very practical implications for human societies of the future.

Zizioulas develops this understanding of person further when he argues that since this notion of person is to be found only in God, human personhood is never satisfied with itself until it becomes an *imago Dei*.[77] Human persons, he says, are called to exist in the way God exists. Living according to his or her *nature* leads the human person to individualism and finally to mortality, whereas living according to the image of God as a *person in communion* leads to *theōsis* (becoming God). Both for God and human beings, "personal identity emerges only from the exercise of love as freedom and of freedom as love."[78]

This radical, biblical, ecclesial vision of persons in communion, which will be explored in greater detail in the following two chapters, is shown by Zizioulas to be intrinsically related to the triune God. His theological vision is founded on the premise that the relational link between God and humanity is in the person: "A personal relationship between created and uncreated cannot happen unless there exists from both sides the characteristics of a person."[79] The persons of the Trinity thus provide a basis for the meaning of the human person:

---

[76] Ibid.
[77] Zizioulas, "Human Capacity," 410–11.
[78] Zizioulas, "Contribution of Cappadocia," 35.
[79] Pergamon, *"To einai tou Theou,"* 27.

> What gives us an identity that does not die is not our nature but our personal relationship with God's undying identity. Only when nature is hypostatic or personal, as is the case with God, does it exist truly and eternally. For it is only then that it acquires uniqueness and becomes an unrepeatable and irreplaceable particularity in the "mode of being" which we find in the Trinity.[80]

This vision provides enormous practical possibilities and implications for the life of the Church in the third millennium. In a period when chaos and uncertainty are a primary and constant experience for so many on this planet, it offers a dynamic vision of personhood and freedom for a future life that begins in the present.

But what about those who do not reach this "mode of being"? This theological vision of personhood could be interpreted to mean that becoming a person and attaining freedom are possible only for those who believe in God and for those who are initiated into the life and worship of the Christian community. However, that is not how I interpret Zizioulas's work. A hermeneutical key to this theology is the Council of Chalcedon (451). Georges Florovsky has noted, "One can evolve the whole body of Orthodox belief out of the Dogma of Chalcedon."[81] If one takes into account the fact that the teaching of this council is at the heart of Orthodox theology and is a central plank in Zizioulas's whole theological vision, a more inclusive interpretation is suggested. This teaching holds that when, in Christ, God became a human being, and uncreated being became one with all created being in a way that there was no mixing or confusion, it became possible for all creation to be "saved." Zizioulas describes this as the capacity to attain full personhood and freedom for eternity.

Initiation into the Christian ecclesial community provides a vision of how this process of coming to freedom and personhood (which in theological terms is also called the process of *divinization*) can be fully enacted. It does not follow, however, as every Christian well knows, that persons who set out on this path arrive at this state of personhood and freedom. Nor does it follow that those who do not choose this particular path are doomed to individualism and mortality. Because of the union effected between humanity and divinity in Christ, the fullness of life is made possible for each human person.

---

[80] John D. Zizioulas, "The Doctrine of the Holy Trinity: The Significance of the Cappadocian Contribution," in *The Trinity Today*, ed. Christoph Schwöbel (Edinburgh: T&T Clark, 1996) 58.

[81] Georges Florovsky, "Patristic Theology and the Ethos of the Orthodox Church," in *Aspects of Church History: Collected Works* (Belmont: Nordland, 1975) 4:24.

In the broadest sense, I believe Zizioulas's articulation of the ecstatic and hypostatic dimensions of personhood can offer direction and hope to all persons who seek to build communion between other persons and with nature. It rings true to a contemporary experience of personhood. It also offers a challenge to the Church in its relationship to the world and to contemporary culture. In speaking about an ethos that the Church can offer to the world, Zizioulas has referred to the prayer from the Divine Liturgy of St. John Chrysostom: "Thine own of Thine own we offer Thee, in all and for all."[82] This suggests that the Church, which Zizioulas believes is most fully itself at the Eucharist, is a sacrament for the world. It is meant to be like a "light on a lampstand" (Matt 5:15) that can reveal what is already there—the *eschaton,* wherein communion is complete—for all of humanity and for all of creation.

Freedom and Personhood "in Christ" and "in the Spirit"

Zizioulas's central concern about the issue of freedom is linked to the question of how a person can be constituted in an ontological reality that is not limited by createdness and therefore by ontological necessity. To address this issue, he turns to patristic christology to show how it is "in Christ" that the human pull to personhood can be fulfilled.[83] He argues that the ultimate challenge to the freedom of the person is the necessity of existence. Here he is referring to the phenomenon of existential angst that arises from the experience "*that* I exist." This is a fundamental human experience that has been described by the mystics throughout the ages.[84] Contemporary mystical theologian William Johnson reflects on it thus:

> One can experience one's incompleteness emotionally or economically or culturally or sexually; and all this is painful. But how terrible to experience it at the deepest level of all, that of existence! For all these other sorrows are partial experiences of one root experience of existential contingency. And this, I believe, is the sorrow of the man who knows not only *what he is* but *that he is.*[85]

---

[82] See for example, Metropolitan John (Zizioulas) of Pergamon, "Ethics Versus Ethos: An Orthodox Approach to the Relation Between Ecology and Ethics," in *The Environment and Ethics: Presentations and Reports, Summer Session on Halki '95,* ed. Deuteron Tarasios (Militos Editions, 1997) 26.

[83] See Pergamon, *"To einai tou Theou,"* 28–30.

[84] See, for example, *The Cloud of Unknowing and the Book of Privy Counselling,* ed. William Johnston, S.J. (New York: Image Books, 1973) ch. 44.

[85] Ibid., 12.

Zizioulas believes that a human person who can do no other than accept his or her existence—*that* she or he is—is not really free. To illustrate this point, he refers to a powerful example from Dostoevsky's *The Possessed*, where Kirilov argues that "every man who desires to attain total freedom must be bold enough to end his life."[86] Zizioulas sees this dilemma as an expression of the tragic side of the quest toward personhood. He is interested, however, in the positive pull that exists within this—the challenge that consists in the possibility of affirming one's existence, not as an inevitable recognition of a given fact, but freely, as an affirmation of self. This, says Zizioulas, is what ultimate freedom as a person means. And it is this, he suggests, that a theology of God can reveal:

> Philosophy can arrive at the confirmation of the reality of the person, but only theology can treat of the genuine, the authentic person, because the authentic person, as absolute ontological freedom, must be "uncreated," that is, unbounded by any "necessity," including its own existence. If such a person does not exist in reality, the concept of person is a presumptuous daydream.[87]

In order to arrive at this "absolute ontological freedom," says Zizioulas, a person needs to be initiated into a way of being that "does not suffer from createdness." According to Zizioulas, that is the meaning of the phrase in John's Gospel about being born "anew," "from above" (John 3:3, 7), and it is this that patristic christology teaches is the good news.[88] It is thus that christology gives the assurance to humanity that the impulse toward personhood is not toward a mask or a tragic figure but toward historical reality.

> Jesus Christ does not justify the title of saviour because he brings the world a beautiful revelation, a sublime teaching about the person, but because He realises in history *the very reality of the person* and makes it the basis and "hypostasis" of the person of every man.[89]

The answer being proposed is thus to be found in the historical reality of Jesus Christ.

The person of Christ according to post-Chalcedonian theology is *one* and is identified with the hypostasis of the Son in the Trinity. In Christ the hypostatic union is a union of two natures, divine and human.

[86] See Zizioulas, *Being as Communion*, 42.
[87] Ibid., 43.
[88] Ibid., 54.
[89] Ibid.

Christology is the assurance to the human person that her or his nature can be "assumed" and hypostasized in a manner free from ontological necessity and that her or his existence can be affirmed as personal on the basis of a relationship with God in Christ. The unity of the human and the divine that was effected in Christ means that the human person is now capable of the freedom and love that exist within the communion of Godself.[90] Because of the incarnation, the human person is capable of eternal life.

Zizioulas argues that the significance of christology springs not simply from each person's individual relationship with Christ, who becomes a model for imitation, but rather from the fact that Christ constitutes the ontological ground of every person. In Christ every woman, child, and man may be saved from the fate of being separated individual entities, and personhood may be restored. It is for this reason that Zizioulas holds that christology must "de-individualize" Christ so that its relevance to anthropology can be recognized and fully valued.[91] This has relevance for all of humanity, but for those baptized into Christ it offers a specific path to life.

When exploring this christological vision, Zizioulas is quick to add that in order for this perspective to be preserved, christology's roots in pneumatology must always be acknowledged. He argues that there is nothing more unbiblical than starting to consider the Holy Spirit only after the figure of Christ has been completed, since the biblical accounts show Christ being constituted by the Holy Spirit. The Spirit should thus not be seen just an assistant to each individual in reaching Christ but as the means by which the person is participant in Christ. Zizioulas argues that it is impossible to obtain any clue to the relation between each human being and Christ in the Spirit "unless the individual dies as such and rises as a person."[92] Being *in* the Spirit brings humanity *into* Christ.

Thus for personhood to be realized, what has been realized in Christ through the hypostatic union needs to happen in each human being. That is the action of the Spirit. As Paul describes in his letters, each one becomes a person by "putting on Christ." Zizioulas adds to this insight by stating:

> And this is what makes Christ the head of a new humanity (or creation) in that he is the first one both chronologically and ontologically to open

---

[90] See ibid., 55–56.
[91] Zizioulas, "Human Capacity," 441.
[92] Ibid., 442.

this possibility of personhood in which the distance of individuals is turned into the communion of persons.[93]

He proposes that it is only through personhood, which involves communion as well as integrity of being, that God and human persons can be clearly distinguished from one another, precisely by affirming their distinct entities in communion. It is in Christ and through the Spirit that God and humanity are united in a communion that clearly posits the identity of each nature.[94]

Persons as "Difference in Communion"

A further existential implication of being in Christ is that difference no longer predicates division but communion. This important insight is developed further by Zizioulas in a paper entitled "Communion and Otherness," delivered to the eighth Orthodox Congress in Western Europe held in Blankenberge, Belgium, in 1993. On that occasion he identified the whole question of the *other* to be a major existential concern within a post-modern Western world. He underlined the seriousness of this issue by suggesting to his fellow Orthodox Christians that:

> fear of the other is pathologically inherent in our existence [and] results in the fear not only of the other but of *all otherness*. . . . We are afraid not simply of a certain other or others, but, even if we accept certain others, we accept them on condition that they are somehow like ourselves. Radical otherness is anathema. Difference itself is a threat.[95]

Thus fear of the other and fear of otherness lead to identifying difference as a cause of division. Personhood, by contrast, perceives difference to be a vital element for any true communion.

This insight connects into a particular dimension of Trinitarian theology. In his address "Communion and Otherness," Zizioulas shows how the triune God provides a model for the proper relation between communion and otherness for both humanity and the Church.[96] He points out that a study of the doctrine of the Trinity reveals that "otherness is *constitutive* of unity, and not consequent upon it. God is not first one and then three, but simultaneously One and Three."[97] Zizioulas

---

[93] Ibid.

[94] Ibid., 447.

[95] Metropolitan John (Zizioulas), "Communion and Otherness," *St. Vladimir's Theological Quarterly* 38, no. 4 (1994) 349–50.

[96] See Zizioulas, "Communion and Otherness," 352.

[97] Ibid., 353.

suggests that it further reveals that otherness in the Trinity is absolute. "The Father, the Son and the Spirit are absolutely different (*diaphora*, none of them being subject to confusion with the other two)." Moreover, and "most significantly," he suggests that in God it is possible for otherness or the particular to be *ontological:* "Each Person in the Holy Trinity is different not by way of difference of qualities but by way of simple affirmation of being who He is."[98]

In another essay published a little earlier (1991), Zizioulas had argued that it is possible for the particular to be ontologically ultimate because of the continual communion between Father, the Son, and the Spirit.[99] Because this relationship is permanent and unbreakable, there is no contradiction between the "one" and the "many." Thus "the particular is raised to the level of ontological primacy, it emerges as being itself," and relationship constitutes an indispensable ontological ingredient.[100] Zizioulas concludes that:

> otherness is inconceivable apart from *relationship*. Father, Son and Spirit are names indicating relationship. No Person can be different unless He is related. Communion does not threaten otherness, rather, it generates it.[101]

Thus relationship is the basis of personhood, and the Trinity, which can be described as an event of communion, is a true source for understanding all relationships and the "other" in relation. Difference is the locus of the Spirit's work, and it is in a lived communion that the uniqueness and difference of each entity are found to be able to come to their full potential and creativity:

> The mystery of being a person lies in the fact that here otherness and communion are not in contradiction but coincide. Truth as communion does not lead to the dissolving of the diversity of beings into one vast ocean of being, but to the affirmation of otherness in and through love.[102]

Zizioulas thus claims that a significant manifestation of the move from individuality to personhood in Christ through the Spirit is the shift in

---

[98] Ibid.

[99] See Zizioulas, "On Being a Person," 41, n. 16. Zizioulas refers here to sources of the basic patristic teaching, which holds that wherever one person of the Trinity is, the others are there too.

[100] Ibid.

[101] Zizioulas, "Communion and Otherness," 353.

[102] Zizioulas, *Being as Communion,* 106.

human beings from seeing *difference* as a source of division to recognizing it as an intrinsic value and as a means of communion. The implications of this insight are enormous. If difference were truly valued by
the various Christian Churches, ecumenism would have an entirely
different face. If one did a thought experiment whereby the peoples of
the world recognized difference of all kinds as an asset instead of a liability, the repercussions would be immense. Imagine what might happen just in the area of race relations in Israel, in Africa, in Australia, in
so many countries of the world.

It is from such conclusions that Zizioulas moves to define love in
ontological terms. Referring to Paul's hymn to love in 1 Corinthians 13
he claims:

> Love is not simply a virtue; it is an ontological category, not simply an
> ethical one. Love is that which will survive into the "age which does
> not end or grow old" when all the gifts which impress us today, such as
> knowledge, prophecy, etc., will pass away.[103]

He speaks of love replacing the ontology of *ousia*, thus attributing to
love the role formerly attributed to substance in classical ontology. He
defines love as a "relationship creating absolute and unique identities."[104] His emphasis on the enduring nature of each person's unique
identity opens up further understandings of what life in the triune God
can mean. It indicates that each person's communion within God does
not involve the surrender or diminishment of the person's uniqueness
but rather enables that uniqueness to come to full fruition. It also suggests that in death personal identity is not relinquished into "the great
matrix of being," as some would propose.[105] On the contrary, Zizioulas
stresses that God and humanity are so united in Christ that the uniqueness of human persons will endure with the divine persons for eternity.

Conclusions

Zizioulas believes that personhood is about the claim to *uniqueness*
in the absolute sense of the term. It is not about qualities or capacities of
any kind—biological, social, or moral. His whole thesis on the ontology
of person rests on the fact that absolute uniqueness is created by the

---

[103] Metropolitan John (Zizioulas) of Pergamon, "The Eucharist and the Kingdom
of God—(Part III)," *Sourozh* (1995) 40.

[104] Zizioulas, "On Being a Person," 42.

[105] See Rosemary Radford Ruether's thesis on personal eschatology in *Sexism
and God-Talk: Toward a Feminist Theology* (Boston: Beacon Press, 1983) 256–58.

continuity of unbroken relationship. Relationships of genuine love are therefore the proper context for the experience of an ontology of personhood. He argues that the more one loves ontologically and truly personally, the less dependent is such loving on the particular qualities of the person loved. Both in the case of the triune God and the human person, the identity of a person emerges through relationship: "This hypostatic fullness as otherness can emerge only through a relationship so constitutive ontologically that relating is not consequent upon being but is being itself."[106] The basis of such an ontology is thus located in an understanding of a personal God whose being is communion in love.

Zizioulas believes that for the Christian, baptism into the ecclesial community is the primary way of enabling personhood in Christ and the Spirit to come to fruition. The ultimate fullness of ecclesial hypostasis, however, continues to be limited by the boundaries of biological hypostasis. Only when death ceases to be "natural" will humanity experience the true ontology of the person. In the meantime the human person seeks to be freed from the necessity of nature by experiencing sacramentally the "new being" as a member of the eucharistic ecclesial community.[107]

In summary, it may be said that John Zizioulas's Trinitarian theology teaches that there is no true being without communion. His vision of the triune God is essentially a vision of persons-in-communion. It is particularly the concept of person arising from Trinitarian theology and his consequent understanding of relation as an ontological category that Zizioulas offers to the contemporary existential quest for the full meaning of personhood and freedom.[108] If the triune God is understood most fundamentally as "persons in communion," then the concept of person certainly is humanity's "most dear and precious good." Such a vision elucidated by Zizioulas not only opens life-giving understandings of the potential of human personhood and freedom that endures eternally, but it also reveals a dynamic and thrilling vision of God. God disclosed as "persons in communion" reveals a totally shared personal life at the heart of the universe.[109] It is my argument that if such a vision, such a symbol of God, were offered to the peoples

---

[106] Zizioulas, "On Being a Person," 46.

[107] Ibid., 43–44.

[108] See, for example, a collection of essays, including a contribution from Zizioulas, in *Persons, Divine, and Human: King's College Essays in Theological Anthropology*, ed. Christoph Schwöbel and Colin Gunton for the Research Institute in Systematic Theology (Edinburgh: T&T Clark, 1991).

[109] See Johnson, *SHE WHO IS*, 222.

of the world through the lives of credible Christian communities, universally and locally, it could conceivably sustain a humanity capable of enabling a peaceful, creative future life on this planet.

While Zizioulas's Trinitarian theology of persons in communion is unambiguously the center point or source of his whole theological system, it incorporates within it, as essential elements, not only an anthropology, christology, and pneumatology, as this chapter has shown, but also an ecclesiology and a cosmology. It is his cosmology—his theology of creation—that will be the primary focus of the next chapter. Zizioulas argues for the necessity for Christianity (the Church) to create an "ethos," arising from a theology of the triune God, by means of which humanity could both discover and be enabled to sustain its dynamic interconnectedness with all creation.

CHAPTER 3

God and Creation

The entire universe is a liturgy, a cosmic liturgy which offers the whole creation before the throne of God.[1]

Thine own of Thine own we offer Thee, in all and for all.[2]

John Zizioulas's election as a member of the Ecumenical Patriarchate of Constantinople and his ordination as Metropolitan of Pergamon in 1986 led to his being more specifically involved in leadership of the Churches of the Orthodox tradition. In the wake of the Seventh Assembly of the World Council of Churches in 1991, with its theme "Come Holy Spirit, Renew the Whole Creation" and the election of His All Holiness Bartholomew as Ecumenical Patriarch, the patriarchate has undertaken a significant public leadership role in drawing attention to the ecological crisis. It has also actively engaged environmentalists, lawyers, scientists, politicians, educators, and other experts in dialogue with theology and the Christian faith in order to address the issue.[3] When speaking to a plenary of the European Parliament in Strasbourg in 1994, Patriarch Bartholomew offered the conviction that:

[1] John Zizioulas, "La vision eucharistique du monde et l'homme contemporain," *Contacts* 19 (1967) 83.

[2] From the Divine Liturgy of St. John Chrysostom.

[3] In the early 1990s, the Ecumenical Patriarchate collaborated with the World Wide Fund for Nature to inaugurate a series of summer seminars designed to promote awareness and action on the environment. The first seminar held in 1994 was entitled "The Environment and Religious Education." In 1995 the topic was "The

the ecological problem of our times demands a radical evaluation of our understanding of how we see the entire world; it demands another interpretation of matter and the world; another perception of the attitude of humankind towards nature, and another understanding of how we acquire and make use of our material goods. Within the measure of our spiritual capacity, the Orthodox Church and theology endeavor to contribute to the necessary dialogue concerning this problem.[4]

Zizioulas's theological contribution to this still-developing initiative of the Orthodox Church has been significant, and it provides a context for the focus of this chapter—his theology of creation.

Zizioulas's theology of creation is most comprehensively spelled out in the lecture series entitled "Preserving God's Creation" and delivered at King's College, London, in January 1989. Other sources include papers he has given on the environmental crisis in connection with the various initiatives taken by the Ecumenical Patriarchate to bring the spiritual and theological dimensions of this issue into the public arena.[5] These all reveal that Zizioulas's vision for an ecologically sustainable world leads to the heart of his Trinitarian theology.

Environment and Ethics," in 1996 "The Environment and Communication," and in 1997 "The Environment and Justice." The participants, numbering each time between fifty and sixty, came from many places, including Europe, the United States, Asia, and Africa, and represented not only Orthodox Churches but also many other major Christian denominations and world faiths, Church-related and environmental organizations, as well as international and local professionals in the various disciplines concerned. Each seminar also included young theologians and environmentalists. In 1995 these same two bodies cooperated to organize a symposium entitled "Revelation and Environment (95–1995 A.D.)" on the island of Patmos. The focus was on the world's seas and oceans. In 1997 "Religions, Science and the Environment—Symposium 11: The Black Sea in Crisis" gathered 150 experts from the fields of religion, science, and environmental management. They participated in an eight-day voyage that included visits to ports in Turkey, Bulgaria, Romania, Ukraine, Russia, Georgia, and Thessaloniki. Metropolitan John (Zizioulas) of Pergamon played a key role as theologian in these initiatives.

[4] Deuteron Tarasios, ed., *The Environment and Ethics: Presentations and Reports, Summer on Halki '95* (Militos Editions, 1997) 35–36.

[5] Metropolitan of Pergamon, "Orthodoxy and Ecological Problems: A Theological Approach," in *The Environment and Religious Education,* ed. Deuteron Tarasios (Militos Editions, 1997) 26–30; Pergamon, "Ethics Versus Ethos: An Orthodox Approach to the Relation Between Ecology and Ethics," in Tarasios, *The Environment and Ethics,* 25–27; Pergamon, "The Environment and Justice: A Theological Approach," my own notes from an unpublished keynote address delivered on June 26, 1997, to the summer session on Halki, entitled "The Environment and Justice."

A Eucharistic Vision of Creation

Zizioulas's very first post-doctoral publication, "The Eucharistic Vision of the World and Contemporary Humanity," was an address he gave under that title to a congress held in Thessalonika in 1966 on the theme "The Orthodox Church and the World." This initial work demonstrates that from the outset Zizioulas has been concerned to reveal the connections between theology and life, particularly contemporary life. He criticizes the dualism of Western theology, which has accepted the separation between the sacred and the secular, and acknowledges that this flaw has crept into Orthodoxy. He argues that it is the liturgy that provides the basis for a positive approach to the world and creation. Within the liturgy the faithful offer the gifts of creation—bread and wine—to God as Eucharist (thanksgiving), and this represents, he claims, a journey of cosmic dimensions. Quoting Ignatius of Antioch, he describes liturgy as a "remedy of immortality," since it ensures that all that has been created can be transformed into its full potential by being brought into God's life:

> This acceptance of the world through the liturgy shows that within a liturgical vision of creation, the world never ceases to be *God's cosmos*. It shows . . . that all that we are, all that we do, all that interests us in the world can and needs to pass through the hands of the celebrant as an offering to God. Not so that it remains as it is, but so that it no longer refrains from being what it is at depth. So that it *becomes* what it *truly* is. . . .[6]

Zizioulas insists that within this liturgical vision of the world, the distinction between natural and supernatural does not exist. The identification between celestial reality and earthly reality means that God ceases to be understood as "beyond" nature. In the person of the Son, God is recognized to be present *with us*. In a similar way, Zizioulas claims that within a eucharistic vision of the world, the dichotomy between time and eternity ceases to exist and that the unity of the past, the present, and the future enables a complete acceptance of the sanctification of time and of history.[7]

In this initial description of his theological vision, Zizioulas also underlines the organic connection between the moral life and a vision of the transfiguration and renewal of creation and humanity *in Christ*. Within such a vision, morality does not consist in a system of legalities and rules; rather, it flows from an ongoing insertion into this religious understanding of the universe and of all reality. Morality is thus perceived to

---

[6] Zizioulas, "Vision eucharistique," 86.
[7] See ibid., 87.

be a consequence of a sacramental transfiguration and an *invitation* into the freedom of the children of God, who continues to bring about the transformation needed.[8] Here, in his early work, Zizioulas links freedom to relationship between persons. Having asked why Christianity has so little to offer the contemporary world, he suggests, with some angst, that it is because Christians offer the world moral dictums, believing that it is sufficient to speak to the world to change it: "We forget that the *Logos* is not words but a *Person;* it is not a voice, but a living presence which is incarnated in the Eucharist, a Eucharist which is above all a gathering and a communion."[9]

The Human Person, Creation, and the Ecological Crisis

Over twenty years later, Zizioulas's began his lecture series on the ecological crisis by stating that this crisis is about "the *very being* of humanity and perhaps of creation as a whole."[10] He agrees with commentators from many disciplines when he warns that if "we follow the present course of events, the prediction of the apocalyptic end of life on our planet at least, is not a matter of prophecy but of sheer inevitability."[11] Zizioulas, however, does not presume that the gravity of the situation will of itself elicit a reasonable response from humankind, because he does not believe that the answer can be found in rationalism:

> People do not give up their standards of living because such a thing is "rational" or "moral." By appealing to human reason we do not necessarily make people better, while moral rules, especially after their dislocation from religious beliefs, prove to be more and more meaningless and unpleasant to modern man.[12]

Zizioulas argues that it is useless to address this urgent task by placing hope in rational and ethical solutions, as Western societies have sought to do. He notes the loss of much of the mythological, the imaginative, and the sacred in the post-Enlightenment world of the West and suggests that what is needed is "a new culture in which the *liturgical dimension* would occupy the central place and perhaps determine the ethical principle."[13]

[8] See ibid., 89–90.

[9] Ibid., 90.

[10] Zizioulas, "Preserving God's Creation: Three Lectures on Theology and Ecology," *King's Theological Review* 12 (1989) 1–5 (hereafter "Creation I"), here 1.

[11] Ibid.

[12] Ibid.

[13] Ibid., 2.

An understanding of the human person as essentially a relational being is central to Zizioulas's constructive vision of the future of the universe. In his address to the first summer seminar on Halki he stated:

> The human being is not an individual but a person, and there is a big difference. An individual is a single entity which can be conceived of in itself without reference to other entities. A person is a unique entity which cannot be conceived of without relation to other entities, not only other humans but to nature as a whole. . . . We should relate to nature not as individuals standing separately but as partakers of nature.[14]

Zizioulas believes that the human person has a key role in creation because she or he has the capacity "to *relate* in such a way as to create events of communion whereby individual beings are liberated from their self-centeredness and thus from their limitations."[15] The individual beings he is referring to here mean all created entities. His vision is that everything is created to find its fulfilment by transcending itself and by coming to completion in God. In order for this to be able to happen, Zizioulas argues that each human person needs to fulfil her or his role as "priest of creation."[16] Zizioulas is aware that "priesthood" can hold pejorative connotations and hastens to clarify that his intention in using this term is to focus on it "carrying with it the characteristic of 'offering,' in the sense of opening up particular beings to a transcending relatedness with the 'other'—an idea more or less corresponding to that of love in the deepest sense."[17]

That is a very powerful concept. It suggests that humanity has a key role in liberating the universe by means of the human person's capacity for transcending relationships. It presumes that there exists an interdependence between humanity and nature and that the human

---

[14] Pergamon, "Orthodoxy and Ecological Problems," 28.

[15] See also John Zizioulas, "Ordination—A Sacrament? An Orthodox Reply," *Concilium* 4 (1972) 35, where Zizioulas makes it clear that relationship "should not be understood in the sense of an abstract and logical *relatio,* but as having a deeply and existential and soteriological meaning."

[16] Zizioulas, "Creation I," 2. Reference to the human person as "priest of creation" first appears much earlier in John Zizioulas; see "Ordination and Communion," *Study Encounter* 6 (1970) 188, 192; also "Human Capacity and Human Incapacity: A Theological Exploration of Personhood," *Scottish Journal of Theology* (1975) 435; "Eucharistic Prayer and Life," *Emmanuel* 85 (1979) 194–95. For a further use of this term, see also A. R. Peacocke in *Creation and the World of Science: The Bampton Lectures 1978* (Oxford: Clarendon Press, 1979) 295–97.

[17] Zizioulas, "Creation I," 2.

person comes to fulfillment and true freedom by becoming the catalyst through which nature, too, is set free from its incompleteness by being brought into communion with other created entities and with God. To convey the full theological meaning of this role, Zizioulas uses the term *anakephalaiosis* ("recapitulation"), which was developed by Irenaeus, the second-century bishop of Lyons. "Bringing to communion" in this context, therefore, does not just mean that humanity brings about a basic relatedness or connection between all the entities of the universe, but rather that in Christ, humanity itself comes to completion by both participating in and enabling a communion of deep, life-giving love within creation.[18]

Zizioulas's answer to *how* this mandate is to be accomplished is that "man has to become a liturgical being before he can hope to overcome his ecological crisis."[19] To the ears of a citizen of a Western postmodernist world, this sounds like a strange remedy indeed! Such an epigrammatic claim (obscured further for many by its sexist expression) needs some serious elaboration if it is to yield the prophetic vision it contains.

Humanity as Priest of Creation

Zizioulas emphasizes that the early theologians taught explicitly that nothing at all existed previous to creation and that no factor whatsoever, apart from God's free intention, contributed to the creation of the world. He reminds us that Christian theology had to make it clear that time and space are categories that came into being together with creation. Space and time are thus understood to determine the world existentially and mark the difference between God and the world, created and uncreated being.[20]

---

[18] Note here that Zizioulas is drawing from the Irenaean tradition through the lens of Maximus the Confessor. The latter taught that humanity, restored in Christ, has a mediating role with the created universe in all its differentiation. Humanity may thus "reintegrate the whole universe and finally bring it into permanent salvific relationship with its Creator." See Lars Thunberg, "The Human Person as Image of God: Eastern Christianity," *Christian Spirituality: Origins to the Twelfth Century,* ed. B. McGinn, J. Meyendorff, and J. Leclerq (New York: Crossroad, 1986) 297, 304, 308. For another perspective of humanity's ultimate and "salvific" relationship with creation, see also Mary Clark, "Inquiry into Personhood," *Review of Metaphysics* 46 (1992) 22.

[19] Zizioulas, "Creation I," 2.

[20] Zizioulas, "Preserving God's Creation: Three Lectures on Theology and Ecology," *King's Theological Review* 12 (1989) 41–45 (hereafter "Creation II"), here 43.

Ancient liturgies, most notably those in the East, included the notion of the sanctification of matter and time. The emphasis in these liturgies was not on the salvation of the individual soul but on the "event of communion with other members of the worshiping community and with the material context of the liturgy."[21] As well as focusing on the offering of the bread and wine, the liturgies were connected with the seasonal conditions, and the physical senses of the participants were actively engaged in the rituals. Zizioulas observes that the earliest eucharistic prayers of the Church, while carrying a Greek sense of the goodness of creation, also include a blessing of the fruits of the earth in ways typical of the Hebrew tradition. They convey a faith in the survival of nature and the survival of humanity.

This liturgical evidence shows that nature occupied a central place in the early Church's consciousness. Zizioulas draws attention to the difference of this stance from paganism, which believed that nature self-perpetuated itself eternally. The liturgies of the early Church, he suggests, demonstrate a belief that creation would only survive if it was "referred to the eternal and unperishable Creator."[22] For that reason humanity, as a liturgical being with the capacity to bring about this act of communion, was deemed to be responsible for the survival of nature. In Christian cosmology the world had no guarantee of survival other than being in communion with *"what is not world by nature . . . namely God as understood in the Bible."*[23] Zizioulas concludes that since it was believed that nature cannot attain this communion by itself, the crucial point in the survival of a contingent world was understood to rest "in the act or the event of its communion with God as totally other than the world."[24]

Zizioulas draws attention to the centrality of the action of the anaphora, or "the lifting up," within the eucharistic liturgies. He argues that this action, whereby humanity gives thanks and offers the gifts of creation to God, is of equal importance to God's act of sending down the Holy Spirit to transform the gifts into the body and blood of Christ.[25] He notes that the ancient naming of this central sacrament as "Eucharist" draws attention to the significance of this practice. To similar effect, the Eucharistic Prayer or Canon of ancient liturgies always

---

[21] Zizioulas, "Creation I," 4.

[22] Ibid., 3.

[23] Ibid.

[24] Ibid.

[25] The Offertory prayers of the Roman Missal containing the restored liturgy of the Eucharist in the post-Vatican II reforms provide an example of this practice reclaimed.

began with thanksgiving for *creation,* and only after this was thanksgiving offered for redemption through Christ. It is here that Zizioulas argues that the priestly aspect of the Eucharist "did not consist in the notion of sacrifice as it came to be understood in the Middle Ages, but in that *offering* back to God His own creation."[26]

In a much earlier address, given in the mid-seventies for the Societas Liturgica, Zizioulas had elaborated more fully his understanding of the action of the anaphora as a function of the priestly role of humanity. He argued:

> It is through its being opened up to infinite existence that creation can overcome the fragmentation and decomposition which leads to the phenomenon of death. In so doing man does nothing but what Christ did as true Adam: he becomes a *priest.* Priesthood is thus identical with offering, with anaphora, not with offering a sacrifice in the senses of self-deprivation or substitution, but in the sense of allowing all that exists in a limited and finite way to enter into the limitless and infinite existence of God. . . . When the church lifts up the gifts of creation, all created existence opens up to the infinite and the hands of the human person become the instruments of eternal life for the entire cosmos.[27]

It is this dimension of priesthood, developed in the early Church, that Zizioulas wants to recover and restore as a way of addressing the ecological problem in our time.

Consistent with his conviction that theology must be situated within the existential quests of humanity in the modern world,[28] Zizioulas identifies two recent intellectual forces—the theory of evolution and the development of quantum mechanics—which he welcomes for having acted as life-giving antibodies to this serious sickness of the modern era. Darwinism, he suggests, has had the salutary effect of placing the human being back to its organic place in nature, while natural philosophy through Einstein and the subsequent schools of quantum physics have signaled the end of the dichotomy between substance and event:

---

[26] Zizioulas, "Creation I," 5. See also A. M. Allchin, in *Man and Nature,* ed. H. W. Montefiore (London: Collins, 1975) 148–49, who describes the Byzantine Liturgy as "an offering of the world to God by man, it is a passing over; in no sense a static thing, but rather a movement from this world to the world to come, from earth to heaven . . . the whole of mankind and indeed the whole universe is conceived to be in some way associated with this movement of offering, this coming to God."

[27] Zizioulas, "The Eucharistic Prayer and Life," *Emmanuel* 85 (1979) 194–95.

[28] See Zizioulas, *Being as Communion,* 26.

Everything that *is* at the same time *happens,* space and time coinciding with one another. The world itself is an event, and cannot be conceived apart from an *act*, one might say a ritual that takes place all the time. In addition, we have the blow on the subject-object structure dealt by quantum mechanics. The observer and the observed form an unbreakable unity, the one influencing the other. The universe in its remotest parts is present in every single part of it.[29]

Zizioulas rejoices that through these developments in the biological and natural sciences, the human being is reinstated to an integral, connected place in creation. He also underscores the urgent need for theology to engage creatively with these scientific developments, and he embarks on this process himself by drawing from the liturgical tradition of the ancient Church.

Zizioulas's re-reading of the tradition focuses on the role that humanity is destined to play through its relationship with creation. For him, this provides the key to how the ecological dilemma is to be addressed. I do not interpret this to mean that he believes that creation does not already have an ongoing relationship with God and that it is somehow dependent on humanity to establish it. Such an interpretation would fail to take account of the significance of the teachings of Chalcedon that are so central to Orthodox theology and to emphases within Zizioulas's own work that illustrate the importance of this teaching. My understanding is that his focus is on the stark existential question of what can address the crisis of planet Earth at risk. His "solution," predictably perhaps, is found at the core of his theological belief. He argues that "it is only by destroying false individualism and replacing it with personhood, i.e., a sense of being in communion with nature, that we can hope to overcome our ecological problems."[30] As mentioned above, he holds no hope that rationality or morality will enable humanity to make the kind of radical changes needed to save the planet. He seeks a more primordial motivation and finds this in humanity's role as priest of creation. His re-reading of the doctrine of creation suggests that only if humanity develops a truly loving *relationship* with creation will it be able to survive.

In order to elaborate on this role of humanity in the salvation of creation, Zizioulas builds on some of the elements of an ontology of person that he has developed previously. For example, in his work *Being as Communion,* he argues that neither philosophy nor any other discipline is capable of uncovering the nature of personhood, because the conditions for an ontology of person exist only in a personal God.

---

[29] Zizioulas, "Creation I," 4.
[30] Pergamon, "Orthodoxy and Ecological Problems," 28.

Only theology, therefore, has the ultimate capacity to address the issue. On this basis he argues in his lectures on the ecological crisis that the authentic person, "as absolute ontological freedom, must be 'uncreated,' that is unbounded by any 'necessity' including its own existence."[31] For him, it is the doctrines concerning Christ that give assurance to the human person that her or his nature can be "assumed" and hypostasized in a manner free from ontological necessity. Irenaeus's theological vision of recapitulation is again evident here: because of the radical communion of human with divine effected by the Christ's incarnation, and through the salvific power of his death and resurrection, each member of the human race can come to freedom (salvation) by becoming fully person through communion with God, other persons, and all creation.[32]

When Zizioulas focuses on the relationship between humanity and the rest of creation, the concept of freedom again surfaces as a key issue. He claims that the radical difference between human beings and animals consists in much more than the factor of rationality, as has been widely held in the West, especially since the Enlightenment. He notes that whereas animals, in pursuit of survival, have proved to be ingenious in adapting to the inherent rationality of nature, the human person does much more. Often "challenged and provoked by the *given*," humanity seeks to create new realities outside existing boundaries. There is a pull within humans that prompts them to become creators themselves and, in this process, causes them to resist being bound by established realities. Zizioulas believes that this pull to break through set limits and established boundaries is a desire for freedom that is a highly significant and specifically human characteristic: "The question of freedom and that of creation out of nothing are interdependent: if one creates out of something, one is presented by something given; if one creates out of nothing, one is free in the absolute sense of the term."[33]

The human person, however, is by definition a creature. Humanity can choose what it likes, but it cannot avoid the reality of givenness. Zizioulas therefore wants to pursue how humanity can be considered free in the absolute sense. He recalls a basic tenet of Christian anthropology which holds that the human person was created "in the image and likeness of God," and he posits that this inevitably must refer to something that characterizes God in an exclusive way. He notes that while humanity must always work with what is given and that this

---

[31] Zizioulas, *Being as Communion*, 43.

[32] See Chapter 2.

[33] Zizioulas, "Preserving God's Creation: Three Lectures on Theology and Ecology," *King's Theological Review* 13 (1990) 1–5 (hereafter "Creation III"), here 2.

"tragic element" is encoded within a human person's being, God's most distinguishing characteristic is the capacity to create out of nothing. It is here that Zizioulas gets to the nub of his proposal: he asks why God would implant within humanity's very being an unfulfillable drive to be free in the absolute sense. He then suggests that the answer to this apparent contradiction has to do with the ultimate survival of creation and with humanity's call to be "the priest of creation."[34]

In order to provide a theological basis for this provocative claim, Zizioulas focuses on the story of the Fall in Genesis. In this story Adam and Eve are depicted as exceeding the limits put on them and seeking to be like God themselves. Zizioulas asks why God would have given them a drive toward absolute freedom if they were to be forbidden to use it. To address this question, he turns to an alternative reading of the Fall that comes from Irenaeus. Contrary to the later Western interpretation promoted particularly by Augustine, namely, that Adam and Eve committed the original sin because they exceeded the limits of their freedom, Irenaeus taught that the story reveals God's placing man and woman in the garden so that they could grow to adulthood by exercising their freedom. According to Irenaeus's interpretation, Adam and Eve are depicted as being deceived and exercising their freedom in the wrong way. He teaches that God became one of us through Christ, not to save us from the guilt of Adam's and Eve's sin, now inherited by all humanity (original sin), but so that humanity could learn the right way to exercise freedom. It was thus, in Christ, that humanity discovered how this urge toward freedom could become the means of drawing all creation into unity *(anakephalaiosis)*.[35]

Zizioulas notes that this reading of the Fall means that instead of teaching that Adam and Eve should have adjusted their drive to freedom to match their creaturely limitations, it is teaching the opposite. It is proposing that the very drive to freedom that is inherent within humanity is God-given and is, in fact, the characteristic that most reflects that we are made in God's image. Moreover, it is Zizioulas's thesis that humanity was given this drive to absolute freedom, the *imago Dei,* not for itself but for creation.[36] He argues that since creation of itself does not possess any natural means of survival, if left to itself it would

---

[34] Ibid., 3.

[35] This alternative reading has coexisted in the tradition alongside classic theology that "saw the Incarnation as the great emergency-measure by which God decided to bring the world back to its original perfection." See H. Berkof, "God in Nature and History," *Study Encounter* 1, o. 3 (Geneva: World Council of Churches, 1965) 6, 7.

[36] See Zizioulas, "Creation III," 3.

inevitably become extinct.[37] The only way it can survive is for it to transcend itself, and this requires a drive toward absolute freedom. The whole creation "waits with eager longing for the revealing of the children of God," so that it too "will be set free from its bondage to decay and will obtain the freedom of the glory of the children of God" (Rom 8:19, 21). The fact that this drive is given to humanity is therefore a cause for celebration, for it is through its connectedness to humanity that creation is to survive. Zizioulas concludes that humanity, by virtue of being made in the image of Godself and therefore with an innate drive to full freedom, "is able to carry with [it] the whole of creation to its transcendence."[38]

Having searched the tradition to discover humanity's role in relation to creation, Zizioulas further addresses the question of *how* humanity can carry out this mission. He draws attention to the fact that intrinsic to the above proposition is the fact that there is a unique tendency within the human person to create a new world. He gives the example of the creative drive of the artist and claims that together with the innate pull toward freedom, this tendency is another essential dimension of each human being made in the image of God. When this tendency is skewed, as is portrayed in the story of the Fall in Genesis, humanity seeks to become God, the ultimate reference point in existence, and uses nature as a possession. An alternative possibility occurs if humanity acts not in an individualistic but in a personal way. In this instance, creation is still used as a source of life—for food, clothing, building, technology—but humanity relates to nature in such a loving way that nature itself acquires what Zizioulas describes as a personal dimension. According to this understanding, "the personal approach makes every being unique and irreplaceable, whereas the individual approach makes of it a number of statistics."[39] The personal approach also enables humanity to relate to creation "as a totality, as a catholicity of interrelated entities . . . which as natural science observes today, is inherent in its very structure."[40]

Zizioulas concedes that it is possible for a human being to act in this personal (respectful) way toward nature without any reference to God. However, he argues that creation was destined to be in such a creative relationship not only with humanity but also with God, and that it is the person of Christ, the new Adam, who reveals humanity's

---

[37] Zizioulas gives no evidence that he is taking into account here contemporary scientific views on the death of the universe.

[38] Zizioulas, "Creation III," 3.

[39] Ibid., 4.

[40] Ibid.

proper relation to the natural world as priest of creation. "We must teach ourselves and our children," he says, "that we are members of a community which regards creation as Christ's body."[41] Zizioulas believes that this involves human persons treating creation in such a way that humanity becomes the link between God and creation, and he points to the two dimensions of personhood (elaborated above in Chapter 2) which enable this to occur:

> One is what we may call its *hypostatic* aspect, through which the world is integrated and embodied in a unified reality. The other is what we call its ecstatic aspect by virtue of which the world by being referred to God and offered . . . as "His own" reaches itself to infinite possibilities.[42]

Here Zizioulas is emphasizing that personhood "implies the 'openness of being,' and even more than that, the *ek-stasis* of being, i.e., a movement toward communion which leads to transcendence of the boundaries of the 'self' and thus to freedom."[43] The essential self of the human person is thus realized only when it stretches beyond itself in creating communion with God, with other persons, and with other entities in creation.

Moreover, it is through this communion that the unique and unrepeatable mode of existence *(hypostasis)* of each person and the uniqueness of each particular entity within creation are realized. As we have seen in his earlier work, Zizioulas has argued the position that "communion does not threaten personal particularity; it is constitutive of it."[44] Here he is focusing on humanity's communion with all creation, and he claims that the way the human person is destined to arrive at the fullness of his or her unique self is through an interactive relationship with creation. This constitutes the basis of what Zizioulas means by humanity's call to priesthood. He understands priesthood to be "a broader existential attitude encompassing all human activities that involves a conscious or even unconscious manifestation of these two aspects [hypostatic and ecstatic] of personhood."[45]

---

[41] Pergamon, "Orthodoxy and Ecological Problems," 30.

[42] Zizioulas, "Creation III," 4.

[43] Zizioulas, "Human Capacity," 408.

[44] Ibid., 408–9.

[45] Zizioulas, "Creation III," 5. See N. Affanassief, *L'Eglise du Saint-Esprit*, quoted in Paul McPartlan, *The Eucharist Makes the Church: Henri de Lubac and John Zizioulas Dialogue* (Edinburgh: T&T Clark, 1993) 229–30. Affanassief also claims that the prime characteristic of Christians is that, while there are specific gifts given to some, *all* are priests and that it is "as a priest that each is most configured to Christ."

Zizioulas is suggesting that the exercise of this priesthood involves the whole of life, not just a ritual action within formal liturgy. It involves relating to creation in such a respectful way that the uniqueness of each entity and the interconnectedness of everything are so recognized and honored that nature is enabled to develop its full potential as a "bearer of life." In another arena Zizioulas refers to this same phenomenon when he states that "God has ordained nature to be elevated to the ultimate status of personhood in Christ."[46] He believes that when humanity relates to nature in such a personal way, the material world, through this communion, is elevated to the level of humanity's existence and itself acquires a personal dimension. Expressed in more specifically theological terms, this exercise of priesthood means humanity chooses to act not in the flawed manner of Adam and Eve but in the way of Christ.

In earlier writings Zizioulas has also made it clear that this understanding of priesthood means that there is actually no such person as a "non-ordained" member of the Church:

> . . . baptism and especially confirmation (chrismation) as an insepa-
> rable aspect of the rite of initiation involves a "laying on of hands" and
> a "seal" . . . [which] leads the baptised person to the eucharistic com-
> munity in order to assume his particular *ordo* there.[47]

He describes the difference between the ordained person and the lay person in terms of "a *specificity of relationship* within the Church";[48] both belong to different orders, and for both ordination is determined by communion rather than by ontology or function.[49] In the context of this understanding of ordination, Zizioulas points to the eucharistic liturgy as the place where the role of humanity as priest linking creation to God is ritualized.[50] The act of offering of the elements to the Creator and receiving them back in order to consume enacts in symbolic sacramental terms the responsibility of the human person for creation:

---

[46] Verbatim from notes I took at a keynote address, "The Environment and Justice: A Theological Approach," delivered by Zizioulas on June 26 to the summer session in Halki in 1997.

[47] Zizioulas, "Ordination—A Sacrament?" 36. See also Metropolitan John, "Eucharist and the Kingdom of God—Part III," 35.

[48] Ibid., 37.

[49] See John Zizioulas, "Ordination and Communion," *Study Encounter* 6 (1970) 190; and Zizioulas, *Being as Communion,* 163–66.

[50] See also Zizioulas, "Vision eucharistique," 85–87, and "The Eucharistic Prayer and Life," 193–95.

All of this involves an *ethos* that the world needs badly in our time. Not an ethic, but an *ethos*. Not a programme, but an attitude and a mentality. Not a legislation, but a culture.[51]

An Ethos for a Restored Ecology

In all the above Zizioulas has been arguing that the ecological crisis is a crisis of culture. He describes it as "a crisis that has to do with the loss of the *sacrality* of nature in our culture."[52] It is difficult to enter into the flow of his thought without being aware of the strong similarities of his theological vision to that of indigenous religions, the wholistic wisdom of which is again being recognized and revalued in this ecological age.[53] Zizioulas, however, seeks to make a firm distinction between how the world is viewed by what he calls "paganism" and by Christianity. The former regards the world as sacred because it is permeated by divine presence and is unaware of its need for transcendence, whereas the Christian is called "not simply to 'preserve' it but to cultivate and embody it in forms of culture which will elevate it to eternal survival." Zizioulas holds that it is particularly within the liturgy of Eucharist that this can take place most powerfully: "In the liturgy matter is not a window to higher things. It is the very substance of a transformed cosmos; it is an end in itself."[54]

Thus while Zizioulas would acknowledge the value of the myths and rituals of many religions because they contribute toward the development of an ethos that promotes the sacrality and therefore the survival of nature,[55] he is arguing that Christianity can offer much more. Through the incarnation, uncreated and created have been irrevocably joined in Christ. What was destined to extinction is now drawn

[51] Zizioulas, "Creation III," 5.

[52] Ibid.

[53] The values and the inherent wholistic wisdom of indigenous peoples for a sustainable universe of the future have also been adopted in a variety of forms by a plethora of New Age practices that have multiplied in recent decades within Western societies. These often do not give evidence of the intrinsic integrity of thought contained in the Christian vision described by Zizioulas or that of indigenous religions. However, they do perhaps give witness to some growing contemporary consensus of humanity's experience of the interrelatedness and sacredness of all creation.

[54] John Zizioulas, "The Church as the Mystical Body of Christ," unpublished paper presented to the annual meeting of the Académie Internationale des Sciences religieuses, Crete, 1985, quoted in McPartlan, *The Eucharist Makes the Church,* 137.

[55] See Peacocke, *Creation and the World of Science,* 270ff., for a discussion of the connection between theology and ecological values.

into relationship with the divine for eternity. Because of the incarnation, humanity is called to live in such a way that its deeply loving relationship with creation is the "offering up" that enables humanity with creation to be drawn into God's life of communion.

While "offering up" refers to a specific action of the ordained minister within the eucharistic liturgy, Zizioulas is essentially referring to a priesthood that is to be exercised by every person. Every person is to participate in the priestly task of "offering," of living and relating to all creation in such a way that each particular being is in turn opened up to a transcending relatedness with the "other," this action "corresponding to that of *love* in the deepest sense."[56] In this way the action of the anaphora within the Eucharist, the lifting up of creation to God the Creator, the Source of all being, is to be played out continually around the planet in the life of every person. In so doing, every person is an *alter Christus*, initiating a priestly action whereby creation, having been offered to God, can be transformed by the action of the Holy Spirit and brought to a fullness beyond its natural capacities. That is the sense in which the human being has to become a liturgical being so that the ecological crisis can be overcome.

That is also a description of how humanity and all creation are drawn into the hypostatic and ecstatic life of the Trinity. The gathering in community to enter into the great mystery of Eucharist, or thanksgiving for creation and salvation in Christ and the Spirit, becomes a transforming moment. Within that moment each person's incorporation into the very life of God is enacted before being spun out again to continue this saving, relational, and priestly action in the world. Hence, Zizioulas's claim that in order to overcome the ecological crisis the human person has to become a liturgical being.

In light of the above, it could equally be said that in order to overcome the ecological crisis, the human person must recognize his or her origin and destiny in the dynamic life of the triune God. Zizioulas's engagement of theology with ecology in order to address the ecological crisis leads inexorably, through an articulation of a theology of creation, to the heart of all that is—to a God revealed as a communion of three divine persons into whom humanity and all creation are drawn:

> Thanks to the economy of the Holy Trinity which has been realised in the person and the work of Christ, "with the cooperation of the Holy Spirit," space and time are capable of receiving transfiguration. . . . the Kingdom of God is not something that will displace material creation, but will transfigure it, cleansing it from those elements which

---

[56] Zizioulas, "Creation I," 2.

bring about corruption and death. The Eucharist gives us the assurance that matter is sacred and worthy of every honour.[57]

The triune God is there as the dynamic ground and underlying premise of his proposal: the personal, unoriginate Origin of all life who in complete freedom creates out of nothing; the Christ, who, in becoming one with humanity, draws all people out of the death of an individualistic misuse of freedom into a loving, relational, liberating connectedness with all creation; the Holy Spirit, who transforms creation, the priestly offering of a redeemed humanity, into the true freedom of a reconciled and eternal communion. Zizioulas is thus steadfast in demonstrating an intrinsic and ultimate relatedness between the Trinity, humanity, and all creation, and in claiming that this relatedness has very practical as well as ontological significance.

It is clear from the above that for Zizioulas, the celebration of the Eucharist within the ecclesial community is of primordial importance. It is the eucharistic gathering of believers led by the bishop that creates the Church as an inclusive community. It also creates an ethos wherein the "individual" is enabled to realize her or his full human capacity by becoming an "ecclesial hypostasis," a person. He claims that it is through the Church that the human person can come to *be* through loving relationships with other human persons, with the divine persons, and with all creation. In so doing, the human person is "saved"—attains freedom—and all created entities are also saved and set free from extinction.

It is this whole liturgical vision that Zizioulas seeks to promote as a "remedy of immortality."[58] The contemporary crisis he is addressing issues from stark, destructive existential realities: water, air, and the very earth itself are being destroyed; species of flora and fauna are becoming extinct at an increasing rate every moment. Zizioulas's solution to this very practical moral dilemma is cast in symbolic language because his primary perspective is eschatological. The outcomes he seeks, however, are eminently pragmatic. He is concerned with saving the water, air, and forests. His eschatological vision assures him that in Christ "all things" *(ta panta)* have already been reconciled; that everything is saved; that the bridge between uncreated and created has been effected. He is not suggesting that humanity has to bring this about; rather, he is arguing that there is an urgent task to be accomplished in the historical

---

[57] Metropolitan John, "Eucharist and the Kingdom of God—Part III," 43–44.

[58] An expression of Ignatius of Antioch. See Zizioulas, "Vision eucharistique," 86.

present: if the ecological crisis is to be addressed in a fundamental way, humanity has to change the way it relates to the rest of creation.

Zizioulas does not believe that moral dictums or mere good sense will effect the kind of primordial change needed. He does believe, however, that the profound eschatological vision at the heart of Christian faith is capable of sustaining a practical conversion that will bring about salvation for creation now and into the future. His argument is that the culture created through the living ethos of a vibrant Christian community, centered on the Eucharist, can provide for this most powerfully. He believes that the liturgy is the key formative source of initiation into a way of being that can shape and transform humanity's relationships and behavior toward every other entity. My reading of his work is that this is the sense in which he holds that a redeemed humanity has a key role in the "salvation" of creation.

The community of the Church is the locus within which such a saving ethos can be created. Zizioulas's theology of Church elaborates his vision further. The essential identity of the Church as *koinōnia*, founded in the persons-in-communion of the triune God, will be examined in the next chapter.

CHAPTER 4

The Church as Communion

The Church is . . . a "mode of existence," a way of being.
The mystery of the Church . . . is deeply bound to the being
of [humanity], to the being of the world, and to the very
being of God.[1]

Early in his work as a theologian Zizioulas consciously identified with the way that the ancient Church interpreted the term "theology"—that theology is used "to denote a grasp of the mystery of divine existence as it was offered to the world and experienced in the ecclesial community."[2] In 1993 he addressed a Faith and Order World Conference in Spain and focused on this mystery of divine existence that is offered to the world and experienced in the ecclesial community. In a keynote address entitled "Church as Communion," Zizioulas claimed that God as Mystery is most fully expressed as three divine persons in an eternal, dynamic communion of love. He sought to show that the biblical and patristic origins of communion, or *koinōnia,* reveal that this concept does not derive from the experience of sociology or of ethics but from faith in a God whose very being is *koinōnia.* He argued that since the God revealed by Jesus Christ and the Holy Spirit is Trinitarian, any authentic theology of Church must be based on the doctrine of the Trinity.

[1] Zizioulas, *Being as Communion: Studies in Personhood and the Church* (New York: St. Vladimir's Seminary Press, 1993) 15.
[2] J. D. Zizioulas, "The Ecumenical Dimensions of Orthodox Theological Education," in *Orthodox Theological Education for the Life and Witness of the Church* (Geneva: World Council of Churches, 1978) 36.

On the basis of such a theological premise, Zizioulas posed a question that includes several essential elements of his ecclesiological agenda:

> If the very being of God in whom we believe is *koinonia*, and if the person of Christ in whose name we human beings and the whole creation are saved is also in his very being *koinonia*, what consequences does this faith entail for our understanding of the Church? How does the notion of *koinonia* affect the Church's identity, her structure and her ministry in the world? . . . Finally, how can the understanding of Church as *koinonia* affect her mission in the world, including her relation with the entire creation?[3]

These questions immediately illustrate the identifying factor of Zizioulas's synthetic theological system, which he makes explicit again and again in his work: God, Church, and cosmos are inextricably interconnected and can only be properly understood if held in relation to one another. None can be properly understood as a separate entity in itself. These questions also suggest that the being of God—how God is in Godself—provides the key to a theological understanding of Church and world and to the connection of one to the other. Zizioulas's vision is that God's very being is relational and that Church and world need to be understood in relational terms.

From its origins, patristic theology taught that the Church is formed in history but that it leads to the vision of God in Godself—the eternal triune God. Zizioulas points out that this "meta-historical, eschatological and iconological dimension of the Church is characteristic of the Eastern tradition, which lives and teaches its theology liturgically."[4] Within such an understanding of Church there is a belief in a continual dialectic of God and the world, of history and the *eschaton*. Ecclesial being and the being of God are experienced as organically interconnected.

In practice, however, Zizioulas admits, Orthodox theology very often places such emphasis on the heavenly realities that it runs the risk of disconnecting the Church from the social and ethical implications of life in the world.[5] By contrast, Western theology tends to situate the Church as an essentially historical phenomenon, and the Western Church can find itself limited by its very engagement with historical

---

[3] Zizioulas, "The Church as Communion," *St. Vladimir's Theological Quarterly* 38 (1994) 6–7.

[4] Zizioulas, *Being as Communion*, 19.

[5] See John Zizioulas, "Eschatology and History," in *Cultures in Dialogue: Documents from a Symposium in Honour of Philip A. Potter*, ed. T. Weiser (Geneva, 1985) 39.

realities.[6] Zizioulas laments "the self-sufficiency in which East and West have indulged after the great schism"[7] and argues that "ecclesial being must never separate itself out from the absolute demands of the being of God—that is its eschatological nature—nor from history."[8] He emphasizes that both need to meet at depth in order for the Church to be able to live out the full mystery.

In 1986 Zizioulas delivered a paper at Chevetogne that was later published as "The Mystery of the Church in the Orthodox Tradition."[9] In this he spells out four basic theological principles that he considers crucial to an understanding of the Church. This chapter will first focus on his elaboration of each of these principles within an overall framework of God and Church understood as communion. The second section of the chapter will explore in more explicit ways how his development of the concept of Church as communion provides the basis for his ecumenical vision of unity between the Churches.

Four Principles of an Ecclesiology of Communion

1. *Trinitarian Theology as the Essential Context for Ecclesiology*

Zizioulas begins his elaboration of the principle that ecclesiology needs to be situated within the context of Trinitarian theology by emphasizing the clear distinction of the persons in the Trinity.[10] He insists that the full distinction and integrity of the Trinitarian persons are essential for an understanding of the Church's own proper identity and destiny. He stresses that the Church's relationship with the Father is necessarily different from its relationship with the Son and draws attention to the distinct characteristics of the Father by focusing on a certain dialectic between Christ and the Father. He shows that in the Eucharist, "when the Church prays to the Father, it is Christ who prays to him for us and with us."[11] Zizioulas also underlines that in the Eucharist there is a total identification of Christ and the Church. The distinctness

---

[6] See ibid., 32. Zizioulas refers to J. Cardinal Daniélou's identification of Western characteristics of Christianity, which include "concern for ethics, a tendency towards practical matters, a preoccupation with history and a juridical approach to the question of salvation."

[7] Ibid.

[8] Zizioulas, *Being as Communion*, 20.

[9] John Zizioulas, "The Mystery of the Church in the Orthodox Tradition," *One in Christ* 24 (1988).

[10] Ibid., 295.

[11] Ibid., 297. Zizioulas notes that this is particularly evident in the Eucharistic Prayers, which from the beginning were addressed to the Father.

of the Father and the Son and the identification of Christ with the Church mean that the Church is drawn into the dynamic relationship between the divine persons by virtue of its identification with Christ. This provides the basis for Zizioulas's claim that the true context for understanding the Church is the very life of the triune God.

Second, Zizioulas argues that in the Spirit, the Church becomes an image of the Trinity itself and therefore is communion by its very nature:

> [The] Spirit as life giver and communion brings the ultimate, the eschaton (Acts 2)—i.e., the eternal life of God—into history. The Church in this way becomes the communion of saints in which the past, the present, and the future are not causally related to each other, but are the one body of Christ in the event of communion.[12]

Through the action of the Spirit, the Church is constituted in the same way as the Trinity—as persons in communion—and the Church's very essence is therefore a dynamic, personal event. Zizioulas expresses this in another way by saying that in the Church, just as in the Trinity itself, "the 'essential' and the 'existential,' nature and person, are not causing each other but are identical with each other."[13] He is arguing that in ecclesiology, as in the Trinity, it is not possible to distinguish between "essence" and "event." The Church can never be understood in a static form, as something that can be defined in some final way. As the Body of Christ, it is always "in relation," and through the advent of the Spirit bringing the eternal life of God into history, it is continually being created as a new event.

For Zizioulas, this theological understanding of the nature of the Church is crucial.[14] Moreover, he sees that this central Trinitarian understanding of the very nature of the Church has clear practical implications for its life and structure. For example, since the Spirit does not create individuals but persons in communion, so a local Church com-

---

[12] John Zizioulas, "The Pneumatological Dimension of the Church," *Communio: International Catholic Review* 1 (1974) 147.

[13] Ibid.

[14] See for example, Zizioulas, "The Doctrine of God the Trinity Today," in *The Forgotten Trinity*, ed. Alasdair I. C. Heron (London: BCC/CCBI, 1991) 27–29; "The Church as Communion," 4–10, 15–16; *Being as Communion*, 110–14; "The Pneumatological Dimension of the Church," *Communio: International Catholic Review* 1 (1974) 147, 151, 157–58; "Orthodox-Protestant Bilateral Conversations: Some Comments," in *The Orthodox Church and the Churches of the Reformation: A Survey of Orthodox-Protestant Dialogues*, Faith and Order Paper 76 (Geneva: World Council of Churches, 1975) 59.

munity constituted by the Spirit does not exist as Church in isolation. However, as the Body of Christ, the local Church in communion with the universal Church is the whole Christ.[15] This, claims Zizioulas, is shown in the structure of the Church in two ways: "(a) by a communion in time through Apostolic Succession, and (b) by a communion in space through conciliarity."[16] Every episcopal ordination is therefore understood not only in continuity with the tradition of faith transmitted from the Apostles but also as a new Pentecostal event in itself that takes place within the eucharistic community, "in which all orders, including the laity, are decisively active as well." In this way apostolic succession and tradition itself are not just passed on historically from one generation to another, they are constantly re-enacted and re-received in the Spirit.[17]

In a similar way, conciliarity, while being understood as "an event taking place through synodical institutions and with reference to a center or centers of unity as provided by history,"[18] also needs to be recognized as a charismatic event arising out of the local Churches and authenticated only through reception. The authority of a council, therefore, does not lie in its historical continuity and juridical correctness but in the *event of communion* which the Spirit creates and which brings conciliarity back to its original community basis. "Essence" and "event" are thus held in tandem and in dynamic relation. Zizioulas reasons that because "truth is not a petrified entity, but a living reality," the decisions of the councils, past, present, or future, all need to be constantly received and re-received in an event of communion created by the Spirit.[19] When the Church is understood in the same way as the triune God, in whom the "essential" and the "existential" are not causing each other but are identical with each other, there is a basis for understanding the need to maintain a communion across time and space within the Church as well as the need to maintain a creative tension between charism and institution, with neither having the ascendancy.

---

[15] See Zizioulas, *Being as Communion*, 24–25, where Zizioulas refers to the work of the well-known thesis of modern Orthodox theologian Nicholas Afanasiev on "eucharistic ecclesiology" and sets out clear distinctions from his own work, the most essential being Afanasiev's claim that wherever the Eucharist takes place, there is the complete "catholic" Church.

[16] Zizioulas, "Pneumatological Dimension of the Church," 149.

[17] See Zizioulas, *Being as Communion*, 207.

[18] Zizioulas, "Pneumatological Dimension of the Church," 149–50.

[19] See J. D. Zizioulas, "Conciliarity and the Way to Unity—An Orthodox Point of View," in *Churches in Conciliar Fellowship* (Geneva: Conference of European Churches, 1978) 24–25.

This principle has significant practical implications. If it were adhered to, the Church would need to revise in a radical way its practice of being faithful to the tradition.

The issue of ministries in the Church is another arena where the practical implications of this theological principle become evident. According to Zizioulas, who draws very directly from 1 Corinthians 12, ministry concerns the various charisms within the Church and is a *"specificity of relationship* within the body."[20] The notion of hierarchy is thus recognized as a necessity to ensure the unity and particularity of the ministries. In order to clarify the meaning of hierarchy, Zizioulas again refers directly to the image of the triune God:

> The hierarchy in the Trinity does not stem from any ontological or moral evaluation within it, but from the unity of life and at the same time the specificity of each person in . . . relationship with other persons; it is the Father as person in particularity of his relation to the two other persons that renders that Trinity both a unity and a diversity. Hierarchy is thus a notion in the idea of personhood.[21]

Here hierarchy means specificity of relationships. It is clear that hierarchy so understood is manifestly different, for example, from some of the ways Roman Catholic dogmatic statements describe "the divinely willed hierarchical Church."[22] Zizioulas claims that the institution of the Church "is not meant to create an objective *auctoritas* for security and obedience, but to provide the means for personal and free existence in communion."[23] All ministries can be authoritative only in the sense that they realize the communion that stems from the communion of God's triune self.[24]

---

[20] Zizioulas, "Pneumatological Dimension of the Church," 151.

[21] Ibid., 151–52. See also Zizioulas, "Ordination and Communion," *Study Encounter* 6 (1970) 191, and Metropolitan John, "The Eucharist and the Kingdom of God," (Part III), trans. Elizabeth Theokritoff, *Sourozh* 58 (1994) 33–35, for further elaborations of this.

[22] See, for example, "Letter to the Bishops of the Catholic Church on some Aspects of the Church understood as Communion," *L'Osservatore Romano,* June 17, 1992. This document was prepared by the Congregation for the Doctrine of the Faith with a view to correcting what it perceived to be "an anti-hierarchical idea of the Church" that occurred in the period after the Second Vatican Council with the reclaiming of the ancient concept of *koinonia* as a fundamental description of Church.

[23] Zizioulas, "Pneumatological Dimension of the Church," 152. See also John D. Zizioulas, "On the Concept of Authority," *The Ecumenical Review* 21 (1969) 162–64.

[24] See Zizioulas, "Pneumatological Dimension of the Church," 164.

That is a very powerful claim. It is drawn directly from the principle that ecclesiology needs to be situated within the context of the Trinitarian God. If the true authority of ministries were judged by their capacity to realize the kind of communion that exists within the triune God—a communion of loving mutual and equal relations where difference is valued as essential for relationality and where hierarchy means specificity of relationships—many of the present structures and practices of authority within the Churches would be identified as not "of God" and therefore without valid authority. This principle, if applied, thus has the capacity to revolutionize the shape and structures of the Churches and also to provide a basis for unity within the one Church of Jesus Christ.

Zizioulas further argues that the Church's structure cannot be conceived as a source of security, since the reality of communion is constantly dependent on the disturbing, transformative intervention of the Holy Spirit:[25]

> The affirmation that Christ is the Truth ceases in the Spirit to point to an objectified and conceptualised truth (the *aletheia* of the Greeks) and makes Truth identical with life and communion, the very life and communion of God. . . . Infallibility thus appears in the Spirit to be a dynamic, circular movement. It does not repose statically on any structure or ministry, but it expresses itself through a certain ministry by a dynamic *perichoresis* in and through the whole body. Thus a layman in his membership in the body, which is by definition charismatic, can point to the Truth by contesting the bishop's deviation from it. Yet if this is done in the Spirit, it can only happen by a constant strengthening of the bond of participation in the community.[26]

The key image of the Church situated within Trinitarian theology thus remains persons in communion. Zizioulas has shown how equality and mutuality through difference within the dynamic perichoretic life of the three divine Persons provides an archetype of how structures within the Church are called to be. All persons, regardless of their "order" within the Church, are thereby considered to have a unique contribution to make to the truth that comes about through full communion. It goes without saying that if Church structures were such that they enabled such participation to occur, they would be very different from most of those presently in place in many of the Churches. Zizioulas

[25] See J. D. Zizioulas, "Informal Groups in the Church: An Orthodox Viewpoint," *Informal Groups in the Church*, ed. R. Metz, trans. M. O'Connell (Pittsburgh: Pickwick Press, 1975) 287.

[26] Zizioulas, "Pneumatological Dimension of the Church," 153–54.

has demonstrated how this thoroughly orthodox and apparently "safe" theological principle that most Christian Churches would endorse[27]— that ecclesiology needs to be situated within the context of Trinitarian theology—has in fact radical and practical implications for ecclesial life and structures.

2. *Ecclesiology Requires a Synthesis Between Christology and Pneumatology*

The second principle that Zizioulas sets out is that ecclesiology requires a synthesis between christology and pneumatology. As has been established, Zizioulas is wholly resistant to a christology that portrays the Holy Spirit as the person of the Trinity whose essential task is merely to assist and guide us in our relationship with Christ: "For some people (even whole traditions)," he says, "the Spirit plays the role of the agent of Christ. He is the janitor who opens the door and lets people into Christ"![28]

Again, Zizioulas appeals to theologians of the early Church who were also bishops—Irenaeus, Athanasius, Cyril of Alexandria, Basil the Great—to illustrate that it was their experience in the life of the communities that helped them reach "the proper synthesis: christology and pneumatology had to exist simultaneously and not as separate or successive phases of God's relation to the world."[29] Referring to the biblical accounts that describe the role of the Spirit in the life of Christ (Matt 1:18-20; Luke 1:35; 4:13), Zizioulas emphasizes that it is the Spirit who actually realizes in history "that which we call Christ, this absolutely relational identity, our Saviour." He thus argues that christology is "constituted pneumatologically":

> The Holy Spirit in making real the Christ-event in history, makes real *at the same time* Christ's personal existence as a body or community. Christ does not exist first as truth and then as communion. . . . All separation between christology and ecclesiology vanishes in the Spirit.[30]

[27] See, for example, "The Constitution and Rules of the World Council of Churches," as amended, New Delhi, 1961. David P. Gaines, *The World Council of Churches: A Study of Its Background and History* (Peterborough, N. H.: Richard R. Smith, 1966) 1:245. See also the Dogmatic Constitution of the Church, *Lumen Gentium* 4.

[28] Zizioulas, "The Mystery of the Church in the Orthodox Tradition," *One in Christ* 24, no. 4 (1988) 295. See also Zizioulas, "On the Concept of Authority," *The Ecumenical Review* 21 (1969) 143.

[29] Ibid., 143–44.

[30] Zizioulas, *Being as Communion*, 110–11.

Exploring the notion of the Spirit as constitutive of the identity of Christ has significant implications for ecclesiology. Since the primary work of the Spirit is "communion"—the opening up of reality to become relational—Zizioulas argues that by being born of the Spirit "Christ is inconceivable as an individual: he becomes automatically a relational being."[31] Christ's very identity is thus conditioned by the existence of the "many," and the Church is part of the definition of Christ.[32] The Spirit breaking into history formed and continues to form what Zizioulas chooses to call the "corporate personality" of Christ.

Zizioulas is concerned that a major stumbling block for ecclesiological discussions in the ecumenical movement arises from the need to have a clear-cut distinction between Christ and the Church. For him, this presupposes an individualistic understanding of Christ that is not the Christ of the Scriptures: "This could not be the spiritual being who incorporates all in himself. He cannot be the firstborn among many brothers or of creation, of whom Colossians and Ephesians speak. The "one" without the "many" is an individual not touched by the Spirit. He cannot be the Christ of our faith."[33]

It is for that reason that Zizioulas makes use of the concept of "corporate personality" proposed by some biblical scholars.[34] Though there is debate among exegetes about the particular meanings of "corporate personality,"[35] Zizioulas's own use of the term is clear. It means for him that the one and the many are mutually constitutive.[36] He draws a parallel between the fact that in the Trinity, the Father is the cause, whereas in the Church, Christ is the cause.[37] In both there is a dynamic, relational

---

[31] Zizioulas, "The Mystery of the Church," 299.

[32] John D. Zizioulas, "The Ecclesiological Presuppositions of the Holy Eucharistic," *Nicolaus* 10 (1982) 342.

[33] Zizioulas, "The Mystery of the Church," 299.

[34] See ibid., and Zizioulas, *Being as Communion*, 146, n. 7; 182, n. 38; 230, n. 63, for references to specific works: S. Pederson, *Israel: Its Life and Culture* (1926); H. Wheeler Robinson, *The Hebrew Conception of Corporate Personality* (1936); A. R. Johnson, *The One and the Many in the Israelite Conception of God* (1942); J. de Fraine, *Adam et son lignage: Etudes sur la "personnalité corporative" dans la Bible* (1959).

[35] See Paul McPartlan, *The Eucharist Makes the Church: Henri de Lubac and John Zizioulas Dialogue* (Edinburgh: T&T Clark, 1993) 171, n. 31. For a contemporary summary of the biblical concept, see also *The New Jerome Biblical Commentary*, ed. R. Brown, J. Fitzmyer, R. Murphy (Englewood Cliffs, N. J.: Prentice Hall, 1990) 77:69–70.

[36] See McPartlan, *The Eucharist Makes the Church*, 179.

[37] See ibid., 185, where McPartlan elaborates on this point of Zizioulas's by arguing that: "the Spirit gives us Christ, that is, the Spirit forms the corporate personality of Christ. The one and the many are *all* the work of the Spirit. The fact that the

communion between the "one" and the "many." All this means for Zizioulas that christology without ecclesiology is inconceivable. He states bluntly: "If the Church disappears from his identity he is no longer Christ, although he will still be the eternal Son."[38] He understands the Church to be "the mystery hidden before all ages" (Col 1:26). The Church is a "gathering," an incorporation of the many who are distinct and often very different into Christ, and therefore into the eternal filial relationship between the Father and the Son.

Earlier Zizioulas noted that in the letters of Paul, the local eucharistic community receives the name *ekklesia* and that the term was used in a dynamic sense, "when you come together as a church" (1 Cor 11:18):

> As a combination of the existing fragmentary liturgical evidence of the first centuries allows us to know, "the whole church" "dwelling in a certain city" would "come together" mainly on a Sunday to "break bread." This *synaxis* would be *the only one* in that particular place in the sense that it would include the *"whole Church."*[39]

Zizioulas claims that although this fact is not usually noted by historians, it is of paramount ecclesiological significance, for it draws a distinction between the Christian and the non-Christian pattern of unity at the time of the early Church. The distinctiveness in the manner of their gathering together lay in who was included at these gatherings. The Christians held that in Christ there was no longer Jew or Greek,[40] male or female,[41] adult or child,[42] rich or poor,[43] master or slave[44]—all were welcome at the eucharistic table. The eucharistic community was thus "in its composition a *catholic community* in the sense that it transcended not only social but also natural divisions."[45] Such an inclusive, catholic community was to be a revelation and a sign of God's reign. Zizioulas is careful to emphasize that "here catholicity is not a moral but a christological reality." It is catholic not because it is a community that aims at certain ethical ideals—being open, inclusive, serving the world and the like—but because in the first place it is "a community

---

many exist by the Spirit and yet are causally dependent upon Christ is aptly expressed by saying that Christ, the 'one,' *gives* the Spirit to the 'many.'"

[38] Zizioulas, "The Mystery of the Church," 300.

[39] Zizioulas, *Being as Communion*, 150.

[40] Gal 3:28; Col 3:11; cf. 1 Cor 12:13.

[41] Gal 3:28.

[42] Matt 19:13.

[43] Jas 2:2-7; 1 Cor 11:20f.

[44] 1 Cor 12:13; Gal 3:28; Eph 6:8.

[45] Zizioulas, *Being as Communion*, 152.

which experiences and reveals the unity of creation *insofar as this unity constitutes a reality in the person of Christ.*"[46]

The catholicity of the eucharistic community was also reflected in its structure. The whole Church gathered at the one altar with the one bishop seated in the place of God and understood as the living image of Christ. "A fundamental function of this 'one bishop' was to express in himself the 'multitude.'"[47] The bishop was the one who drew the diverse many of each local Church into unity. Like the Eucharist itself, the episcopacy is a relational ministry.[48] The function of the bishop was to unite in himself the various elements inherent in the local community's historical existence, and the bishop exercised his episcopal service only within the context of a specific local Church. This action mirrors what occurs when the bishop presides at Eucharist: the elements are transcended and become unified in the one Body of Christ.[49] When the bishops of the early Church met in council or synod, they gathered not as individuals but as local Churches. From its origins the episcopacy was thus also the ministry that was to express and safeguard the Church at a universal level.[50]

It is in Christ that the Church is thus the mystery of the "One" and the "many."[51] And it is the Spirit who constitutes this Body of Christ, the Church. "The Spirit makes the Church be,"[52] says Zizioulas, and therefore he asserts that pneumatology is an ontological category in ecclesiology:

> The Spirit by rendering the Church both a concrete structured community and a relational cosmic event realises through the one divine energy the catholicity of Christ who is the recapitulation of all. It is thus that the unity of the divine economy is fulfilled in its Trinitarian

[46] Ibid., 159.

[47] Ibid., 153. See also Zizioulas, "Ordination and Communion," 191, for further elaboration on the role of the bishop.

[48] See also Zizioulas, "The Early Christian Community," in *Christian Spirituality: Origins to the Twelfth Century*, ed. Bernard McGinn, John Meyendorf, and Jean Leclerq (London: Routledge & Kegan Paul, 1986) 31–35.

[49] See John D. Zizioulas, "Ecclesiological Issues Inherent in the Relations Between Eastern Chalcedonian and Oriental Non-Chalcedonian Churches," in *Does Chalcedon Divide or Unite? Towards a Convergence in Orthodox Christology?* ed. Paulos Gregorios, William H. Lazareth (Geneva: World Council of Churches, 1981) 150.

[50] See J. D. Zizioulas, "Episkopē and Episkopos in the Early Church: A Brief Survey of the Evidence," *Episcopé and Episcopate in Ecumenical Perspective*, Faith and Order Paper 102 (Geneva: World Council of Churches, 1980) 37.

[51] See Zizioulas, "Pneumatological Dimension of the Church," 146.

[52] Zizioulas, *Being as Communion*, 131.

character by being ultimately referred to the Father both by the Son and the Spirit.[53]

Here it is obvious that the Church of which Zizioulas is speaking is not only the pilgrim Church on earth but the final eschatological communion of saints, the future that the Church on earth, in history, experiences in the Eucharist.[54]

It is clear that Zizioulas's second ecclesiological principle is in some sense a particular elaboration of the first. It also relates to the source of the issue that he had diagnosed to be problematical within both Eastern and Western ecclesiology, namely, the lack of a proper synthesis between christology and pneumatology. That is a key issue within Zizioulas's ecclesiology, and some practical implications arising from it will be elaborated below. By claiming that the Spirit constitutes the corporate Christ, he is also emphasizing that it is the Spirit who constitutes both the historical and the eschatological Christ. That leads directly into a third principle that Zizioulas regards as decisive for ecclesiology, namely, that the *eschaton* should be considered as a source of identity that sustains and inspires its ongoing existence in history.

3. The Eschaton *Enters History:* The Eucharist *"Makes the Church"*

Just as Christ, the all-inclusive being, the corporate personality, is an eschatological reality, so too the Church draws its essential identity, suggests Zizioulas, not from history but from the *eschaton*.[55] This third ecclesiological principle that he develops is intrinsically connected to reclaiming the ancient understanding of Eucharist within ecclesiology. In a paper presented to a WCC gathering on "Eschatology and History," Zizioulas refers to the description in the Book of Revelation of the eschatological city establishing God's tabernacle in history. He points out that the way to enter into the mystery of this powerful iconic language is through the liturgy. Zizioulas illustrates how liturgical language transcends the historical event and presents a glimpse of what will be. The Eucharist is presented as "the moment in the Church's life when, through the Holy Spirit, the 'eschaton' enters history."[56] The

---

[53] Zizioulas, "Pneumatological Dimension of the Church," 158.

[54] See McPartlan, *The Eucharist Makes the Church*, 266.

[55] Zizioulas, "The Mystery of the Church," 300.

[56] J. Zizioulas, "L'eucharistie: quelques aspects bibliques," in *L'eucharistie, Eglises en dialogue* 12, ed. J. Zizioulas, J.M.R. Tillard, J. J. von Allmen (Paris: Mame, 1970) 31.

eschaton, he suggests, "respects history not by copying it but by transforming it, and transcending the antimonies and limitations of history."[57] The Spirit breaks in upon humanity and creation and forms the corporate Christ of the last day.[58]

The celebration of the sacraments, and especially the Eucharist, become key moments when the eschatological identity of the Church can be both nourished and take root in history. In the Eucharist the Church becomes "a reflection of the eschatological community of Christ, the Messiah, an image of the Trinitarian life of God." As such it is essentially a relational identity and in terms of human existence must transcend all divisions. Zizioulas argues that "if the Church in its localisation fails to present an image of the Kingdom in this respect it is not Church."[59] From the perspective of the Eucharist, the Church needs to be recognized as "an event, taking place again and again, not a society structurally instituted in a permanent way."[60] Zizioulas hastens to add that this does not mean that the Church should not have institutional structures, but rather that such structures need always to be understood within the context of the Church's true identity, which is eschatological and therefore oriented toward the future and what it will fully become in Christ:

> To my mind, institutions such as episcopacy or the structure of the Eucharistic community or the distinction between laity, priests and bishops, or even conciliarity, stem from the Church as event and Mystery, precisely in the celebration of the Eucharist.[61]

It follows that institutions have to be constantly reconstituted and cannot be taken for granted as historical necessities in their present form.[62]

The necessity for a proper theological (that is, Trinitarian) understanding of the relationship between christology and pneumatology and between history and eschatology is an issue that Zizioulas returns to again and again. He points to very practical distortions that otherwise occur. For instance, he suggests that behind the commonly held position that the Church precedes the Eucharist lies the view that

---

[57] Zizioulas, "Eschatology and History," *Cultures in Dialogue: Documents from a Symposium in Honour of Philip A. Potter,* ed. T. Weiser (Geneva, 1985) 36.

[58] See McPartlan, *The Eucharist Makes the Church,* 264, for a summary of what McPartlan calls Zizioulas's "powerful and precise Pneumatology."

[59] Zizioulas, *Being as Communion,* 254–55.

[60] Zizioulas, "The Mystery of the Church," 301.

[61] Ibid.

[62] Zizioulas, "Eschatology and History," 37.

christology precedes pneumatology and that the institutional or historical aspect of the Church is what causes the Eucharist to exist:

> This position forms part of an Ecclesiology which views the Church as the Body of Christ which is first instituted in itself as an historical entity and then produces the "means of grace" called sacraments, among them primarily the Eucharist . . . if this order is followed, then you must have first the Ministry of the Church who actually *makes* the Eucharist. The Eucharist is a product of the priestly machinery.[63]

During different phases of history, such understandings have led to the loss or serious distortion of the theological and pastoral significance of the Eucharist. Zizioulas's position, firmly anchored within a Trinitarian understanding of ecclesiology, is that the "*Church constitutes the Eucharist while being constituted by it.* Church and Eucharist are interdependent, they coincide, and are even in some sense identical."[64] For Zizioulas, "the expression 'body of Christ' [in the Eucharist] means simultaneously the body of Jesus and the body of the Church."[65] It therefore may be said that "the Eucharist makes the Church."[66]

Again, it is clear that many practical implications flow from this fundamental understanding of how the Church is constituted. For example, because of a shortage of clergy brought about by a magisterium holding on to a tradition of ordaining only celibate males, a huge proportion of the communities within the Roman Catholic Church are now being denied a regular celebration of the Eucharist.[67] If the above principle were understood and adhered to, it would be recognized that those communities, in being denied the possibility of celebrating Eucharist, are also being denied the possibility of becoming the Body of Christ, of literally *being* Church.

---

[63] Zizioulas, "Ecclesiological Presuppositions," 341.

[64] Ibid.

[65] Ibid., 342.

[66] See Metropolitan John, "The Eucharist and the Kingdom of God" (Part III), 33–34. Zizioulas writes with approval of "truly Orthodox dogmatic theologians" who claim that "the Eucharist makes/constitutes the Church." He refers specifically to the work of G. Florovsky (1948) and I. Karmires (1973). See also the basic thesis within McPartlan, *The Eucharist Makes the Church.* This doctoral dissertation establishes a dialogue between Henri de Lubac and John Zizioulas and argues that both these theologians base their respective ecclesiologies on this claim.

[67] See an editorial in the international Catholic weekly *The Tablet*, September 21, 1996, which refers to what it calls "a staggering statistic," namely, that more than half of the 900 million Roman Catholics in today's world do not have access to the Eucharist each Sunday.

The identity between Christ and the Church that Zizioulas empha-sizes could lead to the presumption that for him there is no distinction between the Christ of glory and the pilgrim, sinful Church of history.[68] However, as McPartlan points out, Zizioulas argues that full identifica-tion of the Church with Christ only occurs momentarily during the celebration of the Eucharist, since "the Eucharist is the only occasion in history when these two coincide."[69] McPartlan writes: "The thrust of Zizioulas's 'strong eschatological emphasis' is . . . to make the *momen-tary* identification of the earthly community around the bishop with the heavenly Church around Christ. It is precisely this regularly experi-enced identification which repeatedly prompts the Church *in via* to conversion."[70]

There is a strong rhythm to this repeated eucharistic action, which McPartlan likens to a beating heart. Each week there is a gathering in one place of an inclusive local community to hear the Word, to offer up the gifts of creation. There is the calling down of the Holy Spirit to transform the gifts of bread and wine, symbols of the life of the com-munity, into the body and blood of Christ. The people of God thus be-comes one with the whole Christ, the *ecclesia sanctorum*, before being scattered once more to live out different charisms and ministries and to be priests of creation in the world. Within the rhythm of this weekly gathering "there is identification between Christ and the eschatological Church and distance between that corporate entity and each local Church around its bishop. . . . The Eucharist gathers the latter and makes it into the former."[71]

It is thus the celebration of the Eucharist that best enables the *escha-ton* to become a source of identity for the Church and to sustain its ongoing existence in history. As Zizioulas spells out in his *Being as Communion*, the eucharistic community is the Body of Christ par excel-lence, "simply because it incarnates and realises our communion with the very life and communion of the Trinity in a way that preserves the eschatological character of truth while making it an integral part of his-tory."[72]

---

[68] See Gaëtan Baillargeon, *Perspectives orthodoxes sur l'Eglise-communion: L'oeuvre de Jean Zizioulas* (Montréal: Editions Paulines, 1989) 255–58.

[69] Zizioulas, "Ecclesiological Presuppositions," 342.

[70] McPartlan, *The Eucharist Makes the Church*, 266. See also 265–70 for a spirited defense of Zizioulas's position in response to Baillargeon's critique that Zizioulas does not sufficiently allow for a distinction between Christ and the sinful Church *in via*.

[71] Ibid., 287.

[72] Zizioulas, *Being as Communion*, 114.

4. *Ecclesiology Has a Cosmic Dimension*

Just as boundaries within the Western mind have to be stretched to assimilate the Orthodox situating of the Church's identity so centrally within the *eschaton*, so a similar stretching has to occur to accommodate Zizioulas's theology situating the significance of the Church within the entire cosmos. He writes:

> Christology had very early to become "cosmic" (cf. the epistles to the Ephesians and the Colossians), so as to make the person of Christ not only the "first born among many brethren" . . . but also the one in whom "all things *(ta panta)*" are brought into existence *(entistai)* and are constituted *(sunentemen)* (Col 1:16-17). The mystery of Christ as the "head" of the new humanity is thus extended to include the entire cosmos and the same is true of the Church as mystery (cf. Col 1:18).[73]

As has been discussed in Chapter 3, Zizioulas believes that the human person has a critical role to play as priest in the salvation of the cosmos. The context in which he presented this vision initially suggested an anthropocentric view of the world.[74] However, his more recent work demonstrates a shift to a cosmic-centered view: "We must move from an anthropomonistic ethics to a cosmic ethics. Human beings are a part of the natural cosmos, and thus their salvation is a part of the salvation of the cosmos."[75] He still holds, however, that humanity has a key role to play. He believes that the action of "offering up" creation to God requires that the human person be simultaneously in loving relation to all created entities and in union with the person of Christ, "since Christ as incarnate Son constitutes *the* priest of creation."

---

[73] Zizioulas, "The Mystery of the Church," 301.

[74] See John D. Zizioulas, "Preserving God's Creation: Three Lectures on Theology and Ecology," *King's Theological Review* 12 (1989) 1–5; 41–45; 13 (1990) 1–5. Within contemporary cosmological and ecological discourse, such a claim can carry negative understandings as it is linked to humanity's ruthless destruction of planet Earth. For example, see Thomas Berry, *The Dream of the Earth* (San Francisco: Sierra Club Books, 1988) 209. Berry describes human beings as "the most pernicious mode of earthly being" and as "the affliction of the world, its demonic presence." See also Denis Edwards, *Jesus the Wisdom of God: An Ecological Theology* (New York: Orbis Books, 1995) 154–56, for a more moderate stance but which still argues against an anthropocentric view to the extent that it means that everything is centered on human beings. Edwards argues that all created things have an intrinsic value in themselves because of their relationship with the triune God.

[75] Pergamon, "Ethics Versus Ethos: An Orthodox Approach to the Relation Between Ecology and Ethics," in *The Environment and Ethics: Presentations and Reports, Summer Session on Halki '95,* ed. Deuteron Tarasios (Militos Editions, 1997) 26.

Zizioulas wants to emphasize here that he believes that the cosmic dimension of the Church is based on the freedom of the human person.[76] The human person freely assumes the connection with creation and refers it to God. In Zizioulas's mind this enables a certain dialectic to exist between humanity and creation, while allowing humanity to be the focus of unity between God and creation in Christ. It is particularly in the Eucharist, which constitutes the Church gathered in one place, that this dialectic is enacted:

> The eucharist . . . sanctifies the space in which we live by transforming it from being a place of division into a place of unity and by referring to God all the fruits of our labour and of the earth. In celebrating the Eucharist, the local Church is established in a particular place and leads humanity to treat creation with respect and preserves humanity from alienation from itself and the natural world.[77]

Today the very existence of the eucharistic community continues to show that it is the work of the Holy Spirit in history to bring all the disparate entities of creation together in Christ. In the Eucharist the Church also anticipates sacramentally the ultimate saving of the whole creation from death (1 Cor 15:26).

God understood as *koinōnia* also has important implications for understanding the Church's relationship to the world. If *koinōnia* is the key paradigm for the relationship of God, Church, and world, then the mandate to proclaim the Good News throughout the world can be understood as an inculturation of the gospel in the world. Zizioulas proposes that the task of theology becomes one of seeking "ways of *relating* the Gospel to the existential needs of the world and to whatever is human."[78] He suggests that the longings of humankind thus become the starting point of mission.[79] Once these longings are identified, the gospel and revelation are brought into dialogue with them.

As I have explored in more detail in Chapter 3, it is within this mission to the world that Zizioulas singles out a particularly urgent task for the Church in these times, namely, alleviating the ecological crisis. Having conceded that sensitivity to the environment and to the integrity

[76] Zizioulas, "The Mystery of the Church," 302.

[77] J. Zizioulas, "L'Eucharistie, foyer de l'Eglise locale," unpublished lecture to the Conference on *"Les paroisses dans L'Eglise d'aujourd'hui,"* Louvaine-la Neuve, September 14–16, 1981, p. 14.

[78] Zizioulas, "The Church as Communion," 13.

[79] There is an obvious link here with the ecclesiology emerging from the Roman Catholic Church through the Second Vatican Council. See especially *Gaudium et Spes,* no. 1.

of creation has not traditionally been part of the Church's mission, he urges that it now must be.[80] He has argued for the need of the Church "to become conscious of and to proclaim in the strongest terms the fact that there is an intrinsic *koinōnia* between the human being and its natural environment, a *koinōnia* that must be brought into the Church's very being in order to receive its fullness."[81] Since God chose the way of communion in order to transform the world by being personally and existentially involved in the world, the Church has no choice but to do the same.[82]

Moreover, since the role of the Church is not primarily to receive and perpetuate ideas and doctrine as such, but rather to do with life and love, the very life and love of God,[83] Zizioulas is emphatic that it "should be understood absolutely and without any reservations" that this transcendence of all divisions is "the ultimate essence" of the catholicity of the Church:

> It covers all areas and all dimensions of existence whether human or cosmic, historical or eschatological, spiritual or material, social or individual . . . no dualistic dichotomies can be accepted. Man and the world form a unity of harmony and so do the various dimensions of man's own existence. . . . There is a constant interrelation between the Church and the world, the world being God's creation and never ceasing to belong to Him and the Church being the community which through the descent of the Holy Spirit transcends in herself the world and offers it to God in the Eucharist.[84]

Thus this principle that claims and elaborates a cosmic dimension of the Church draws attention to the intrinsic interrelatedness of God, Church, and world, which in turn points to the interrelatedness of each of the above principles. All are in "communio." The Church can only be authentically Church if understood within the context of the triune God; Christ and the Spirit have different but equal and essential roles in drawing humanity and the whole of creation into relationship with the Father. Both history and eschatology contribute to the identity of the Church, and that takes place especially in the Eucharist, in and through which humanity offers creation to God and with it is drawn

[80] Zizioulas addressed this specific issue at some length in the three lectures given at King's College, London, in 1989.

[81] Zizioulas, "The Church as Communion," 13.

[82] See Zizioulas, "Ordination and Communion," 192.

[83] See John D. Zizioulas, "The Theological Problem of 'Reception,'" *One in Christ* 21 (1985) 191.

[84] Zizioulas, *Being as Communion*, 162.

into God's life of communion. Within such a powerful ethos of union and communion, the historical disunity of the Christian Churches stands out as anomalous and scandalous.

An Ecumenical Vision of the Church

The call to unity between the Churches has been addressed by Zizioulas's life and ministry in many different ways. At the international forum of the World Council of Churches held at Santiago de Compostela in the last decade of the twentieth century, we see him drawing from his two great strengths: his academic research into the theology and history of the early Church and his pastoral experience during three decades of ecumenical dialogue at national and international levels. Here Zizioulas presents his vision of the Church as communion in a manner that is congruent with his theological vision. His focus is clearly toward the future as he engages the central truths of the Christian faith with urgent, practical issues of Church unity and offers a dynamic contribution to the ecumenical agenda.[85]

A consistent strand in Zizioulas's approach to ecumenism is belief that what he calls a confessionalistic approach to the problem of Church unity is unhelpful, since it is based on the premise that "truth is essentially a matter of propositions."[86] In a similar vein, Zizioulas notes that the challenge of ecumenism—the issue of there being one Church in the world, although there exist many Churches[87]—is an issue that is often tackled as an institutional "problem" that can be solved by good will and structural reform. He argues that the critical and difficult question of ecumenism must first of all be addressed theologically. He claims that a "sound doctrine of God as Trinity and of the divine economy of Christ in relation to the work of the Holy Spirit" is the sine qua non for an ecclesiology of communion and therefore of any true unity

---

[85] As with the BCC Commission Study, Zizioulas's impact on the work of this international forum is very obvious. The fruits of his contribution are recorded in different accounts of this assembly. See Gerard Kelly, "On the Way to Fuller Koinonia: The Fifth World Conference on Faith and Order," *Pacifica* 8 (1995) 155–73; Susan Hardman Moore "Towards Koinonia in Faith, Life and Witness," *The Ecumenical Review* 47 (1995) 3–11; Mary Tanner, "Cautious Affirmation and New Direction: A First Assessment of the Fifth World Conference on Faith and Order," *The Way* 34 (1994) 317–18. See also Thomas F. Best and Gunther Gassman, eds., *On the Way to Fuller Koinonia: Official Report of the Fifth World Conference of Faith and Order* (Geneva: WCC Publications, 1994) 127, 231–32, 240–41.

[86] Zizioulas, "Ecumenical Dimensions of Orthodox Theological Education," 35.

[87] See Best and Gassman, *Official Report,* for a note of appreciation expressed in the plenary assembly of Zizioulas's articulation of this particular issue.

between the Churches.[88] His consequent advocacy for Trinitarian theology to be placed more fully on the agenda of the Faith and Order Commission demonstrated his belief that these doctrines are not just dogmatic formulations for theologians but that, precisely because they point to the living, personal mystery of divine existence, they have profound practical implications for the life of the Church and the world.

In his paper "The Church as Communion," Zizioulas took the opportunity to explore the practical issues of authority, structure, and ministry as a means of contributing to the growth in communion between the Churches. My interest in pursuing his exploration of these existential realities through the lens of the Church as communion is prompted by the fact that they also reveal dimensions of the Trinitarian Mystery active at the center of the Church's life. For that reason in the next section we will take up Zizioulas's exploration of the issues of *authority and reception* and *ecclesial structures* under the rubric of the Church as communion and within the wider context of his ecumenical contributions on these issues.

Authority and Reception

As mentioned above, the issue of authority is a key issue both within and between the Churches in these times. In Zizioulas's work it is constantly linked to the theological principle of "reception." Because his understanding of Church is so thoroughly based on *koinōnia*—the dynamic, mutual relationship between different persons, the many gathered into the one Christ—it is not surprising that he understands tradition as a relational dynamic: "a reinterpreted and re-received reality in the light of the particular context into which it is transmitted."[89] According to this understanding, tradition is not primarily a formal transmission of teaching and life. In an ecclesiology of communion, time is not broken down into past, present, and future, and the true criterion of authority and tradition becomes what the world will be like in the fullness of God's reign. To underline this point, Zizioulas quotes one of his favorite sayings of his seventh-century mentor Maximus the Confessor: "The things of the past are shadow, those of the present *eikon*, the truth is to be found in the things of the future."[90] As has been discussed above in the section on eschatology, the orientation of tradition needs to be understood not as primarily directed towards the past but toward the future. If tradition is essentially concerned with the

[88] Zizioulas, "The Church as Communion," 15.
[89] Ibid., 13.
[90] Ibid., 14.

creation of communion, it necessarily involves a continual openness to becoming what *will* be.

The principle of reception and re-reception is intrinsically related to this understanding of authority and tradition. It is also an important practical consequence of the Church understood as communion and is therefore an issue that often occurs in Zizioulas's work.[91] He stresses the point that "the Church *was born* out of an ongoing process of reception" and notes that in our era, when the ecumenical movement is of critical importance, "the highest form of reception . . . is that of *mutual ecclesial recognition* and not simply of agreement of doctrine."[92] However, it is the classical idea of reception deeply embedded in the tradition of both the Orthodox and Roman Catholic Churches that perhaps illustrates most powerfully the dynamic, creative, and future-oriented potential of the Church understood as *koinōnia*. Zizioulas notes two fundamental aspects of reception that are important for today:

> The first is that the Church *receives;* she receives from God through Christ in the Holy Spirit; but she receives also from the world, its history, its culture, even its tragic experiences and failures for she is the body of the crucified Lord. . . . the second aspect is that the Church *is received* . . . the Church should be *offering herself to the world for reception.*[93]

What is received in the first place is God's love made incarnate in Jesus and given to us in the Holy Spirit. Both the message and the medium of the gift given are personal and relational. Zizioulas is emphatic about the significance of this crucial but often obscured point: "Whatever we may add to the meaning of reception as theologians, as Church historians and as canon lawyers, we should not obscure, ignore or destroy this fact. The Church exists in order to give what she has received as the love of God for the world."[94] Thus while the Church also receives as part of the living tradition the historical facts of Jesus' life, death and resurrection and then also receives the creeds that the people of God confess to be a true statement of the acts of God among us, the central reality is that above all the Church receives God as persons in communion.[95] Since it is God's love that is offered, through Christ in the Spirit, God does not impose the reception of this gift. God as love

[91] See particularly Zizioulas, "The Theological Problem of 'Reception,'" 187–93.

[92] Ibid., 187–88.

[93] Ibid., 189.

[94] Ibid., 190. See following also for a discussion for the use of "received" in Paul and Hebrews.

[95] See 1 Cor 11:23.

personified offers Godself freely and therefore may be rejected: "The Spirit is freedom, and reception of anything that is the content (the 'what') of reception cannot be imposed, on anyone by anyone. Truth is not authoritarian; it is authoritative by springing from an event of communion."[96]

This obvious but highly significant observation is often completely obscured by the way that authority is in fact exercised in the Churches. However, wisdom accrued from many different interdisciplinary sources corroborates the fact that any authentic communion between persons can occur most fully through an event of communion in a climate of freedom. Coercion does not enable truth to be received in its fullness.

The second fundamental aspect of reception that Zizioulas stresses is that the Church receives from the world, from its history, its cultures, its sufferings. The Church is the body of the crucified Christ. The world itself, if received, thus shapes the Church. That has all kinds of implications. In Chapter 3 it was noted how developments in the biological and natural sciences have contributed to what Zizioulas describes as reinstating humanity to an integral, connected place in creation. Another example of the Churches' learning from developments within contemporary scholarship is the recognition of the critical significance of the inculturation of the gospel if reception is to be able to take place. Zizioulas stresses freedom as an essential element of reception by different cultures: "Different people receive the gospel and Christ himself in different ways. There should be freedom of expression and variety of cultural forms in the reception. This is one of the reasons that make it necessary for reception to pass always through the local Church."[97]

It has thus been recognized that unless those entrusted with the proclamation of the Good News are first able to receive God's deeds that have already been at work in each culture by the work of the Holy Spirit, the capacity to offer the Good News of God's personal and unconditional love will be seriously impeded. The implementation of the principle of the Church's need to receive from the world's histories and cultures has scarcely begun. Its full enactment will ensure that the Church will become a truly global reality and be enabled to receive the fullness of the gospel message through a prism of all the rich and variegated cultures of humankind.

It follows from what has been said that authority in the Church resides not in any office of itself but in the event of communion created by the Spirit as the Spirit forms believers into the Body of Christ, both

[96] Zizioulas, "The Theological Problem of 'Reception,'" 191.
[97] Ibid., 192.

locally and universally. In practice this means, for example, that while for Roman Catholics and Orthodox the highest form of authority resides in the ecumenical council, both Churches acknowledge that no council is authoritative simply as an institution. Reception of a council's decisions by the local Churches must occur for such decisions to be authoritative.[98] Moreover, reception finally takes place within the context of the eucharistic communion of each local Church, with the one bishop guaranteeing both that the reception is in line with previous communities going back to apostolic times and that the reception is held in common with the rest of the ecclesial communities of the world.[99] The authority of ecumenical councils also lies in the fact that their decisions can make existential sense for generations.[100]

Thus Zizioulas's exploration of authority within the context of a theology of communion reveals the essential elements of his theological vision. It is Godself offered freely as Love personified in Christ and through the Spirit that the Church is invited to "receive" and in turn to offer this gift in freedom to the many of the world for reception. In every instance the relationships involved are to mirror those within the triune God. They are to be mutual and equal, with the uniqueness of each entity fully respected. It is thus through the very diversity of the local Churches that the universality of the Good News of God's reign is to reach all peoples and cultures.

Ecclesial Structures: Local and Universal

Such a vision prompts immediate questions about the kinds of ecclesial structures that would enable it to be realized. If the Church is communion, then relationality must be the sine qua non in its structures.[101] In exploring how the Church looks in the light of this principle,

---

[98] See Zizioulas, "The Church as Communion," 12.

[99] See Zizioulas, "The Theological Problem of 'Reception,'" 191–92.

[100] See Zizioulas, "Conciliarity and the Way to Unity," 25. For a more detailed description of how Zizioulas understands this ongoing process of "re-reception," see also Zizioulas, "The Teaching of the 2nd Ecumenical Council on the Holy Spirit in Historical and Ecumenical Perspective," in *Credo in Spiritum Sanctum*, ed. J. S. Martins (Rome: Libreria Editrice Vaticana, 1983) 1:29–54. This paper, given at a conference in Rome to mark the fifteen-hundredth anniversary of the Council of Constantinople, is "such an attempt towards a *re-reception* of the 2nd Ecumenical Council in a way that would imply faithfulness to the past without enslavement to its mere formulations and wordings," 30.

[101] See Metropolitan John, "The Eucharist and the Kingdom of God" (Part III), 32–37, for an elaboration of "the structure of the Church's 'institution.'"

Zizioulas distinguishes two levels of structure: the local and the universal. On a local level, he argues that an ecclesiology of communion would mean that no Christian can exist as an individual, and he recalls an old Latin saying, *unus christianus nullus christianus,* to stress the point that the way to God passes through the neighbor.[102] He also emphasizes the interdependence of the different members of the community and that no member of the Church, regardless of his or her position, can say to another "I need you not" (1 Cor 12). All are needed precisely because they are different and bring a range of diverse gifts to the whole body. In this he is again underlining inclusivity as an essential and defining characteristic of the Christian community.

Here Zizioulas also addresses the question of the limits to diversity. Noting the obvious implications for ecumenism, he asks whether communion sanctions diversity in an unconditional way. In response, he suggests as a working principle that the Church "must be structured in such a way that unity does not destroy diversity and diversity does not destroy unity."[103] He acknowledges that the application of such a principle is difficult but moves directly to one of the central claims of his theological-historical research: that of the role of the bishop in effecting unity in the Church.[104] To ensure communion, "all diversity in the community must somehow pass through a ministry of unity" and that within the local Church the one bishop, as presider of the Eucharist, is the primary minister of unity. He simultaneously reaffirms, however, that "this one minister should be part of the community and not stand above it as an authority in itself. . . . There is a *perichoresis* of ministries and this applies also to the ministry of unity."[105]

Thus a key component in Zizioulas's vision of the structures of Church as communion is the ministry of *episcopē.*[106] As developed above in the section on the corporate Christ, the bishop is the "one" who in the local Church brings the "many" into unity. Zizioulas again appeals to the experience of the Church of the first centuries:

[102] See Zizioulas, "The Church as Communion," 8.

[103] Ibid., 9.

[104] Note that Zizioulas's doctoral thesis devotes substantive sections to establish the scriptural and patristic bases for the role of the bishop in establishing the unity of the Church. See Pergame (Zizioulas), *L'Eucharistie, l'evêque et l'église durant les trois premiers siècles,* trans. Jean-Louis Parlierne (Paris: Theophanie, Desclee de Brouwer, 1994) 73–190.

[105] Zizioulas, "The Church as Communion," 10.

[106] Note that John Paul II in his 1995 encyclical *Ut Unum Sint,* 94, claims that the role of the Pope "consists precisely in 'keeping watch' *(episkopein),* like a sentinel, so that, through the effort of the Pastors, the true voice of Christ the Shepherd may be heard in all the particular Churches."

By opting for a *single* person in the community who would assume the ministry of the *episkopē* precisely in the form of the eucharistic presidency, the early Church found a way to minister to the needs of catholicity on the local level. The natural and social world in which the Church lives involves divisions of all kinds (sex, race, age, profession, class, etc.). These have to be transcended in Christ and the eucharistic gathering was always understood as the event which brings about the transcendence. The turning of the president of the eucharistic assembly into the minister of unity was found then to be essential.[107]

Zizioulas is insistent, however, that within the local Church the bishop's primary role should not in any way be understood as that of administrator of the diocese.[108] It is as presider of the Eucharist that the essential ministry of the bishop must be understood—the diversity of persons and gifts are all offered to God through Christ in the Spirit. As in his theology of creation and his addressing the ecological crisis, Zizioulas here implies that it is not a set of rules or an ethic that will bring about unity; it is the creation of an ethos that is needed. He is suggesting that the practical and often vexing issues of governance of a local ecclesial community can best be addressed if the minister of unity is the one who leads the community in the worship of a triune God of communion. The power of the symbol of episcopal office is to be brought into full play. The bishop is to personify Christ in the leadership of the local community.

This same principle of relationality applies to the structure of the Church at regional and universal levels. Even though Orthodox ecclesiology is based on the idea that "wherever there is the Eucharist there is the Church in its fullness as the Body of Christ,"[109] Zizioulas is also clear that "one community isolated from the rest of the communities cannot claim any ecclesial status. There is one Church in the world, although there are many Churches at the same time."[110] It is here that Zizioulas stresses again the critical and practical import of a "proper synthesis" between christology and pneumatology. If pneumatology is neglected (as has been the case in the Roman Catholic Church), undue submission of the local Church to the universal structure occurs. In this instance the magisterium assumes powers that exceed its true authority, and the local Churches collude by failing to claim their authentic

---

[107] Zizioulas, "Episkopé and Episkopos in the Early Church," 41.

[108] See the preface to the second edition of Pergame, *L'Eucharistie, l'evêque et l'église,* 10, where Zizioulas warns of the dangers of this growing phenomenon in the Church.

[109] Zizioulas, *Being as Communion,* 247.

[110] Zizioulas, "The Church as Communion," 10.

identity as Church. If christology is neglected (as has happened in some of the evangelical Pentecostal Churches), the local Church becomes unrelated to the one Church of God in the world. Zizioulas claims that: "if we attach to Christology and Pneumatology an equal importance, we are bound to attribute full catholicity to each local Church (the *totus Christus*) and at the same time seek ways of safeguarding the oneness of the Church on a universal level."[111]

In a formal address to the Lambeth Conference in 1988, Zizioulas spoke strongly about the importance of the role of a central authority within the Church, which he believes to be "a question of faith and not just of order." He stated that a "Church which is not able to speak with one mouth is not a true image of the body of Christ."[112] In 1993, in his address to the Faith and Order world conference at Santiago de Compostela, he further suggested that appropriate understandings of both the synodal system and the ministry of primacy provide ways for the proper balance between christology and pneumatology to be acted out. He appealed to the structures of the early Church as a model for consideration:

> . . . in each region the heads of the local Churches—the bishops—must recognize one of them—the bishop of the capital city—as primus (protos) and do nothing without him. The latter, however, must do nothing without these bishops, so that [according to canon 34 of the "Apostolic Canons"] the Triune God may be glorified.[113]

Such a model provides, he suggests, the possibility for the structures of both synodality and primacy to function in an interrelated way that ensures the integrity and catholicity of the local Church while providing for the whole Church to speak with one voice.

In spelling out some of the implications of the principle of the Church as communion for ecclesial structures, both local and universal, Zizioulas thus claims *relationality* as the key criterion. The keystone of his exploration of the concept of *koinōnia* thus derives essentially from faith, from the fact that God's very being is *koinōnia*. Because God is Trinitarian and a relational being and because the Church is the "*ecclesia* of God," the Church itself must reflect in its very being the way God exists—the way of personal communion. "The demand that we should 'become as God is' (Luke 2:36 and parallels) or that we should be 'par-

---

[111] Ibid.

[112] Metropolitan John (Zizioulas) of Pergamos, "Address to the 1988 Lambeth Conference," *Sourozh* 35 (1989) 32. Zizioulas was co-chairman of the Anglican-Orthodox Joint Doctrinal Commission at this time.

[113] Zizioulas, "The Church as Communion," 11.

takers of divine nature' (2 Peter 1:4) implies that the Church cannot exist and function without reference to the holy Trinity, which is the way God is. . . ."[114] Zizioulas's fundamental challenge to the ecumenical movement is that the whole Church—local, regional, universal— must be *koinōnia*, because that is how God is.

Conclusion

This exploration of Zizioulas's theological system in these four chapters has come the full circle: God, world, Church, God. At every turn it has become clear that such is the synthetic and organic nature of his theology, that to study his Trinitarian theology is to study his whole theological system. Every aspect of it springs from or leads to the Trinity and reveals the dynamic, relational life of different but equal persons-in-communion as the center point.

I have been arguing that the symbol of God as Trinity has something very significant to offer the existential quest of humanity at this time. The above unfolding of Zizioulas's neopatristic synthesis, drawing as it does from East and West, demonstrates that this contemporary Greek theologian has much to offer to the retrieval of this ancient symbol that is at the center of Christian faith and worship. It demonstrates that for the Christian Churches, the path of Trinitarian theology can open up a way to genuine unity through radical transformation and renewal of all the Churches based on relationship with God as persons in communion. It challenges the Churches to find their unity and reconciliation literally within the triune God, who is the source and the goal of their identity and mission.

For a world struggling to find significant common symbols amid the bewildering new and chaotic realities of life, Zizioulas's elaboration of the Christian symbol of the triune God also has much to offer. His Trinitarian theology focuses on the dynamic, divine, personal life of freedom at the heart of the universe into which humanity and all of creation are invited. This vision of the Trinity provides a glimpse of uniqueness and personal difference flourishing in an inclusive climate of mutual love and communion. This vision of God assures a world that is fearful of its very continuing existence that concepts that are so central to contemporary concern—freedom, person, and relationship— have dimensions that are eternal.

In Part Three Zizioulas's theology of the Trinity will be elaborated further as it is brought into mutual critical correlation with another rich source of insight for the task of retrieval of the triune God—the

---

[114] Ibid., 7.

Trinitarian theology of Roman Catholic feminist theologian Elizabeth Johnson.

PART TWO

The Trinitarian Theology of Elizabeth Johnson

CHAPTER 5

Renaming the Trinitarian God

The symbol of God functions. The symbol of God functions. The symbol of God functions.

For Elizabeth Johnson, "the right way to speak about God" is an issue of "unsurpassed importance."[1] She observes that "the symbol of God functions as the primary symbol of the whole religious system, the ultimate point of reference for understanding experience, life and the world." She suggests that the language a faith community uses about God implicitly represents its values and at the same time "powerfully molds the corporate identity of the community and directs its praxis." She further notes that the symbol of God is of equal significance for the individual person: "As a focus of absolute trust, one to whom you can give yourself without fear of betrayal, the holy mystery of God undergirds and implicitly gives direction to all of a believing person's enterprises, principles, choices, systems of values, and relationships."[2]

Johnson is drawn to examine how right speech about God is linked with the contemporary critical issue of the "pervasive exclusion of women from the realm of public symbol formation and decision-making."[3] Her steady focus on the practical impact of the symbol of God uncovers how this central symbol has functioned for millennia to

---

[1] Elizabeth Johnson, *SHE WHO IS: The Mystery of God in Feminist Theological Discourse* (New York: Crossroad, 1992) 11.

[2] Ibid., 2.

[3] Ibid.

"support an imaginative and structural world that excludes or subordinates women" and how, in turn, this "undermines women's human
dignity as equally created in the image of God."[4] The seriousness and
urgency of this situation are emphasized in the opening pages of Johnson's work on the mystery of God, *SHE WHO IS*, when she repeats, almost in mantric fashion, the sentence: "The symbol of God functions."[5]
She uses this sentence like a flashing red light to alert the reader to the
fact that this is a truth that would be dangerous to ignore. She warns
that "what is at stake is the truth about God, inseparable from the situation of human beings, and the identity and mission of the faith community itself."[6]

Many other theologians, and particularly feminist theologians,
have identified the power of language for naming God as a critical
issue.[7] Johnson's question concerning the right way to speak about God
can be situated as part of the rising swell of the women's movement
within society and the church. It can also be situated within the growing concern of all people who have begun to recognize the profound
implications of speech about God both for the future of life on this
planet and for the human person's capacity to know and relate to God.
Related to this has also been a notable body of work that addresses the
specific problems of naming the triune God.[8] The exclusive naming of

[4] Ibid., 3.

[5] Ibid.

[6] Ibid., 6.

[7] See Mary Daly, *Beyond God the Father: Toward a Philosophy of Women's Liberation*
(Boston: Beacon Press, 1973); Rosemary Radford Ruether, *Sexism and God-Talk:
Toward a Feminist Theology* (Boston: Beacon Press, 1983); Elisabeth Schüssler
Fiorenza, *In Memory of Her: A Feminist Theological Reconstruction of Christian Origins*
(New York: Crossroad, 1983); Sallie McFague, *Models of God: Theology for an Ecologi-
cal, Nuclear Age* (London: SCM Press, 1987); Anne E. Carr, *Transforming Grace: Chris-
tian Tradition and Women's Experience* (San Francisco: Harper & Row, 1988); Sandra
M. Schneiders, *Women and the Word: The Gender of God in the New Testament and the
Spirituality of Women* (New York/Mahwah, N.J.: Paulist Press, 1986); Anna Case-
Winters, *God's Power: Traditional Understandings and Contemporary Challenges* (Louisville, Ky.: Westminster/John Knox Press, 1990).

[8] See Mary Collins, "Naming God in Public Prayer," *Worship* 59 (1985) 291–304;
Catherine Mowry LaCugna, "The Baptismal Formula, Feminist Objections and
Trinitarian Theology," *Journal of Ecumenical Studies* 26 (1989) 235–50, and "God in
Communion with Us," in *Freeing Theology: The Essentials of Theology in Feminist Per-
spective*, ed. Catherine Mowry LaCugna (New York: HarperSanFrancisco, 1993)
83–114; Carr *Transforming Grace*, 134–57; Rebecca Oxford Carpenter, "Gender and
Trinity," *Theology Today* 41 (1984) 7–25; David S. Cunningham, "On Translating the
Divine Name," *Theological Studies* 56 (1995) 415–40; Ruth Duck, *Gender and the Name
of God: The Trinitarian Baptismal Formula* (New York: Pilgrim Press, 1991); Gail

the Trinity as Father, Son, and Holy Spirit is problematic because of the dynamic, relational nature of the Trinitarian symbol—the names of the triune persons reveal their respective identities. Catherine LaCugna spells out some of the reasons why this is "one of the thorniest pastoral and theological problems":

> There is far from a consensus on whether God's name as Father, Son, and Holy Spirit is revealed and cannot be changed, or whether it can be changed, on what basis, in what contexts, or by whom. Baptism into the triune name of God presents a special problem, because some churches will not recognize the validity of another church's baptism if there is any deviation from the formula given in Matthew 28:19.[9]

It follows that any constructive work on renaming the Trinitarian symbol will be complex and difficult. Until now it has primarily been women who have been motivated strongly enough to address it.[10]

Rebecca Chopp has noted that "feminist theology is not a mere corrective enterprise in Christianity. Rather it is reformulation of Christianity in which among other things, the good news of Christianity emancipates and transforms the world."[11] Johnson's work of renaming

---

Ramshaw, *God Beyond Gender: Feminist Christian God-Language* (Minneapolis: Fortress Press, 1995), and "De Divinis Nominibus: The Gender of God," *Worship* 56 (1982) 117–31, and "Naming the Trinity: Orthodoxy and Inclusivity," *Worship* 60 (1986) 491–98; Marjorie Suchocki, "The Unmale God: Reconsidering the Trinity," *Quarterly Review* 3 (1983) 34–49; Elaine M. Wainwright, "What's in a Name? The Word Which Binds/The Word Which Frees," *Freedom and Entrapment: Women Thinking Theology,* ed. Maryanne Confoy, Dorothy Lee, and Joan Nowotny (North Blackburn, Victoria: Dove, 1995) 100–20; Patricia Wilson-Kastner, "The Trinity," in *Faith, Feminism and the Christ* (Philadelphia: Fortress Press, 1983) 121–37; Barbara Brown Zikmund, "The Trinity and Women's Experience," *The Christian Century* 104 (April 15, 1987) 354–56.

[9] LaCugna, "God in Communion with Us," 99.

[10] This is not to imply that feminist theology has only spoken to women or that male theologians have not supported its concerns in the realm of God-language and integrated its insights into mainstream theology. In 1991, for example, the *Journal of Feminist Studies in Religion* invited eight male theologians to reflect on the influence of feminist theory on their theological work. See Francis Schüssler Fiorenza, John B. Cobb Jr., Peter C. Hodgson, Gordon D. Kaufman, Wayne Proudfoot, Mark Kline Taylor, David Tracy, and Vincent L. Wimbush, "The Influence of Feminist Theory on My Theological Work," *Journal of Feminist Studies in Religion* 7, no. 1 (Spring, 1991) 102–29. In the various responses there is an agreement that many areas of contemporary theology, such as language about God, christology, anthropology, creation, ecclesiology, ministry have been seriously changed by feminist theology.

[11] Rebecca S. Chopp, *The Power to Speak: Feminism, Language, God* (New York: Crossroad, 1991) 21.

the Trinitarian God has this strong constructive dimension. It is essentially about reformulation, but it is also about emancipation and transformation. Her method is to bring elements of women's experience into dialogue with retrievable elements of the Christian tradition. She describes her work of exploration as "one way of speaking about one core, religious symbol," by attempting "to braid a footbridge between the ledges of classical and feminist Christian wisdom."[12]

This chapter traces Johnson's constructive method. It outlines her search of the tradition to discover "rules for speaking about God" that have evolved over time within Christianity. It explores the biblical, christological, and mariological sources retrieved by Johnson for the purpose of uncovering strands of the tradition that are redemptively congruent with women's experience and then sets out Johnson's alternative constructive proposal for renaming the triune God.

Rules for Speaking About God

One of Johnson's particular gifts is her capacity to identify sources of wisdom within classical Christianity which have been held consistently by the teaching Church but which in fact have not been practiced consistently. For example, from the beginnings of Christianity there has developed a body of teaching regarding the possibilities and limits of human knowing and speaking about God. This accrued wisdom has always held an honored place within the tradition, but such were/are the forces of patriarchy at work within society and the Church that they have rarely been applied to critique the exclusive male language for God used in theology and worship. In order to provide a sound framework for her work of critique, retrieval and reconstruction, Johnson appeals to this classical wisdom to speak rightly about God.

Divine Incomprehensibility

A central plank of this framework is the doctrine of divine incomprehensibility. Johnson recalls some of the key tenets of this dogma:

> The holiness and utter transcendence of God present throughout all creation have always been an absolutely central affirmation of the Jewish tradition and its grafted branch, Christian faith. God as God, ground, support, and goal of all, is illimitable mystery who, while immanently present, cannot be measured, manipulated or controlled. . . . God's unlikeness to the corporal and spiritual world is total . . . it is proper to

---

[12] Johnson, *SHE WHO IS*, 12.

God as God to transcend all similarity to creatures, and thus never to be known comprehensively or essentially as God.[13]

Johnson points out, however, that both theology and preaching often use God-language that is in fact too certain and distinct. She refers to Hans Urs von Balthasar's observation in the early eighties that there was scarcely a work in dogmatics that gives proper attention to the incomprehensibility of God.[14] Theologians can and do forget what both Hebrew and Christian Scriptures hold as central, namely, that God is essentially mystery in the profoundest sense. The first commandment underlines God's otherness, and abundant references throughout the Torah and the prophetic and wisdom writings spell out that the holy name YHWH signifies God's presence, not essence, and that the latter is unfathomable (Exod 3:14).[15] Similarly, the God revealed by Jesus the Christ "bears witness to the strong and consistent belief that God cannot be exhaustively known but even in revelation remains the mystery surrounding the world."[16]

In the early Christian era, Greek philosophy taught that the ultimate origin of all must be totally different from the world of multiplicity and change, and that therefore human concepts are limited in their capacity to convey divine reality. This appealed to Christian theologians trying to express the biblical theme that God is unknown but present. Johnson notes, however, that the dogmatic formulations of christology and the Trinity of the first centuries in fact tended to become definitions instead of remaining pointers toward the Divine Mystery. This was in spite of the fact of the strong insistence on the incomprehensibility and transcendence of God on the part of so many of the theologians of the East, such as Athanasius and the Cappadocians, who were involved in the formulation of the dogmas. In the West, Augustine's influential work powerfully expressed the ineffability of God and therefore supported the need to use many names in expressing the divine nature. Augustine was clear in his caution that "if you have understood, then this is not God."[17] He taught that since God is love,

---

[13] Ibid., 104–5.

[14] See Johnson, "The Incomprehensibility of God and the Image of God Male and Female," *Theological Studies* 45 (1984) 441–42. Johnson refers to Hans Urs von Balthasar, "The Unknown God," in *The von Balthasar Reader,* ed. M. Kehl and W. Löser (New York: Crossroad, 1982) 184.

[15] See Johnson, *SHE WHO IS,* 106. See also Johnson, "The Incomprehensibility of God," 445–48, for a fuller exploration of biblical sources that reveal both incomprehensibility and female imaging of God.

[16] Ibid., 107.

[17] Augustine, *Sermon* 52, ch. 1, no. 16.

we can best taste something of God through loving.[18] Johnson summarizes: "What we receive from early Christian theology is a pattern of positive affirmation, coupled with agnosticism of definition, both essential to the truth about God. In the end, we are united to God as to an unknown, savoring God only through love."[19]

Eventually, at the Fourth Lateran Council in 1215, this theological tradition of divine incomprehensibility found its way into official Church teaching. At this council an important axiom for language about God was hammered out. The council promulgated that "between Creator and creature no similarity can be expressed without implying that the dissimilarity between them is even greater."[20] This teaching was developed further by the university theologians of the thirteenth century, who taught that human speech about God is neither univocal nor equivocal but analogical.[21] Referring back to the earlier Christian sources including Chrysostom, Augustine, John Damascene, and Pseudo-Dionysius, the great Scholastic theologian Thomas Aquinas taught that "the perfection of all our knowledge about God is said to be a knowing of the unknown, for then supremely is our mind found to know God when it most perfectly knows that the being of God transcends everything whatever that can be apprehended in this life."[22] This teaching is so consistent that it survived even the defining certainties of the First Vatican Council (1869–1870). In speaking about rationalism, this council held that:

> Divine mysteries of their very nature so excel the created intellect that even when they have been given in revelation and accepted in faith, that very faith still keeps them veiled in a sort of obscurity, as long as 'we are exiled from the Lord' in this mortal life, 'for we walk by faith and not by sight' (2 Cor 5:6-7).[23]

In tracing the thread of teaching about the incomprehensibility of God over the centuries, Johnson observes a clarity in the steady con-

---

[18] See Johnson, *SHE WHO IS*, 108, which refers to *De Trinitate* 8.8.12.

[19] Ibid.

[20] H. Denzinger and A. Schönmetzer, *Enchiridion Symbolorum: Definitionum et Declarationum de Rebus Fidei et Morum*, 35th rev. ed. (Barcinone: Herder, 1973) 806; henceforth referred to as DS. See J. Neuner and J. Dupuis, eds., *The Christian Faith in the Doctrinal Documents of the Catholic Church* (New York: Alba House, 1981) 109. Quoted in Johnson, *SHE WHO IS*, 109.

[21] See Johnson, *SHE WHO IS*, 109.

[22] Aquinas, *In Boethii De Trinitate*, 1, 2, ad 1. Quoted in Johnson, *SHE WHO IS*, 110.

[23] DS 3016, in Neuner and Dupuis, *The Christian Faith*, 45–46 (*Dei Filius*, chap. 4). Quoted in Johnson, *SHE WHO IS*, 112.

sensus that emerges. This teaching demonstrates that "absolutizing any particular expression as if it were adequate to divine reality is tantamount to a diminishment of the truth about God."[24] This consensus of belief endures into the contemporary period, when the agnosticism characterized by the "death of God" movement and a post-modern sensibility provide what Johnson describes as a "new spiritual climate" that also gives credence to this truth of divine hiddenness. She refers, for example, to William Hill's description of the "positive deepening of darkness" in biblical revelation of God's Trinitarian nature and to Karl Rahner's thesis that God's inexhaustibility is the very condition for the possibility of the human spirit's self-transcendence in knowledge and love. Johnson's conclusion to her survey of this teaching on divine incomprehensibility is very clear: this steady stream of tradition encapsulates a deep wisdom that teaches that no images, including exclusive male symbols, in themselves, can convey that which is finally inexpressible, the Holy Mystery of God.

Analogy

This first "rule" for speaking about God immediately raises the issue of how it is possible to say anything about God. Johnson draws from another resilient strand within the tradition and identifies the teaching on analogy as a primary way that was used to enable appropriate speech about God. She describes early Christian theology addressing the problem of affirmations about God being interpreted as literal by requiring a threefold movement of affirmation, negation, and eminence. She emphasizes that in this process "the play of the mind is subtle":

> A word whose meaning is known and prized from human experience is first affirmed about God. The word is then critically negated to remove any association with creaturely modes of being. Finally the word is predicated of God in a supereminent way that transcends all cognitive capabilities. . . . Every concept and symbol must go through this purifying double negation, to assure its own legitimacy.[25]

Johnson's own assessment of this process is that through it "an unspeakably rich and vivifying reality is intuited while God remains incomprehensible." She reminds us that the "knowing" of God accomplished in the analogical process is a "dynamic of relational knowing"

[24] Johnson, *SHE WHO IS*, 112.
[25] Ibid., 113. The strong influence of Thomas Aquinas's thought is very obvious in Johnson's articulation of "Rules for Speaking about God."

that occurs, not through a concept, but in an intuitive leap of the human spirit that holds together the paradox of God's incomprehensibility and the revelation of God's faithful presence to creation.[26] Johnson refers to Aquinas, a major source of teaching on the various uses of analogy, who argued that analogy shapes every category of words used to speak about God. She instances terms that are metaphorical (God is rock), relational (Creator, Redeemer), negative (infinite, immutable, impassible), as well as terms that point to characteristics of Godself (God is good, personal, exists). Aquinas holds that "all affirmations we can make about God are not so much that our minds may rest in them, nor of such a sort that God does not transcend them."[27]

Johnson describes how the history of theology shows that soon after the development of teaching on analogy was achieved in the medieval schools, the same pattern of forgetting that occurred with the teaching on divine incomprehensibility was repeated. With the growth of nominalism and with the ecclesiastical need to proclaim unambiguous certainties reasserting itself, the primary importance of the negating power of analogy was neglected. Consequently, with the Reformation there were good grounds for disputing the use of analogy as it was then practiced.[28] It was only in the twentieth century, with the Catholic return to the historical sources, that the subtleties of analogy, including its negative component, have been restored. Johnson refers particularly to the contributions of Karl Rahner and David Tracy, who made significant contributions to the recovery of analogy and the "nonliteral although still meaningful character of its speech about God."[29]

Many Names

A third rule that Johnson focuses on from within the tradition's teaching on language for God is the acknowledgment of the necessity of giving to God *many names.* There is nothing subtle about this aspect of the tradition. The use of many names for God is a practice that was

[26] See ibid., 113–14.

[27] Aquinas, *De divinibus nominibus* 1, 2. Quoted in Johnson, *SHE WHO IS*, 115. See also 297, n. 24, where references are provided to Aquinas's mature treatment of analogy in *Summa Theologiae* I, q. 12–13.

[28] See Johnson, *SHE WHO IS*, 116, for references to the strong critiques of Luther and, in this century, Barth and Pannenberg.

[29] Ibid. See Karl Rahner, "The Experiences of a Catholic Theologian," *Communio: International Catholic Review* 11, no. 4 (1984) 404–7, for a moving account, made not long before his death, of this great theologian's reflections on the teaching of analogy.

well established within the Hebrew Scriptures and applied from the beginnings of Christianity. Johnson draws from the variety of discourses within the Bible—narrative, prophecy, command, wisdom writings, hymns of celebration and lament[30]—and the plethora of images that they contain. She recalls how those various discourses provide an abundance of many very different images, female as well as male. They are taken from personal relationships, from crafts and professions, from the animal world, from cosmic realities. She also provides examples of other descriptive terms that have emerged from within post-biblical Christian theological discourse: "source and goal of all, the ground of our being, the depth of reality, the beyond in our midst, the absolute future, ultimate mystery, being itself."[31]

Then, besides Christian traditional sources, Johnson explores the rich and varied heritage from other religious traditions—Jewish, Islamic, indigenous.[32] The range of possibilities seems almost endless. These litanies of images, when listed alongside each other, provide a glimpse of an ever-expanding horizon of provocative and powerful symbols for the divine. From such an exploration one is shaken into recognizing with Johnson that "Western language of recent centuries appears thin and pallid when brought into contact with this polyphony resulting from the human search for appropriate names for God."[33] The very limited use of mainly male images has seriously confined who God can be for humanity. It has limited our capacity to engage with the divine. The entire Christian tradition, as well as all traditions that seek God, bears incontrovertible witness to the need for the use of many names for God.

Johnson's scanning of biblical sources and classical legacy has thus located three basic rules in the tradition for speech about God. She concludes her search by applying her findings to her primary theological concern:

> The classical themes of the incomprehensibility of God, the analogical nature of religious language, and the necessity of many names for God are a heritage most useful to women's desire to emancipate speech about God. They shift the debate from the narrow focus on one or two patriarchal symbols to a field at once more ancient and more living.[34]

---

[30] See ibid., 118, 292, n. 35, for reference to the work of Paul Ricoeur in this area.
[31] Ibid.
[32] See ibid., 118–20, for many examples of different names for God.
[33] Ibid., 120.
[34] Ibid.

Resources Within the Tradition for
Renaming the Trinitarian God

Johnson's constructive contribution to renaming the triune God draws from three major sources within the tradition. These are christology, mariology, and the Wisdom tradition in the Scriptures. It should be noted that Johnson herself does not apply in any major way the research she has done on Mary to her task of renaming the Trinitarian God. However, I find the results of her research in this area so compelling that I believe including it in this context strengthens the creative proposal she offers in *SHE WHO IS*. In this section I will trace Johnson's retrieval of each of these three theological sources and demonstrate how they contribute to her constructive work.

Christology

Johnson claims that christology was central in shaping the doctrine of God. She recalls how the earliest records of the Christian story reveal that the distinctively Christian doctrine of God took shape from within the debate about the question of Jesus Christ:

> Was he or was he not equal in essence to the God who created heaven and earth? Once an affirmative answer was given and Jesus was confessed by the Council of Nicaea to be *homoousios* with the Father, something new had been said about the one true God. . . . This new affirmation, itself the result of the experience of Christ in the living faith and praxis of the church, made a rethinking of the inherited doctrine of God necessary. The outcome was an explicitly developed doctrine of the Trinity, the specific Christian conception of God won from reflection on the person of Jesus Christ.[35]

The identity of Jesus Christ is again a live one, just as it was in the early Church. Johnson joins her voice to that of many theologians who are claiming that emerging new understandings of Jesus Christ are again "revolutionizing" the traditional doctrine of God.[36] The widespread awakening to the limits of classical metaphysics, coupled with the renewal of christology that has been revitalized by significant developments in biblical studies, has led theologians to explore implications for the doctrine of the Trinity. The method that the classical

---

[35] Elizabeth A. Johnson, "Christology's Impact on the Doctrine of God," *Heythrop Journal* 26 (1985) 143.

[36] See ibid. and also 160, n. 2, where Johnson provides references to various contemporary theologians who are claiming a "revolution" in the doctrine of God.

approach adopted was to start with the doctrine of God and to move to a reflection on the mystery of the incarnation. It was thus almost inevitable that characteristics of the classical idea of God—omniscience, omnipotence, impassibility—were superimposed on the historical Jesus and the Christ of faith. In contemporary theology the direction is being reversed. Johnson notes that "what in effect is being produced is a theology of God from below, with christology forming one of its major sources."[37]

Other feminist theologians make this same claim. Gail Ramshaw, for example, who also addresses the issue of the naming of the Trinity, is emphatic that "the central Christian question in the naming of God [is]: who is Jesus in relation to God?"[38] And Catherine Mowry LaCugna, similarly seeking solutions to the naming of the Trinity, claims that "the self-revelation of God in Christ remains the only sure source for overcoming distortions in theology and Church practice, because it is only by living *in Christ* that we meet the living God whom Jesus proclaimed and through Christ are faithful to the true, living God."[39]

In her article entitled "Christology's Impact on the Doctrine of God," published in 1985, Johnson notes that approaching the theology of God "from below" has affected at least three significant aspects of Trinitarian theology: the concept of the divine nature, the relation of God to the world and to history, and the divine attribute of immutability. She explores each one of these. First, she shows how, when freed from the concepts of philosophical monotheism, "the one true God is seen to exist in a triune self-related dynamic" rather than being conceived of as having a single divine nature that is somehow an entity in itself. Moreover, within this relational understanding of God's being, she affirms that "all talk of God as Trinity is ultimately talk of God as love."[40]

Second, by reflecting on the historical particularity of Jesus in relationship to Godself, Johnson concludes that in Jesus Christ, the being of God cannot be separated from relatedness to the world and its history. Put positively, this leads to growth in appreciation that "there is room in God for us, scope in God for the world and humanity."[41]

Third, she claims that reflection on the incarnation from below also leads to an acceptance of the notion of God's "becoming." This replaces the concept of classical theism of God as immutable and is understood

---

[37] Ibid., 159.
[38] Ramshaw, "Naming the Trinity," 492.
[39] LaCugna, "God in Communion with Us," 105.
[40] Johnson, "Christology," 146–47.
[41] Ibid., 148.

as "the movement of the fullness of being, pure actuality overflowing with life and love." Thus, drawing from current christologies, Johnson concludes that the story of Jesus reveals a God who is intrinsically relational in Godself and to the world in a way that is personal and life-giving.[42]

In a further move of "thinking God from the death-resurrection of Jesus," Johnson notes that "the application of critical methodology to scripture has given a new concreteness to this event and moved its significance to the centre of christology."[43] It is now appreciated that Jesus was killed as a public criminal as a result of his fidelity to his mission of proclaiming the kingdom of God and that his resurrection was a turning point in his history. This leads to a revision of the classical theistic attribute of impassibility. The death-resurrection event reveals God as victorious love relating in solidarity with suffering humanity.[44] Further, Johnson demonstrates that "thinking God from the ministry of Jesus," particularly from the perspectives of contemporary liberation and feminist christologies, reveals a God who seeks liberation and wholeness for humanity and all of creation.[45]

Thus Johnson finds within current christological thinking the basis for a reclaimed symbol of Christ and of God that can be liberating for women. There remains, however, a major problem for women. Jesus' maleness has been implicitly transferred to God's own being and has ensured that God is essentially understood as male. Johnson points out that "this view is intensified by the almost exclusive use of father-son metaphors to interpret Jesus' relationship with God"[46]—"Who has seen me has seen the Father" (John 14:9).[47] Consequently, as Rosemary Ruether attests, "the unwarranted idea develops that there is a necessary ontological connection between the maleness of Jesus' historical person and the maleness of Logos as male offspring and disclosure of a male God."[48] Johnson argues that this problem arises, not because Jesus of Nazareth was a male person, but because this one particularity of sex, unlike any of his other historical particularities, has been constantly emphasized

[42] Ibid., 149.

[43] Ibid., 149.

[44] See ibid., 150–54, for a discussion of the christologies of Moltmann, Kasper, Schillebeeckx.

[45] See ibid., 154–58.

[46] Elizabeth A. Johnson, "Redeeming the Name of Christ," in LaCugna, *Freeing Theology*, 119.

[47] See also Johnson, *SHE WHO IS*, 152, and Elizabeth A. Johnson, "The Maleness of Christ," *The Special Nature of Women?* ed. Anne Carr and Elisabeth Schüssler Fiorenza (Philadelphia: Concilium/Trinity Press, 1991) 108.

[48] Ruether, *Sexism and God-Talk*, 117.

and made essential to his identity as the Christ. She is also clear about the serious consequences of this phenomenon. It has meant that "of all the doctrines of the Church christology is the one most used to suppress and exclude women."[49]

For those reasons Johnson argues that Christ is a key symbol that must be freed from its distorted, sexist accretions if the doctrine of God is to be successfully reclaimed as Good News for women. To do this, she goes to the heart of the matter—she returns to the origins of the formulation of christological doctrine and appeals to the teaching of the Council of Chalcedon (451 C.E.). In response to the controversies of the first centuries concerning his identity, Jesus the Christ was proclaimed by this council to be *vere Deus, vere homo*—true God and true human being. The council taught that the one and the same Christ is one *hypostasis* (person) made known in two natures, human and divine, and that between the human nature and the divine nature there is no mixing or confusion. Each nature keeps its own properties. If the logic of this authoritative teaching is followed, then none of Jesus' human characteristics can be mixed or confused with his divinity. However, as Johnson describes, that is not what happened in fact. Instead, "the androcentric imagination occasions a certain leakage of Jesus' human maleness into the divine nature, so that maleness appears to be of the essence of the God made known in Christ."[50] Johnson's argument is that if the clarity of this doctrinal teaching were to be fully reclaimed, the Christ symbol would de facto be freed from its exclusive maleness.

In a second appeal to christological dogma, Johnson recalls the early Christian dictum: "What is not assumed is not redeemed, but what is assumed is saved by union with God."[51] This axiom originated in Irenaeus's work on recapitulation and was refashioned and refined by Athanasius and Gregory Nazianzen.[52] It emerged from the pondering of the mystery of the incarnation by the Christian communities,

---

[49] Johnson, *SHE WHO IS*, 151. See also Rita N. Brock, "The Feminist Redemption of Christ," in *Christian Feminism: Visions of a New Humanity*, ed. Judith Weidman (San Francisco: Harper & Row, 1984) 55–74; Rosemary Radford Ruether, "The Liberation of Christology from Patriarchy," *New Blackfriars* 66 (1985) 324–35; Carr, *Transforming Grace*, 158–79. For post-Christian feminists the maleness of the symbol of Christ is a primary reason that Christianity is judged to be destructive to the human cause. See Daly, *Beyond God the Father*, 69–97; Daphne Hampson, *Theology and Feminism* (Oxford: Blackwell, 1990) 53, 76; Naomi Goldenburg, *The Changing of Gods: Feminism and the End of Traditional Religions* (Boston: Beacon Press, 1979) 4.

[50] Johnson, *SHE WHO IS*, 152.

[51] See ibid., 153.

[52] See Richard P. McBrien, *Catholicism: Study Edition* (New York: HarperSanFrancisco, 1981) 446.

and it grew from the insight that it is Christ's solidarity with all humanity that ensures our salvation. Thus, when in 325 C.E. the Nicene Creed confessed *Et homo factus est* ("became a human being"), it acknowledged "the universal relevance of the incarnation by use of the inclusive *homo*."[53] Johnson reminds the reader that if the credal formula were instead *et vir* [adult male] *factus est,* as in fact it has often been interpreted, then clearly the creed would have taught that women are not saved but only men. That was never the intention of these teachings and has never been taught by the Church. The formal teaching has always been unambiguous that Christ became one with humanity and that all women and men are therefore saved.

Thus, by revisiting those early christological formulas, Johnson points to the value of reinterpreting the symbol of Christ so as to "allow its ancient inclusivity to shine through."[54] She claims that "these texts in their historical context make clear that it is not Jesus' maleness that is doctrinally important but his humanity in solidarity with the whole suffering human race. The intent of the christological doctrine was and continues to be inclusive."[55] Her conclusion is that there is an inherent liberating truth in those foundational Christian dogmas that the "androcentric imagination" has held bound. She demonstrates that if accurately interpreted, they can, in conjunction with liberating insights from contemporary studies in christology, become part of a secure framework upon which to build a doctrine of God that reveals the God of Jesus Christ upholding the full humanity of women.

Mariology

In the case of christological dogma, Johnson uses women's experience of exclusion from images for God as a focus for her search for elements within the tradition that can contribute positively to a full disclosure of the revelation of God. Her work reveals that central elements of christological teaching have been covered over, obscured, or forgotten by a succession of patriarchal cultures ascendant within the Church. In the case of a second source, the living tradition of popular devotion to Mary, Johnson's research reveals that the opposite is true. It shows that for centuries humankind has instinctively refused to let go of the female face of God. The popular devotion of the faithful, despite the attempt to maintain correct mariological doctrine in official teach-

---

[53] Johnson, "Redeeming the Name of Christ," 120.
[54] Johnson, *SHE WHO IS*, 154.
[55] Ibid., 165.

ing and scholarly discourse,[56] escaped the restrictions of patriarchy by covertly projecting divine female attributes onto the most important female figure within the Church, Mary of Nazareth.

In 1989 Johnson published what became a significant article entitled "Mary and the Female Face of God."[57] She showed that many scholars from diverse disciplines have proposed that one of the primary reasons for the extraordinary growth of devotion to Mary throughout history lies in the symbolic power of her image precisely because it is female. Johnson rightly observes that without this devotion to Mary, there would be no female imaging within the mainline Christian perception of God as Father, Son, and Spirit:

> Female images of God, arguably necessary for the full expression of the mystery of God but suppressed from official formulations, have migrated to the figure of this woman. Mary has been the icon of God. For innumerable believers she has functioned to reveal divine love as merciful, close, interested, always ready to hear and respond to human needs, trustworthy, and profoundly attractive. . . . Consequently, in devotion to her as compassionate mother who will not let one of her children be lost, what is actually being mediated is a most appealing experience of God.[58]

In other words, since there was no way to express the fullness of humanity's experience of God without using female images, they very soon were displaced onto Mary, the Mother of God.

Johnson shows how scholars of early Christian history have found clear links between early mariological devotion and the cults of the Great Mother in the Mediterranean world into which Christianity was moving. Jean Daniélou, for example, in his classic study of this adaptation,

---

[56] See, for example, Elizabeth A. Johnson, "Marian Devotion and the Western Church," in *Christian Spirituality: High Middle Ages and Reformation*, ed. J. Raitt, B. McGinn, and J. Meyendorff (New York: Crossroad, 1987) 395.

[57] Elizabeth A. Johnson, "Mary and the Female Face of God," *Theological Studies* 50 (1989) 500–26. See also "Mary as Mediatrix," in *The One Mediator, the Saints and Mary*, ed. H. Anderson (Minneapolis: Augsburg, 1992) 311–26; "Saints and Mary," in *Systematic Theology: Roman Catholic Perspectives*, vol. 2, ed. Francis Schüssler Fiorenza and John P. Galvin (Minneapolis: Fortress Press, 1991); "The Marian Tradition and the Reality of Women," *Horizons* 12, no. 1 (1985) 116–35; "The Symbolic Character of Theological Statements about Mary," *Journal of Ecumenical Studies* 22, no. 2 (Spring, 1985) 312–35. Johnson is working on a substantive project in mariology that will provide a companion volume for her *Friends of God and Prophets: A Feminist Theological Reading of the Communion of Saints*.

[58] Johnson, "Mary and the Female Face of God," 501.

suggests that officials of the Church allowed this assimilation to occur because it was an excellent missionary strategy in a world where female deities were so highly honored. He concludes that the power of the Marian cult lay in the fact that it corresponds to the aspirations of the human heart, functioning in psychologically parallel ways to the Great Mother.[59]

Johnson cites how historians have also identified many specific ways in which the adaptation of worship from female deities to Mary occurred. Temples and shrines, particularly places in nature—wooded grottoes, springs, mountains, lakes—were rededicated to Mary, the Mother of God. Notable examples of this were found in Rome, Athens, Chartres, Ephesus. Similarly, images of Mary were decorated in the blue cloak and the turret of the goddess and Marian images were frequently linked with the moon and the stars, with water and wind. Mary was often depicted seated on a royal throne presenting her child to the world, an iconography patterned on images of the goddess Isis with her son Horus. And in hymns reminiscent of the hymns of praise to Isis, Mary was praised with titles and attributes of female deities—all-holy, merciful, wise, the universal mother, protector of sailors at sea.[60]

Studies in medieval European history reveal extensive growth in popular devotion to Mary, and by the time of the Reformation "her figure had taken on divinised attributes and functions borrowed not from the ancient Goddess but from the Christian Trinity itself."[61] Over time omniscience and power over heaven, earth, and hell were attributed to Mary. Biblical references to God the Father were also ascribed to her. For example, she loved the world so much that she gave her only Son (John 3:16). Johnson comments that similar parallels were made between Mary and Christ in nature, grace, and glory: "As coredemptrix, she merited salvation; as mediatrix, she obtained grace for sinners; as queen and mother of mercy she dispensed it herself." Johnson demonstrates that "all of this power resided in Mary as a maternal woman, who could be trusted to understand and cope with human weakness better than a somewhat testy God the Father or a righteous Jesus Christ."[62] Such was the role of Mary's mercy in medieval times that

---

[59] Jean Daniélou, "Le culte marial et le paganisme," in *Maria: Etudes de la sainte Vierge*, ed. D'Hubert de Manoir (Paris: Beauchesne, 1949) 159–81.

[60] See Johnson, "Mary and the Female Face of God," 506. For a more detailed reference to Chartres, see also Johnson, "Marian Devotion and the Western Church," 398–400.

[61] Johnson, "Mary and the Female Face of God," 507. See also Johnson, "Marian Devotion and the Western Church," 407.

[62] Johnson, "Mary and the Female Face of God," 509. For a description of the development of this phenomenon within the medieval period, see Johnson, "Marian

theologians wrote of her what biblical authors had written of Christ: "In her the fullness of the Godhead dwelt corporeally (Col 2:9); of her fullness we have all received (Jn 1:16); because she had emptied herself, God had highly exalted her, so that at her name every knee should bow (Phil 2:5-11)."[63] Thus Johnson shows how from being "the handmaid of the Lord whose key relationship was with Christ, Mary became Our Lady, an acting subject with an equally important relationship to the individual seeking to attain salvation."[64] Earlier last century Yves Congar judged that a deficient christology led to such power being attributed to Mary. When the divinity of Jesus was emphasized out of proportion to his humanity, the human Mary seemed more approachable, and when God's just judgment was emphasized to the detriment of Christ's mercy, Mary as Mother of Mercy took his place.[65]

Johnson notes how in more recent times, in this post-conciliar period, Catholic scholars have been open to the Protestant critique that in the Catholic tradition, Mary has been substituted in a particular way for the action of the Holy Spirit. Critical surveys of devotional literature by a number of scholars, including Yves Congar, René Laurentin, and Cardinal Leon Suenens, reveal that Catholics have said of Mary that "she forms Christ in them, that she is spiritually present to guide and inspire, that she is the link between themselves and Christ, and that one goes to Jesus through her. Furthermore, Mary is called intercessor, mediatrix, helper, advocate, defender, consoler, counsellor."[66] Johnson points out that all these names or attributes properly belong to the Spirit of God.

Summarizing her explorations of the historical origins of the Marian tradition, its medieval excesses and post-Reformation developments, Johnson concludes that "roughly corresponding to each of these three periods, the Marian figure has taken on the characteristics of the creating, saving and sanctifying God, functioning in some degree in a compensatory way vis-à-vis the three divine persons of Father, Son and Spirit."[67] She also makes clear from other diverse sources, such as the history of the development of doctrine, Reformation theology, feminist and liberation theology, the psychology of religion, and the social sciences, that Marian theology and devotion have adopted female language and

---

Devotion and the Western Church," 400–4, and within post-Reformation Catholicism, see Johnson, "Mary as Mediatrix," 314–18.

[63] Johnson, "Mary and the Female Face of God," 509.

[64] Johnson, "Marian Devotion and the Western Church," 394.

[65] See Johnson, "Mary as Mediatrix," 324.

[66] Johnson, "Mary and the Female Face of God," 511.

[67] Ibid., 513.

symbols that properly belong to God. Johnson demonstrates that such studies make it very obvious that this language and these symbols need to be restored to where they belong.

Johnson's work of retrieving the female face of God from Mary of Nazareth opens a window on what is in fact a living tradition that has prevailed for centuries, albeit for the most part unconsciously and covertly. To maintain the metaphor, her research, by drawing back the curtain from this living tradition, reveals in a fascinating way that the people of God, despite official dictums to the contrary, have almost continuously sought to worship God in female form. Johnson's research reveals that God is pleaded with, trusted, and worshiped in female form as Mother of Mercy, ever-compassionate "Refuge of Sinners," and unrelentingly reliable Advocate and Mediatrix. That is to say, a living spirituality of the triune God in female form has been functioning all this time, hidden under Mary's mantle![68]

Historically, it seems that as soon as official worship and theological discourse moved toward exclusively male expression, this female alternative began to emerge under the respectable guise of devotion to the Mother of Jesus. If one argues that symbols acquire power from below, from the devotion of the heart,[69] and that it is the imagination which really governs our experience of God, then this living tradition reclaimed by Johnson for what it truly is—worship of God in female form—must be counted along with a renewed christology as an important resource and raison d'être for renaming the triune God in our times.

The Wisdom Tradition of the Bible

A further ancient source that Johnson actively harnesses for the renaming of the triune God also comes from the first century of Christianity and was connected to the christological task of seeking to understand the fullness of Jesus' identity as the anointed one of God:

> In the process of giving expression to their experience of the saving significance of Jesus and to his ultimate origin in God's gracious goodness, first-century Christians combed the Jewish religious tradition and Hellenistic culture for interpretive elements. One of the first to be pressed

[68] This is vividly recorded in a widespread iconography of the Madonna of Mercy, sometimes called the Madonna of the Protective Mantle. See, for example, the statue "Madonna of Mercy" from the Museo Nazionale, Florence, and "Vierge ouvrante," Musée des Thermes et de l'Hôtel de Cluny, Paris. The latter is also a Trinitarian symbol in which the Marian figure replaces the Holy Spirit.

[69] See Johnson, "Marian Devotion and the Western Church," 395.

into service was the Jewish figure of personified Wisdom (*Hokmah* in Hebrew, *Sophia* in Greek), that female figure of the late Old Testament and inter-testamental literature whose words, functions and attributes were quite quickly transferred to Jesus.[70]

In recent decades biblical scholars have noted that wisdom writings had been neglected in favor of the historical and prophetic books of the Bible, and they have reaffirmed that "the wisdom tradition reflects a genuine, primary element of biblical faith itself."[71] Elizabeth Schüssler Fiorenza, in her work *In Memory of Her*, built upon contemporary scholarship in wisdom literature when she argued that the earliest Jesus traditions came to describe God in a woman's Gestalt as divine *Sophia*.[72] Following on from this work, in 1985 Johnson published a major piece of research on Jesus as the Wisdom of God. Recognizing that pre-existence, incarnation, and divinity were all significant implications for the use of wisdom categories in christology, she set out to "probe whether it is possible with the help of the imagery, concepts and vocabulary of the wisdom tradition to think through a full christology which is faithful to the hard-won insights of the tradition's faith proclamation at the same time that it breaks out of the usual androcentric pattern."[73] Because the vision of the wisdom tradition depicts the whole of life, even the stuff of everyday life, to be the arena of God's sacred action, Johnson also recognized the potential of wisdom christology to provide an alternative to the dualistic opposition between God and the world that is inscribed in classical patriarchal theology and christology.[74]

---

[70] Elizabeth A. Johnson, "Jesus, the Wisdom of God: A Biblical Basis for a Non-Androcentric Christology," *Ephemerides Theologicae Lovanienses* 61, no. 4 (1985) 261.

[71] Elizabeth A. Johnson, "Wisdom Was Made Flesh and Pitched Her Tent Among Us," in *Reconstructing the Christ Symbol: Essays in Feminist Christology*, ed. Maryanne Stevens (New York/Mahwah, N.J.: Paulist Press, 1993) 97–98. See also 114, n. 1, where Johnson refers to surveys of scholarly literature on this topic: Ulrich Wilckens, "Sophia," in Gerhard Kittel, ed., *Theological Dictionary of the New Testament*, trans. and ed. Geoffrey Bromiley (Grand Rapids, Mich.: Wm. B. Eerdmans, 1964–1976) 7:465–528; R. B. Scott, "The Study of Wisdom Literature," *Interpretation* 24 (1970) 20–45; Roland Murphy, *The Tree of Life: An Exploration of Biblical Wisdom Literature*, Anchor Bible Reference Library (New York: Doubleday, 1990).

[72] In her course on feminist theology at the University of Notre Dame in the summer of 1995, Elizabeth Johnson noted, however, that it was Mark Johnson, a young Harvard scholar in the seventies, who "opened up the floodgates" on this concept with his doctoral study in Wisdom christology.

[73] Johnson, "Jesus, the Wisdom of God," 263.

[74] See Johnson, *SHE WHO IS*, 98–99.

From the study of biblical wisdom writings, it becomes clear that the composite picture of personified Wisdom is the most developed personification of God's presence and activity in the Hebrew Scriptures. It is more developed than Spirit, Torah, Shekinah, or Word. *Sophia* first appears in the Book of Job as a hidden treasure whose whereabouts are known only to God (Job 28). In the Book of Proverbs she is a street preacher and a prophet who cries out in public places with a message of reproach, punishment, and promise. She is depicted as a giver of life and proclaims, "Whoever finds me finds life" (8:35). In the great poem of Proverbs 8:22-31, she is related to the act of creation. *Sophia* existed before the beginning of creation as the first of God's works. In Proverbs 9 she is depicted as having built a house and prepared a table. She then sends her servants out to the streets with the invitation: "Come, eat of my bread, and drink of the wine I have mixed" (9:5). The major wisdom poems of Proverbs all present a personified, transcendent figure who searches out human beings to test and challenge them.

In the Book of Sirach the personification of *Sophia* unfolds further. There is a steady call to learn her ways and to benefit from her instruction, which leads to life. In the great song of self-praise, which is in the form of a hymn of self-praise of a deity, she describes her origins at the beginning of creation and her participation in it (Sir 24:3-6); her pitching of her tent in Israel, where she flourished (vv. 8-19); and finally, her momentous identification with the Torah (v. 23). Thus "the universal and cosmic *Sophia* becomes particularly associated with the history of Israel and its precious covenant law."[75]

Throughout the Book of the Wisdom of Solomon (written not by Solomon but most likely by an Alexandrian Jewish writer of the first century B.C.E.) attributes omnipotence to *Sophia*: "She can do all things" and "renew all things" (Wis 7:27). In fact, "in every generation, she passes into holy souls and makes them friends of God and prophets" (7:27). Then the extraordinary chapter 10 reinterprets the whole story of Israel's salvation history, from the first human being to the Exodus, as the deeds of *Sophia*. Johnson draws attention to the fact that the startling factor of this story is that all those saving deeds have been described previously as the deeds of Yahweh, the unnameable, incomprehensible, all-powerful, saving, and only God of Israel! Further, in the Book of Baruch, *Sophia* appears on earth and lives among human beings (Bar 3:38) while again being identified with the Torah.

Johnson's research thus demonstrates how contemporary biblical exegesis reveals that there is a growing consensus that "Sophia is a

---

[75] Ibid., 89.

female personification of God's own being in creative and saving involvement with the world."[76] She shows that the primary reason supporting this interpretation is the functional equivalence between the deeds of *Sophia* and those of the God of Israel. Some of the most profound christological assertions in the New Testament are made in the categories of personified Wisdom. That will be illustrated in the next section of this chapter when Johnson's proposal for naming the "second person" of the Trinity is explored in some detail. I anticipate this by noting here that Paul is the first New Testament writer to make the connection in the startling juxtaposition of Christ crucified as the *Sophia* of God: "For Jews demand signs and Greeks desire wisdom, but we proclaim Christ crucified, a stumbling block to Jews and foolishness to Gentiles, but to those who are the called, both Jews and Greeks, Christ, the power of God and the wisdom of God" (1 Cor 1:22-24). Among the Synoptic Gospels, Matthew's portrayal of Jesus as *Sophia* is the most fully developed, while John's Gospel is the one in which wisdom categories most influence the portrait of Jesus as the Christ.[77]

This transfer of wisdom understandings into the Christian Scriptures had profound theological consequences. It enabled the embryonic Christian communities "to attribute cosmic significance to the crucified Jesus, relating him to creation and governance of the world [Col 1:5; 1 Cor 8:6]. It was also the vehicle for the developing insight into Jesus' ontological relationship with God."[78] Johnson's work focuses on the significance of the fact that one of the primary sources of the doctrines of the incarnation and the Trinity came from the identification of Jesus with this female gestalt of God. She spells out some of the implications of this fact, which has been obscured from theological discourse for so long:

> Whoever espouses a wisdom christology is asserting that Jesus is the human being Sophia became; that Sophia in all her fullness was in him so that he manifests the depth of divine mystery in creative and graciously saving involvement in the world. The fluidity of gender symbolism evidenced in biblical christology breaks the stranglehold of androcentric thinking that circles around the maleness of Jesus. Wisdom

[76] Ibid., 91. It should be noted that Johnson makes this claim within a context of describing four other interpretations of the theological significance of *Sophia*. Johnson's work is a feminist retrieval of *Sophia*, which draws from and is supported by significant biblical scholars who are not working from a specifically feminist perspective. See, for example, Raymond Brown, *The Gospel According to John, I–XII* (Garden City, N.Y.: Doubleday, 1966) cxxv.

[77] Ibid., 95–98.

[78] Ibid., 98.

christology reflects the depths of the mystery of God and points the
way to an inclusive christology in female symbols.[79]

Because christological reflection occurred within the social context of
patriarchal cultures and because christology found formal expression
primarily within Greek metaphysical categories, it developed incorpo-
rating almost exclusively the masculine symbols of Logos or Son,[80] and
most of this female wisdom imagery passed to the figure of Mary of
Nazareth.[81] Johnson's constructive work therefore seeks to ensure that
in these times the rich source of wisdom categories can again be applied to *Hagia Sophia*, Holy Wisdom, as a primary image of the mystery
of Christ, thus building toward an inclusive symbol of the Trinity while
Mary is able to be restored to her proper place within the communion
of saints.[82]

A Proposal for an Alternative Naming of the Trinity

Johnson's goal in her work of retrieval of the symbol of God as
Trinity is to enable it to function in ways that are redemptive for women
and for all humanity. Her research into christology, mariology, and the
wisdom tradition in the Scriptures provides a foundation within the
Christian tradition upon which to build her creative feminist work of
renaming the triune God. Some basic linguistic options are needed,
however, to provide a framework for her proposal. She suggests that "a
certain liability attends the very word God" because of the history of its
use in androcentric theology. Nevertheless, she makes a case for its
continued use, taking a gamble that if it is situated within a "new
semantic field," it will be released from its androcentric past.[83] Johnson

[79] Ibid., 99.

[80] See ibid., 97–98, 152, and Johnson, "Jesus, the Wisdom of God," 284–89, for a
discussion of how and why this critical move took place.

[81] See Johnson, *SHE WHO IS*, 100.

[82] Elizabeth Johnson's next work on Mary will be situated within the context of
the symbol of the communion of saints.

[83] See Johnson, *SHE WHO IS*, 42–44, for a discussion of this option, which
McFague also makes. Other options chosen have been Goddess, God/ess (for theological, not liturgical, use), God, chosen by Carol Christ, Rosemary Ruether, and
Elizabeth Schüssler Fiorenza, respectively. See Carol P. Christ, "Why Women Need
the Goddess: Phenomenological, Psychological, and Political Reflections," *Woman-
spirit Rising*, ed. Carol Christ and Judith Plaskow (San Francisco: Harper & Row,
1979) 273–87; Ruether, *Sexism and God-Talk*, 46; Elisabeth Schüssler Fiorenza, *Jesus:
Miriam's Child, Sophia's Prophet: Critical Issues in Feminist Christology* (New York:
Continuum, 1994) 191, n. 3.

also opts for the use of female symbols for naming God rather than applying feminine traits or dimensions to God, as other theologians grap-
pling with the same difficulties have done.[84] She argues that the ideal
for use of language for God is "male and female terms used equiva-
lently, as well as the use of cosmic and metaphysical symbols." However, because of the sheer weight of present androcentric bias and the
all-encompassing nature of the prevailing patriarchal culture, she believes that this is not a viable option in these times:

> Male and female images simply have not been nor are they even
> now, equivalent. Female religious symbols of the divine are under-
> developed, peripheral, considered secondarily if at all in Christian lan-
> guage and the practice it continues to shape, much like women through
> whose image they point to God. In my judgement, extended theological
> speaking about God in female images, or long draughts of this new
> wine, are a condition for the very possibility of equivalent imaging of
> God in religious speech.[85]

That is, while her ideal is equivalent usage of female and male images,
Johnson argues that because the overwhelming weight of usage of language for the Trinity has been on the side of the male imagery of father
and son, at this point we need "a strong dose of explicitly female imagery to break the unconscious sway that male Trinitarian imagery
holds over the imaginations of even the most sophisticated thinkers."[86]
She is not seeking to replace the use of all male images with all female
images as an end in itself; rather, she sees it as an intermediate strategy
for beginning to redress the present practice, which, as has been argued
above, has such damaging consequences for humanity and creation.
The need to use female images for God is, therefore, a primary reason
for her proposal that the one triune God be named Holy Wisdom,
Sophia, under the titles Spirit-Sophia, Jesus-Sophia, and Mother-Sophia.

Just as one can only gradually come to know Israel's unnameable
God by pondering and entering into YHWH's mighty deeds, so one is

---

[84] See Johnson, *SHE WHO IS,* 44–56, and "The Incomprehensibility of God,"
454–65, for a full discussion of this phenomenon. Yves Congar, Leonardo Boff, and
Donald Gelpi, for example, all make a case for identifying the Spirit with the feminine. Johnson's choice here has been clearly influenced by the critical studies and
discussions of gender that have proliferated since the late 1940s. Most scholars
would now subscribe to some notion of the social construction of gender. For a recent comprehensive overview of contemporary gender studies and their significance for theology, see Elaine Graham, *Making the Difference: Gender, Personhood and
Theology* (Minneapolis: Fortress Press, 1996).

[85] Johnson, *SHE WHO IS,* 56–57.

[86] Ibid., 212.

invited through Johnson's work to know God as *Sophia* in her many guises as creator, renewing impulse, and author of saving events. Johnson's cumulative method is to gather all such insights that accrue from this fertile *Sophia* source as retrieved via a feminist hermeneutic and to apply them to a female imaging of the Trinity. A guiding principle for this attempt to retrieve the power of the Trinitarian symbol is the central place she gives to the experience of women.

Spirit-Sophia

Johnson begins her proposal for renaming God with the Holy Spirit. The Spirit is the first person of the Trinity we encounter, and Johnson wants to emphasize her presence within all experience and the whole world:

> There is no exclusive zone, no special realm, which alone may be called religious. Rather since the Spirit is creator and giver of life, life itself with all its complexities, abundance, threat, misery, and joy becomes a primary mediation of the dialectic of presence and absence of divine mystery. The historical world becomes a sacrament of divine presence and activity.[87]

Since *Sophia's* universal presence filling the world is analogous to the Holy Spirit, Johnson proposes the name "Spirit-Sophia." She suggests that the Spirit can be likened to *Sophia* because the Spirit too "is more mobile than any motion; because of her pureness she pervades and penetrates all things" (Wis 7:24). The name Spirit-Sophia emphasizes the Spirit's continuing creative action in the world.[88] The Spirit, like *Sophia*, sets people on the right path: "Who has learned your counsel, unless you have given wisdom and sent your holy spirit from on high?" (Wis 9:17). These and other sources within the wisdom texts strengthen the fittingness of speaking about the Spirit in female imagery. Johnson chooses to focus on ways in which the Spirit vivifies, renews, and graces, and in so doing she draws attention to the affinity of such language with feminist values.[89]

In the Nicene-Constantinopolitan Creed the Spirit is called "giver of life," giving witness to the fact that the Spirit is experienced as one who vivifies. Through Spirit-Sophia the whole cosmos comes into being and remains in being. Creation is portrayed as an unfolding event, and God's energizing presence is spoken of in a variety of metaphors:

[87] Ibid., 124.
[88] See ibid., 121–23.
[89] Ibid., 94.

the Spirit dwells within all things (Wis 12:1); she encompasses all life (Acts 17:28); she pervades the universe and holds all things together (Wis 1:7). "All creatures from the personal self to the consentient cosmos are mutually related and exist in an interplay of communion thanks to her presence . . . the Spirit being at once the source of individuation and community, of autonomy and relation."[90]

The Spirit also renews creation. Given the flux of the world, renewal is experienced as an ever-present need. The psalmist recalls that it is the Spirit who initiates and transforms: "When you send forth your Spirit, they are created; and you renew the face of the earth" (Ps 104:30). Johnson identifies responsible care for the earth's life as action that aligns human beings in cooperative accord with the renewing dynamism of God's Spirit, a partnership crucial for the very future of the cosmos. Similarly, the biblical prophetic tradition is consistently linked with the doing of justice (Isa 61:1-2; Luke 4:18-19). The power of Spirit-Sophia can be recognized in the impulse and work to renew social and political structures and in action taken to counter debilitating and life-denying oppressions such as racism and sexism. Johnson recalls that even the present arrangement of the Bible urges the believer to recognize the Spirit as the one who not only initiates creation but who will finally make all things new (Rev 21:5).[91] The Spirit is thus experienced as one who renews and empowers.

The world of the specifically religious is also the arena of Spirit-Sophia's presence. While the offer of grace is universal, and Johnson encourages the widest possible recognition of the Spirit's creative impulse, she notes that it is the religions "which thematise this offer in narrative and ritual, thereby clearly focussing on the Spirit's deeds of drawing all creation toward the holiness of God."[92] Biblical narratives give steady evidence of Jewish and then Christian communities recognizing, naming and celebrating the constant presence and activity of the Spirit among believers. The Spirit is experienced as one who graces.

Johnson's naming of the Spirit as Spirit-Sophia is strengthened by her later writings on the Holy Spirit, in which she draws further from both classical and feminist sources.[93] These, along with her focus on the role of the Spirit and its connection with creation, will be explored in

[90] Ibid., 134.

[91] Ibid., 138.

[92] Ibid., 139.

[93] See Elizabeth A. Johnson, "God Poured Out: Recovering the Holy Spirit," *Praying* 60 (May–June, 1994); "Heaven and Earth Are Filled with Your Glory," in *Finding God in All Things,* ed. Michael Himes and Stephen Pope (New York: Crossroad, 1996); *Women, Earth and Creator Spirit* (New York: Paulist Press, 1993).

much greater depth in Chapter 7. I am emphasizing here that in *SHE WHO IS*, Johnson signals her beginning to redress the neglect of the Spirit within the meager Western pneumatological tradition by her choice to describe the Spirit as the first person of the Trinity and by her naming this person Spirit-Sophia. This name connects the rich resonances of the wisdom tradition with the Holy Spirit and opens up new understandings of the Trinitarian God. This female wisdom image functions to restore the awareness that the Spirit is "the mystery of God closer to us than we are to ourselves, drawing near and passing by in quickening, liberating compassion."[94]

Jesus-Sophia

From this broad canvas of the operations of the Spirit in the whole of creation, Johnson moves the focus to center on God who becomes one with the very flesh of humanity—the one she names "Jesus-Sophia." After tracing how the Christ symbol was co-opted by the patriarchal culture of the Greco-Roman world, Johnson draws on sources from tradition and engages them with insights from contemporary learning in order to construct a genuinely liberating christology. One insight she focuses on is the need to revision anthropology so that the traditional dualistic interpretation of Christ can be overcome. She sounds a note of realism concerning the context of this constructive task:

> The social location of the distorted interpretation of Jesus' maleness in the Christian tradition is an ecclesial community where official voice, vote and visibility belong by law only to men. Rising into intellectual expressions that support the status quo, this patriarchy is bedrock for the androcentric construction of gender differences shaping the misuse of maleness in christology.[95]

However, having noted the power of this patriarchal anthropology that has held sway for so long, she surveys various alternative models and opts for one in which human nature might be celebrated in an interdependence of multiple differences. This model recognizes that all persons are constituted by a number of anthropological constants, essential elements that are intrinsic to their identity. These constants include "bodiliness and hence sex and race; relation to the earth, other persons and social groupings; economic, political, and cultural location and the like."[96]

[94] Johnson, *SHE WHO IS*, 131.

[95] Ibid., 154.

[96] Ibid., 155. Johnson refers here to Edward Schillebeeckx, *Christ: The Experience of Jesus as Lord*, trans. John Bowden (New York: Seabury, 1980) 731–43.

She argues that the various combinations of these elements are constitutive of the humanity of every person. In this multipolar model, sexuality takes its place as one of the many dimensions of the human person instead of being made the primary touchstone of personal identity. Also, within this framework differences and diversity can be recognized as creative resources for the community instead of being perceived as obstacles and handicaps. This multipolar anthropology that Johnson proposes allows christology to locate Jesus' maleness as intrinsically important for his own personal historical identity and for the prophetic challenge of his ministry. However, within such a model his maleness is not theologically determinative of his identity as the Christ or normative for the identity of the Christian community.[97]

This anthropology provides an important part of the framework for Johnson's christology and for her naming of Jesus-Sophia by retelling of the Gospel story of Jesus of Nazareth through the prism of the wisdom tradition. This retelling recognizes Jesus as *Sophia* incarnate and evokes *Sophia's* characteristics of graciousness, creativity, and passion for justice as keys to interpreting the mission of Jesus. Among the Synoptic Gospels, Matthew's in particular depicts Jesus as *Sophia's* child who befriends the outcast, who communicates her prophetic message, and who proves her right even when criticized by others. Jesus laments over Jerusalem, speaking a wisdom oracle that depicts him as a caring mother bird before withdrawing like *Sophia* from the city that rejects him (Matt 32:37-39). He offers *Sophia's* invitation "Come to me" to the weary and promises rest (Matt 11:28), and like *Sophia*, he urges the heavy-burdened to take his yoke upon them (Matt 11:29-30).

John's whole Gospel is also suffused with wisdom themes. The prologue of his Gospel actually presents the prehistory of Jesus as the story of *Sophia* who was present in the beginning with God. In John's portrayal, Jesus, like *Sophia*, calls out in a loud voice in public places, uttering blessing and threat (John 7:28, 37). Like her, he speaks in long discourses using the first person singular pronoun in the "I am" statements (John 6:51; 10:14; 11:25). Both Jesus and *Sophia* are identified with Torah, which reveals the path to light and life for all. As with *Sophia*, whoever loves Jesus is beloved by God (John 14:23) and enters into a relationship of mutual friends (John 15:15).[98]

Johnson's refocusing of the story of Jesus of Nazareth in the Gospels of Matthew and John through the lens of the personified *Sophia* opens

[97] Johnson, *SHE WHO IS*, 155–56.

[98] See ibid., pp. 94–100 and 157. Johnson refers here to the extended treatment of this theme by Elisabeth Schüssler Fiorenza, *In Memory of Her*, 118–59. See also Johnson, "Jesus, the Wisdom of God," for her own full exploration of Jesus as *Sophia*.

up a whole new appreciation of the Christ symbol. It provides the believer's imagination with a rich source of female imagery for entering into the mystery of the pre-existent One who was with God from the beginning, who came and lived among us, and who through the Spirit continues with relentless energy to seek us out to invite us to her table, to communion with God. It provides a hermeneutical key for interpreting Jesus' words and deeds, his death and resurrection.

In a particular way, in both these Gospel accounts and in Pauline theology, the cross in all its dimensions of violence, suffering, and love becomes the parable that enacts Sophia-God's participation in a suffering world. The cross challenges the validity of power made normative by dominance and submission. Christ crucified and risen, the Wisdom of God, reveals the truth that divine justice "leavens the world in a way different from the techniques of dominating violence. The victory of shalom is won not by the sword of the warrior god but by the awesome power of compassionate love, in and through solidarity with those who suffer."[99] The symbol of Jesus-Sophia thus discloses an understanding of power as relational, an understanding that is significant for the task of retrieving the doctrine of the Trinity.[100]

Biblical metaphors such as the Pauline body of Christ (1 Cor 12:12-27) and the Johannine branches abiding in the vine (John 15:1-11) amplify the reality of Christ to include all redeemed humanity. Furthermore, the christology of the cosmic hymns (Col 1:15) expands the notion of Christ to include the entire universe. These sources make it clear that the biblical symbol of Christ cannot be restricted to the historical person Jesus. Like Zizioulas, Johnson is unequivocal on this issue. She vigorously affirms that "Christ is a pneumatological reality, a creation of the Spirit . . . all are one in Christ Jesus (1 Cor 12; Gal 3:28)."[101] Interconnections within the whole cosmos are inherent within the wisdom tradition, and the name Jesus-Sophia draws attention to the fact that as the embodiment of *Sophia,* Jesus the Christ's redeeming care is portrayed as extending to all creatures and to the whole earth itself. Wisdom discourse also directs faith toward a global, ecumenical perspective that is able to be inclusive of other religious paths. Thus feminist theological speech about Jesus the Wisdom of God serves to shift the focus of reflection from maleness to the intrinsic significance of the whole Christ.

At the end of her exploration of the constructive dimensions of Jesus as the *Sophia* of God, Johnson, again like Zizioulas, stresses that

---

[99] Johnson, *SHE WHO IS,* 159.
[100] See Chapter 6 below for a redefinition of power.
[101] Johnson, *SHE WHO IS,* 162.

through the doctrine of the incarnation, "human bodiliness is manifest as irreplaceable sacrament of mutual communion between heaven and earth, not only in Jesus' case but ontologically for all." Jesus' solidarity with the suffering reveals the way that Sophia-God is engaged with the world, and Jesus' inclusive relationality embodies *Sophia's* outreach across the universe. "Herein is glimpsed the nature of divine relatedness to the world as a whole: not a distant, dominating transcendence, but otherness that freely draws near, bringing new life, sustaining all loves."[102] The name Jesus-Sophia thus throws light not only on the divine person who "became flesh and dwelt among us" but also on the very *koinōnia* of Godself.

Mother-Sophia

The third person of the Trinity that Johnson renames is "Mother-Sophia," the "unoriginate origin and the goal of the whole universe."[103] Virtually every religious tradition has sought to find answers to the question of origin. It seems to be a universal experience of human persons that ultimately we cannot credit our existence or the being there of this world to our own devices. Johnson observes that when human beings try to articulate this "absolute point of origin that is no point, the primordial, free, hidden depths of absolute mystery, it speaks always about an unoriginate source of all there is."[104] It is this "source of all there is" that she describes as Mother-Sophia—Holy Wisdom and mother of the universe. She argues that since the most fundamental human relationship is that of parent and child, it should function as the primary analogue. And since it is women whose bodies actually bear children and women who have most often been the ones to nurture and raise them, language of God as mother carries a unique power. The Jewish and Christian Scriptures recognize the importance of the mother-child relationship when they co-opt the metaphors of pregnancy and birth, feeding, training, protecting to refer to God's creative relationship to the world.[105]

Why, then, Johnson asks, do we not speak of God as Mother? Through her feminist lens she observes that omitting maternal imagery in official and unofficial speech about God is a hallmark of our heritage. By contrast, she notes that the words "We believe in one God, the Father, the Almighty, maker of heaven and earth" are repeated week

---

[102] Ibid., 168–69.
[103] Ibid., 169.
[104] Ibid., 179.
[105] See ibid., 171.

after week, over centuries, as Christians recite the Nicene Creed and "bear witness to the grip that the image of the one, all-powerful father who makes the world, has had on the Christian imagination."[106] Johnson claims that it is not simply the case that this overliteralized metaphor, Father, which so monopolizes Christian language about God, just happened by default. She suggests that this eclipse was part of the deliberate strategy of the emergence of patriarchy as the dominant ideology within the Christian community. "Religious imagery and social practice mutually influence each other, and the move to an all-male hierarchical priesthood necessitated exclusively male, ruling images for God."[107] Conversely, that is why efforts to change God language arouse such deep feelings and why such change is difficult to accomplish. Changing Father God to Mother God threatens the prevailing social order.

Another difficulty that besets the use of mother as an analogy for God is, according to Johnson, the social construction of motherhood in institutions shaped by patriarchy. She refers specifically to the work of Adrienne Rich, who differentiates between the institution of motherhood and women's experience of motherhood. Rich describes women's experience of motherhood as "the potential relation of any woman to her powers of reproduction and children" and argues that the institution of motherhood "aims at ensuring that potential and—all women—shall remain under male control" through cultural, ideological, political, economic, social, medical, and religious structures.[108] Feminist studies have shown the necessity of honoring the distinctive nature of women's embodiment while also critiquing patriarchal ideology, which both idealizes motherhood and relegates the role of mother to the private order.

However, despite those acknowledged difficulties with the concept of motherhood, Johnson proposes that this universal and primordial relationship is still an excellent metaphor for language about God the Creator of heaven and earth and of all that is seen and unseen. She notes that it "connotes interdependence and mutuality of life at the deepest level, a quality of intimacy and familiarity that is genuinely person creating."[109] To support this claim from a further source, she gives examples of biblical metaphors explicitly conveying God's ma-

---

[106] Ibid., 172–73.

[107] Ibid., 173.

[108] Adrienne Rich in *Of Woman Born: Motherhood as Experience and Institution* (New York: W. W. Norton, 1986), quoted in Johnson, *SHE WHO IS*, 176. See also 297, n. 10, where Johnson makes reference to other feminist work on this issue.

[109] Johnson, *SHE WHO IS*, 178.

ternal, compassionate power. In Isaiah 42:14 she cries out in painful labor to deliver a new creation of justice. She suckles the newborn, comforts, teaches, fiercely protects, and never forgets the child of her womb (Isa 46:3-4; 66:13; 49:15; Hos 11:3-4; 13:8). This biblical maternal symbol, contrary to the idea in classical theism of God's lack of real relation to the world, vividly depicts a God intensely involved with creation.[110]

In speaking about God as Mother-Creator, Sallie McFague brings to light the toughness inherent in maternal experience and makes a connection between motherly care and justice.[111] Johnson takes up this aspect of mother love brought forward by McFague by reflecting on the tenacious work for justice by women living under oppressive government regimes. Further, she suggests that liberation theologies need to extend their scope to include concern for ecology and nuclear disarmament. "Human beings must become guardians of the world, as good parents of a large household that includes vulnerable but necessary non-human creatures with their own beauty, value and integrity."[112] Hence the significance of God the Mother, Creator of heaven and earth, who images wholistic concern for universal justice. Such a paradigm for God as Mother is dangerous language, claims Johnson, because it powerfully combines compassion with justice and summons those "born of God" to a transformed moral ethic of mercy united with justice.[113]

Maternity, with its all-embracing immanence, shapes a new understanding of divine relationality, mystery and liberation. The mother image discloses an intrinsic relatedness between God and the world, a loving relationality that belongs to the very essence of being a mother and never ends: "Speaking about God as mother fixes as bedrock the idea that relationship is a constitutive way in which divine freedom enacts itself."[114] The universal experience of dwelling in a mother's womb opens up an appreciation that in God too we live and move and have our being. Johnson thus claims that the symbol of God as Mother, as in the case of Spirit-Sophia and Jesus-Sophia, uncovers new understandings for divine immanence and transcendence and so transforms some of the deficiencies of classical theism.

However, strangely, what Johnson does not do in her exposition of Mother-Sophia is attempt to make any kind of case for the identification

---

[110] See ibid., 179–80.
[111] McFague, *Models of God*, 113.
[112] Johnson, *SHE WHO IS*, 183.
[113] Ibid., 185.
[114] Ibid.

of the biblical phenomenon of *Sophia* with Mother. Earlier in *SHE WHO IS*, she connects language for the one God with *Sophia*. She refers to a "way of speaking about the mystery of God in female symbol [as] the biblical figure of Wisdom."[115] She also alludes to *Sophia's* connection with creation as portrayed in the Book of Proverbs,[116] but she does not develop this in relation to Mother-Sophia. With Spirit-Sophia she provides a very convincing case for the identification between Spirit and *Sophia*, and with Jesus-Sophia she calls upon a depth of very reputable biblical scholarship to support her claim, but with Mother-Sophia she makes a full and convincing case for naming God as Mother from life and from biblical sources as a whole, while the specific Mother/Sophia connection remains essentially unsupported.

Johnson has demonstrated, however, that central aspects of classical Trinitarian doctrine are in fact strongly compatible with language about God in female metaphor from an explicitly feminist theological stance. Moreover, as her work on mariology has revealed, the history of devotion to Mary discloses that there has been a powerful living tradition of worshiping the Trinity by means of the prolific female images of "Our Lady," the Madonna whose countless titles covertly carry the worship humanity instinctively seeks to give God imaged in female form. Naming the unoriginate origin of all life as Mother-Sophia enables this profoundly human intuition to be honored while seeking to ground it in the rich theological source of the wisdom tradition.

Conclusion

Johnson's constructive proposal for renaming the Trinity using female images is situated within an emerging body of feminist theological discourse and rests upon firm theological foundations from both contemporary and traditional sources. By placing focus on the Spirit as the starting point of her Trinitarian theology, Johnson seeks to redress the neglect of pneumatology within Western theology while also honoring an insight from women's experience, which prefers to begin from the experiential rather than from the speculative. This also has a bearing on her christology, expressed in the naming of Jesus-Sophia. Her emphasis is that "Christ is a pneumatological reality, a creation of the Spirit . . . [and that] all are one in Christ."[117] Johnson's work in christology, and particularly wisdom christology, emerges as a key component in her proposal. She demonstrates that the complex issue of the

[115] Ibid., 86.
[116] Ibid., 88.
[117] Ibid., 162.

maleness of the Christ symbol has been an unnecessary stumbling block in the evolution of the doctrine of God and in the evolution of the naming of the Trinity in Christian worship. She shows how the very cognitive dissonance created by the mixed gender name of Jesus-Sophia can help free Trinitarian discourse and worship from the idolatrous and exclusive father-son namings and lead the believer to God, Holy Mystery who is finally above all names.[118] And finally, by appealing to the primordial experience of every human being within her or his mother's womb, Johnson proposes to name the person of the Trinity who is "unoriginate origin" and "source of all there is" as Mother-Sophia. She argues that the name Father has held exclusive sway for too long and that this most fundamental human relationship of parent and child can continue to function as the primary analogue with liberating and creative effect as Holy Wisdom, Mother-Sophia.

The movement into this Trinitarian proposal is from Spirit-Sophia, the Giver of life, who renews, graces, and makes us one "in Christ"; Jesus-Sophia, through whom we are joined with all humanity, all creation; and with the ultimate Source of our origin, Mother-Sophia, in whom relationship and freedom are one. The *Sophia*/Wisdom naming of Johnson's proposal ensures a constant focus on divine engagement with the whole cosmos.

In summary, this chapter has shown that Johnson's method of weaving the retrievable strands from classical theology with both the Scriptures and feminist insight has led to her renaming the mystery of Sophia-Trinity. The next chapter will pursue her exploration of the renaming of God and her claim that "the Trinity provides a symbolic picture of a totally shared life at the heart of the universe."[119] It will also explore her naming of God as *SHE WHO IS* and of the suffering God as Compassion Poured Out.

---

[118] Another classic example of this dissonance is Julian of Norwich's use of the name Mother Jesus, who in the Eucharist feeds us from his breasts.

[119] Johnson, *SHE WHO IS*, 222.

CHAPTER 6

SHE WHO IS:
The Being of the Trinitarian God and Suffering

At the heart of holy mystery is not monarchy but community;
not an absolute ruler, but threefold koinonia.[1]

Elizabeth Johnson's Trinitarian theology offers a significant contribution to the retrieval of the symbol of the Trinity not only because she addresses the critical question of the full humanity of women but also because she places suffering at the center of her discourse. Johnson traces the links between suffering and a constructive exploration of God named SHE WHO IS. She argues that a theology of the mystery of God as communion needs to take account of the suffering in the world. In this chapter I examine Johnson's description of the triune God as Mystery of Relation and explore her proposal to name the one God SHE WHO IS and her bringing this image into dialogue with suffering in the world.

Triune God: Mystery of Relation

In her constructive proposal to speak about the Trinity as a "Mystery of Relation," Johnson recalls that "this symbol of holy mystery arises from the historical experience of salvation . . . it is a symbol that develops historically out of the religious experience of the gracious

---

[1] Johnson, *SHE WHO IS: The Mystery of God in Feminist Theological Discourse* (New York: Crossroad, 1992) 216.

God who encountered Jews then Gentiles through Jesus of Nazareth in the power of the Spirit."[2] She establishes the basis for her exploration of God in Godself by specifically reminding the reader of the essential link between the economic and the immanent Trinity:

> . . . the triadic character of our religious experience indicates a three-fold character even of God's own way of being God. The concrete ways that God is given to us in history point to three interrelated ways of existing within God's own being. God really corresponds to the way we have encountered divine mystery in time.[3]

By "religious experience" here Johnson is referring to the multiple attested experiences of salvation history. Like Zizioulas, she resists the argument of some contemporary theologians who hold that it is impossible for human beings to talk about the inner life of God at all.[4] She suggests that much would be lost if we ceased speaking altogether of the immanent triune God.[5] She holds, however, that the "God who saves—this *is* God" and also affirms that "God's relation to the world is grounded in God's own being capable of such a relation."[6] While constantly asserting the need to remember the classic rules for speaking about God—that God is finally incomprehensible, that language about God is analogical, and that there is need for many names for the divine—Johnson seeks out language to describe God *in se.*[7] She suggests, for example, that by meditating on Holy Wisdom's approach in incarnation and grace (in ways described in the last chapter):

> we are enabled to speak about the reality of her own inner relatedness in terms of the livingness of unoriginate Mother, her beloved Child, and the Spirit of their mutual love; or the vitality of Wisdom's abyss, her personal word and her energy; or Sophia's eternal communion in

---

[2] Ibid., 197–98.

[3] Ibid., 200.

[4] See J. D. Zizioulas, "The Doctrine of God the Trinity Today: Suggestions for an Ecumenical Study," in *The Forgotten Trinity* 3: *A Selection of Papers Presented to the BCC Study Commission on Trinitarian Doctrine Today,* ed. Alasdair I. C. Heron (London: British Council of Churches, 1991) 23–24. He argues that "the Immanent Trinity is not exhausted by the Economic Trinity."

[5] Johnson, *SHE WHO IS,* 200.

[6] Ibid., 201. In the latter affirmation Johnson quotes from Catherine LaCugna, "Reconceiving the Trinity as the Mystery of Salvation," *Scottish Journal of Theology* 38 (1985) 13. There is, however, a distinction between Johnson's position and LaCugna's. LaCugna resists speaking of God *in se.*

[7] See Johnson, *SHE WHO IS,* 201–5.

personal mystery, hidden, uttered and bestowed; or the relations of Spirit, Wisdom, and Mother in encircling movement.[8]

Further, she argues that if the God disclosed by Jesus and the Spirit truly reveals how God is in Godself, there is ground for a profound hope precisely because the God so revealed is a compassionate God of communion engaged with the world and may be symbolized as "a totally shared life at the heart of the universe."[9] She proposes that "the thought to which [the symbol of the Trinity] gives rise evokes a sense of ultimate reality highly consonant with the feminist values of *mutuality, relation, equality and community in diversity*."[10] An exploration of these divine characteristics and their interconnectedness, along with her retrieval of the concept of *perichoresis*,[11] provides the core of her constructive proposal to name the triune God as a Mystery of Relation. This section will focus on those components of Johnson's core proposal. She pursues them from the perspective of women's experience, seeking to release new meanings from the ancient Trinitarian dogma of unity in diversity with its mutual and equal relations.

Mutual Relation, Radical Equality and Community in Diversity

Trinitarian theology, based as it is in the biblical story of salvation, has consistently taught that what constitutes the three divine persons is their relationality. It holds that relationality both constitutes each Trinitarian person as unique and distinguishes one from another. From this basis of understanding, the Trinity can be described as "a mystery of real, mutual relations." In her work of retrieving the triune symbol, Johnson focuses this in a particular way. She writes: "At the heart of holy mystery is not monarchy but community; not an absolute ruler, but a threefold *koinonia*."[12]

In order to tap some of the wealth of the image of the triune God as divine *koinōnia* or communion, Johnson draws from women's experience and concentrates on the phenomenon of mutual relation, exploring it specifically through the metaphor of the mutuality experienced in genuine friendship.[13] She acknowledges that classical theology has

---

[8] Ibid., 215.

[9] Ibid., 222.

[10] Ibid., 211.

[11] See the next section for a definition.

[12] Johnson, *SHE WHO IS*, 216.

[13] Sallie McFague and Anne Carr have also explored the metaphor of "friend" as a way to name the Trinitarian God. See McFague, *Models of God: Theology for an*

hesitated to use friendship to model Trinitarian relationships for fear that the persons become indistinct. However, she appeals to the feminist retrieval of the experience of friendship in arguing its relevance as a theological metaphor that can evoke mutual indwelling in the fullness of personal autonomy.[14] Friendship, she rightly claims, is the most free, the least possessive of mutual relationships. It can cross age, sex, ethnic, and every other kind of social barrier and is able to be open to the inclusion of others. Rather than blurring a person's uniqueness, the powerful experience of true friendship reveals that through friendship the particularity of each person is enhanced, and the different gifts of each are enabled to flourish. The experience of friendship reveals that there is a sense in which genuine friends truly "dwell within each other, in each other's hearts and minds and lives." She observes:

> The better the friendship the more potent its capacity to generate creativity and hope, as experiences of trust, care, delight, forgiveness, and passion for common interests and ideas flow back and forth. In addition to person-creating power, the love of mature friendship has the potential to press beyond its own circle to offer blessing to others. Befriending the brokenhearted, the poor, or the damaged earth with its threatened creatures are but some of the ways the strength of this relation can overflow.[15]

All these dimensions of the experience of friendship point to its power as a metaphor for the mutuality of divine communion.

Further, Johnson points out that Jewish and Christian faith traditions both convey a strong basic sense of God's friendliness toward the world. For example, the wisdom tradition in the Bible reveals *Sophia* at work enabling the gift of friendship: "In every generation she passes into holy souls and makes them friends of God and prophets" (Wis 7:27). This is focused in a particular and telling way in the Christian testament through Jesus, who insists on calling his followers not servants but friends (John 15:15). "Jesus-Sophia is the incarnation of divine friendship, hosting meals of inclusive table community and being hospitable to people of all kinds."[16] The friendship so fostered drew people not only to himself but into the mutual knowledge and indwelling characteristic of Jesus' own relation to God (John 17:21).

Ecological, Nuclear Age (London: SCM Press, 1987) 157–80, and for a bibliography on friendship see 218, n. 22. See also Anne E. Carr, *Transforming Grace: Christian Tradition and Women's Experience* (San Francisco: Harper & Row, 1988) 143–44, 150, 213.

[14] See Johnson, *SHE WHO IS*, 235.
[15] Ibid.
[16] Ibid., 217.

Within the Gospel narratives, prevailing concepts of patriarchal power, understood as "power over," are subverted by Jesus-Sophia's words and deeds as he is depicted modeling what genuine mutuality can mean (Matt 15:21-28; Mark 14:3-9; Luke 19:1-10; John 4:5-42). Gospel images of mutuality and friendship can therefore be understood to disclose something essential of Godself. Johnson claims that:

> the love of friendship is the very essence of God. Hidden Abyss, Word and Spirit mutually indwell in a companionable communion of unimaginable strength. In Simone Weil's evocative words, "Pure friendship is an image of the original and perfect friendship that belongs to the Trinity, and is the very essence of God." In this living friendliness the hypostases are not determined by their point of origin or rank in the order of procession but exist in each other in genuine mutuality.[17]

Johnson thus argues that modeling the triune symbol on women's experience of relations of friendship can provide an alternative structure to the hierarchical pattern of relationship expressed in the exclusive male imagery of the classical model of Father, Son, and Spirit.

A second key dimension of any understanding of God as a mystery of relation is a belief in the radical equality of the divine persons. As indicated above, the doctrine of the Trinity has always taught that the triune symbol communicates the idea that the wholeness and equality of each person in relation are essential to Godself. The long battle over subordinationism left the tradition with the explicit affirmation that the persons of the Trinity, the subsistent relations, are radically equal to, though distinctly different from, each other. The very nature of the divine relations is such that the uniqueness of each person comes about and is revealed by being in equal relationship. Johnson notes that on this point classical doctrine and feminist insight "vigorously coalesce."[18] The Trinitarian symbol of a community of equals is completely compatible with the feminist vision that personal uniqueness can flourish through profound companionship that respects differences and values them equally:

> The trinitarian symbol intimates a community of equals . . . [and] points to patterns of differentiation that are non-hierarchical, and to forms of relating that do not involve dominance. It models the ideal, reflected in so many studies of women's ways of being in the world, of a relational bonding that enables the growth of persons as genuine

---

[17] Ibid., 218. See Simone Weil, *Waiting for God*, trans. Emma Craufurd (New York: Harper & Row, 1973) 208.

[18] Ibid., 219.

subjects of history in and through the matrix of community, and the flourishing of community in and through the praxis of its members.[19]

In this ideal vision of a life of creative mutual communion that is mirrored in the symbol of the Trinity, the distinctiveness of each person is enabled and enhanced by the power of relationship that both respects and values differences. This vision, so valued in feminist hopes for the future, is of community in diversity. It is significant to note here that such an understanding of person, described here as a feminist ideal and modeled by the persons in communion of the Holy Trinity, is something that John Zizioulas has developed at depth. It is at the very heart of his Trinitarian theology.[20]

Perichoresis

When Johnson addresses the question of how best to image these divine attributes of mutual relation, radical equality, and community and diversity, she notes that "divine unity itself must be understood in interrelational fashion."[21] She therefore appeals to the ancient yet ever new concept from Eastern theology—*perichoresis*. This concept was first used by Gregory Nazianzen to help express the way in which the divine and human natures in the one person of Christ coinhere in one another without the integrity of either being diminished by the presence of the other. It was later used in the eighth century by the Greek theologian John Damascene to speak of the dynamic and vital character of each divine person and to communicate the way in which the three divine persons mutually dwell in one another while remaining distinct from one another.[22]

The word *perichoresis* means "being-in-one-another, permeation without confusion."[23] It "signifies a cyclical movement, a revolving action, such as the revolution of a wheel" and "evokes a coinherence of

---

[19] Ibid.

[20] See Chapter 2.

[21] Johnson, *SHE WHO IS*, 220.

[22] See Thomas F. Torrance, *The Christian Doctrine of God: One Being Three Persons* (Edinburgh: T&T Clark, 1996) 102.

[23] Catherine Mowry LaCugna, *God for Us: The Trinity and Christian Life* (New York: HarperSanFrancisco, 1991) 271. See also 270, where LaCugna claims that the idea of *perichoresis* emerged as a substitute for the earlier patristic notion that the unity of God belongs to the person of the Father. She contends that when the doctrine of the Father's monarchy was weakened by the Cappadocian doctrine of intradivine relations, the idea of *perichoresis* took its place.

the three persons, an encircling of each one around the others."[24] As Johnson records, the term can be interpreted in two ways. The Latin translation of the term as *circuminsessio,* from the words "sitting" and "seat" *(sedere, sessio),* has a static sense meaning something dwelling or resting within another. The other translation into Latin as *circumincessio,* from *incedere,* meaning "to proceed," "to walk," indicates a more dynamic interweaving of things with each other.[25] The word in its original Greek has a particular advantage as an image of the Trinity because the word *perichoreō,* meaning "to encompass," is very much like the verb "to dance round" or "to dance in a ring," *perichoreuō.* And although the latter has no etymological link with *perichoresis,* it conjures up a dynamic Trinitarian image of an eternal, divine round dance.[26] Johnson herself suggests a further advantage in extending this nuance of the metaphor to include the art form of contemporary dance choreography. Her spinning out of this image conveys something of a contemporary scientific perspective of the random, chaotic nature of a complex universe and the interrelationship of all things:

> Dancers whirl and intertwine in unusual patterns; the floor is circled in seemingly chaotic ways; the rhythms are diverse . . . resolution is achieved unexpectedly. Music, light and shadow, color and wonderfully supple motion coalesce in dancing that is not smoothly predictable and repetitive as in a round dance, and yet is just as highly disciplined. Its order is more complex.[27]

The concept of *perichoresis* appeals to Johnson because perichoretic movement suggests the idea of all three distinct persons existing in each other in an exuberant movement of equal relations. She believes that portraying an exchange of life that "constitutes the permanent, active, divine *koinōnia*" is an excellent model for human interaction in freedom.[28]

---

[24] Johnson, *SHE WHO IS,* 220. Johnson refers here to a range of sources.

[25] See ibid.

[26] See ibid., where Johnson refers to Edmund Hill, *The Mystery of the Trinity* (London: Chapman, 1985) 59–60.

[27] Ibid., 220–21.

[28] Ibid. Several other contemporary theologians have appealed to the image of *perichoresis* for similar reasons. See Jürgen Moltmann, *The Trinity and the Kingdom of God* (New York: Harper & Row, 1981) 174–76; Leonardo Boff, *Trinity and Society* (Maryknoll, N.Y.: Orbis Books, 1988) 5–7, 134–54. See also Torrance, *The Christian Doctrine of God,* 102–3, 168–73; Walter Kasper, *The God of Jesus Christ,* trans. Matthew J. O'Connell (New York: Crossroad, 1991) 283–85.

Johnson continually stresses that no one way of speaking about or imaging this divine mystery will ever be adequate. She recalls the use of geometric figures to convey the Trinitarian mystery. Because classical Trinitarian theology of the East teaches that divinity proceeds from the Father through the Son to the Spirit and so to the world, the Trinity has been illustrated by a straight line. The Western teaching, in contrast, has been most often imaged by a triangle or a circle, emphasizing the place of the Spirit proceeding from both Father and Son and referring all back to the Father.

Johnson proposes that a more apt shape for these times is the triple helix. Borrowing from biological science, she notes that the double helix as the carrier of the genetic code of all human life is "one of the most mysterious, powerful shapes in all creation. The strands of the helix do not originate from each other but are simply there together, not statically but moving in a dance of separation and recombination, which creates new persons."[29] She suggests that the image of a triple helix intensifies this life-giving movement and therefore "connotes the unfathomable richness of holy triune mystery, inwardly related as a unity of equal movements, each of whom is distinct and all of whom together are one source of life, new just order, and quickening surprise in an infinite mix."[30]

Thus, drawing on this dynamic image of new and ongoing life from contemporary science, along with the metaphor of redeeming friendship and the ancient image of *perichoresis*, Johnson summarizes her description of the triune God as Mystery of Relation in poetic cadence:

> The circular dynamism within God spirals inward, outward, forward toward the coming of a world into existence, not out of necessity but out of the free exuberance of overflowing friendship. Spun off and included as a partner in the dance of life, the world for all its brokenness and evil is destined to reflect the triune reality, and already does embody it in those sacramental, anticipatory moments of friendship, healing and justice breaking through.[31]

Based upon redemptive experiences of God as Communion, this description is an attempt to convey, through the limits of language, the triune Mystery of Relation spilling over in love to engage in freedom with a resilient and often rebellious and broken world.

---

[29] Johnson, *SHE WHO IS*, 221.
[30] Ibid.
[31] Ibid., 222.

One Living God: SHE WHO IS

God's Relationship with the World

The question of God's being inevitably raises the critical issue of God's relationship with the world. I will therefore address some of the conundrums that this issue has raised within theological discourse, and Johnson's response to them, as a way of providing a basis for her constructive exploration of *God's being* and her proposal to name God SHE WHO IS.

As noted above, classical theism in the West has characteristically separated the question of the nature of divine being from the historical experience of the mystery of God as triune. The practical result has been that Western theology has often conveyed an imaginative picture of four elements in the study of God—one divine nature and three divine persons. Moreover, as Johnson writes:

> . . . classical thought classifies relation in the category of accident, thereby rendering it unsuitable for predication about divine nature in which nothing accidental inheres. Thus while the persons may be relational, relationship with the world is banned from God's essential nature. The relation between God and the world is said to be "real" on the world's side towards God but not "real" in a mutual way from God to the world.[32]

Unfortunately, it is this image of a non-relational God that has endured from the rich legacy of the great medieval Scholastic tradition. The profound, complex, and finely nuanced theologies of God articulated by such saints and scholars as Richard of St. Victor, Bonaventure, and Thomas Aquinas tended to be reduced to a portrayal of a God who is potent, all-sufficient, unrelated to and unaffected by the world. This occurred through simplistic interpretations of theological manuals that were largely divorced from the biblical sources and were read through the powerful prevailing lens of patriarchy. It is this image of the one God which in turn became a model of the ultimate patriarchal ideal—the solitary, powerful dominant male—and which has been firmly rejected by the post-Enlightenment world. Johnson refers to Walter Kasper's description of "a solitary narcissistic being who suffers from his own completeness"[33] to convey the depth of repugnance expressed today in response to such a God.

Johnson's own exploration of divine being begins from another place. Starting from women's experience, which values the mutuality engendered by relationships of equality and networks of companionable friendship, she turns to an alternative image of the "perfection" of the one God. She appeals to:

> another interpretation of fullness of being that includes rather than excludes genuine reciprocal relations with others who are different; another pattern of life that values compassionate connectedness over separation; another understanding of power that sees its optimum operation to be in collegial and empowering actions.[34]

Thus, although valuing the Scholastic tradition expressed in the creative theological synthesis of Thomas Aquinas, Johnson, along with many contemporary theologians, does not accept the picture of a God who has no real relation to the world. As we have seen in her bid to retrieve the concept of *perichoresis* to convey not only God's relationship in Godself but also God's relationship with creation, her understanding of the relationship between God and the world is that it is a relationship of mutuality.

Before putting aside the Scholastic teaching on a God who has no real relation to the world to pursue this alternative, Johnson draws attention to one critical aspect of traditional teaching that she believes must be retained. It is the emphasis on God's freedom in personal relation. She underlines that the notion of God's freedom must remain at the center of any alternative attempts to describe Godself, and she links this theological principle to the experience of women's choice to be active subjects of history. Reflection on this experience of women also reveals that any genuine relationship between persons can occur only if it is freely chosen.

Like Zizioulas,[35] Johnson points to clear practical connections between understandings of God's freedom and relationality and an emerging contemporary anthropology:

> What is slowly coming to light is a new construal of the notion of person, neither as a self-encapsulated ego [as in dominant males within patriarchal society] nor a diffuse self denied [as in females and oppressed males within patriarchy], but self-hood on the model of relational autonomy. Discourse about God from the perspective of women's experience, therefore, names toward a relational God who loves in freedom.[36]

---

[34] Ibid.
[35] See Chapter 2.
[36] Johnson, *SHE WHO IS*, 226.

This, then, is how God can be named as the one God: a relational God who loves in freedom.

Speaking of the being of a God who loves in freedom raises the issue of how God's mutual relation with creation can be understood. Echoing the author of the Letter to the Ephesians, who refers to the one God "who is above all and through all and in all" (Eph 4:6), Johnson points to the plethora of Christian language—biblical, liturgical, catechetical, theological—that speaks of divine presence and action in the world.[37] This language has consistently conveyed the idea that the very transcendence of the one relational God means that God is not limited by any finite category and is therefore capable of radical immanence. Sophia-God is intimately related to everything that exists and dwells at the heart of the world.

As I have noted above, post-Enlightenment discourse about God was prompted to pursue the question of how the world can be understood to be likewise present in God, of how the indwelling of God in the world can be understood as reciprocal.[38] For classical theism there is no such question. From God's side there is no real relation with anything created, because that would entail diminishment of divinity. For classical pantheism real relation is not possible for opposite reasons— God and the world are understood to be virtually identical, and because there is no differentiation between God and the world, there can be no real relation. In contrast to both of these positions and in company with a number of contemporary Christian theologians, Johnson adopts a third position known as panentheism. She describes this as "a model of free reciprocal relation: God in the world and the world in God while each remains radically distinct. The relation is mutual while differences remain and are respected."[39] As God is in God's own being, so God is within the world and the world is within God. She thus comes to speak of God and the world existing "in mutual, if assymetrical relation."[40]

This understanding of God's relationship with creation leads to a further question of how within the fullness of being of the infinite God there can be room for anything finite to exist. In order to address this issue, Johnson refers to the kabbalistic doctrine of God's self-limitation in creation. This discussion has recently been taken up into Christian theological reflection through the notion of the divine *kenosis* enacted in Christ Jesus (Phil 2:6-8) and explores the concept that in the act of

[37] See ibid., 228–29.
[38] See ibid., 230.
[39] Ibid., 231.
[40] Ibid., 228.

creating, divinity withdraws, that "God makes room for creation by constricting divine presence and power."[41] Johnson draws attention to the fittingness of female imagery to convey this concept of a kenotic, self-limiting God. She notes:

> . . . to be so structured that you have room inside yourself for another to dwell is quintessentially a female experience. To have another actually living and moving and having being in yourself is likewise the province of women. So too is the experience of contraction as a condition for bringing others to life in their own integrity.[42]

As with all metaphors, however, the use of maternal metaphors has its limits, and Johnson again suggests that the metaphor of friendship (explored above) should be brought into play to supplement those maternal images and to evoke the mutual indwelling of God and the world in the fullness of personal autonomy.[43]

Johnson is clear that the point of any of the theological constructions put forward to convey the triune mystery is to find words for the multiple experiences of salvation and liberation that continue to occur within the Christian community. Her aim is "to articulate the radical livingness of God's holy mystery encountered in multifaceted ways."[44] And she argues that it is the consistent witness of those experiences of salvation that finally precludes the patriarchal idea of God as a self-enclosed absolute: "Instead, Sophia-God's holy mystery is spoken about as a self-communicating mystery of relation, an unimaginable, open communion in herself that opens out freely to include even what is not herself."[45] She thus adopts a panentheistic model of God's relationship with the world. God is understood as choosing to limit Godself in order to make room for creation and to enable a mutual indwelling of free reciprocal relation that is constantly open to new life.

Divine Being in Communion: SHE WHO IS

Johnson's attempt to articulate the "radical livingness of God's holy mystery" leads her to an exploration of God's being. In expressions remarkably similar to those used by Zizioulas, she acknowledges

---

[41] Ibid., 233. Johnson here refers specifically to the works of Thomistic scholar William Hill and to Jürgen Moltmann.

[42] Ibid., 234.

[43] Ibid., 235.

[44] Ibid., 222.

[45] Ibid.

that "divine unity exists as an intrinsic *koinōnia* of love" and that "being in communion constitutes God's very essence."[46] Building on this premise, she seeks to use the ontological language of being to new benefit:

> I suggest that the ontological language of being has the advantage of providing an all-inclusive category for reality at large, leaving nothing out and thereby entailing that the cosmos does not slip from view by too heavy a concentration on the human dilemma . . . It is thus a code word for God as source of the whole universe, past and present, and yet to come, and as power that continuously resists evil.[47]

It is this notion of being, which evokes "a most dynamic and living although elusive reality, the act of being-there of things," that Johnson believes has a contribution to make to feminist discourse about God. Tuning directly into the power of Aquinas's thought, she suggests that the language of being so understood can communicate that "all things are on fire with existence by participation in God's holy being which is unquenchable." When applying the language of being to God, Johnson reminds the reader that "the being of God that we are speaking of is essentially love. God's being is identical with an act of communion."[48]

It is through this lens of understanding being that Johnson focuses on the powerful story of encounter between Moses and God described in the Book of Exodus. The story tells of a compassionate God who has heard the cry of the enslaved Israelites, who "knows" their sufferings and seeks to deliver them into freedom (Exod 3:7-8). And the self-identifying name that God gives on this occasion to the bewildered Moses is YHWH—I AM WHO I AM. Johnson notes that biblical commentators are unanimous in their criticism of the anachronistic tendency to read a philosophical meaning back into this text. However, she also notes that from the time of the Septuagint translation onward, the idea that the name YHWH discloses the ontological nature of God gained credence in Jewish circles and was widely used in early Christian theology.[49] Thus Aquinas was drawing from a revered ancient tradition

---

[46] Ibid., 227–28.

[47] Ibid., 237.

[48] Ibid., 238. For another contemporary retrieval of Aquinas's concept of being, see Anthony Kelly's transposition of divine "Being" to "Being-in-Love" elaborated in Kelly, *The Trinity of Love* (Wilmington, Del.: Michael Glazier, 1989), and in *An Expanding Theology: Faith in a World of Connections* (Newtown, N.S.W.: E. J. Dwyer, 1993).

[49] See ibid., 242. See also p. 302, n. 38, where Johnson refers to Kasper, *God of Jesus Christ*, 147–52, for a history of how the name became a metaphysical definition.

when he sought to support his claim that God's very nature is to be, by consciously making a connection between philosophy and Scripture and appealing to a metaphysical interpretation of this text from Exodus. He sought to communicate a God of pure transcendent being in whom the whole created universe participates and argued that the name QUI EST is the most appropriate name for God—*Ergo hoc nomen, "qui est," est maxime proprium nomen Dei.*[50]

Johnson observes that the Latin construction QUI EST is composed of a singular pronoun and a singular verb, with the pronoun being masculine to agree with its referent, the masculine word for God, *Deus*, and that this can be literally translated as "who is" or "the one who is." She therefore argues that since God is not intrinsically male and that if the referent became Sophia-God, this highly influential text, which carries the meaning of a divine relational being who energizes the world, could be translated with a feminist gloss as SHE WHO IS. Moreover, because this name is suggestive of the God revealed in the narrative of the burning bush, it also functions to bring to mind a personal, compassionate, faithful God who sustains a loving relation with humanity and all creation. "Symbolized by a fire that does not destroy, this one will be known by the words and deeds of liberation and covenant that follow. SHE WHO IS, the one whose very nature is sheer aliveness, is the profoundly relational source of being of the whole universe."[51]

Thus the biblical story of liberation from Exodus is key to Johnson's proposal to name the triune God as SHE WHO IS. Quoting Johannes Baptist Metz, she recalls that "the pure idea of God is in reality, an abbreviation, a shorthand for stories without which there is no Christian truth in this idea of God."[52] This name, then, as an abbreviation of the saving story of Exodus, can powerfully evoke the mystery of God in solidarity with the oppressed. It can convey the mystery of a God who is dynamically present to the needy and active to free all that is bound. Moreover, by connecting with the aspect of the story that shows a reluctant Moses enlisted in a collaborative work of liberation, naming God as SHE WHO IS also conveys a call to humanity for mutuality with her in the task of saving the world. Thus:

> alive in the *koinonia* of SHE WHO IS, women and men are called to be friends of God and prophets. . . . This way of speaking crafts a partnership amid the ambiguity of history: SHE WHO IS, Holy Wisdom

---

[50] See Thomas Aquinas, *Summa Theologiae* I, q. 13, a. 11.

[51] Johnson, *SHE WHO IS*, 243.

[52] Ibid., 244. See Johannes Baptist Metz, "Theology Today: New Crises and New Visions," *Catholic Theological Society of America Proceedings* 49 (1985) 7.

herself, lives as the transcendent matrix who underlies and supports all existence and potential for new being, all resistance to oppression and the powers that destroy, while women and men [like Moses], through all the ambivalence of their own fidelity, share in her power of love to create, struggle, and hope on behalf of the new creation in the face of suffering and evil.[53]

Naming the one God SHE WHO IS thus communicates God's dynamic being as *koinōnia*, as a mystery of relation at the heart of the universe; it communicates the image of a God who dwells within, giving life to all that is. Conversely, it also communicates the image of a powerful personal female presence who makes room for a real and reciprocal relation with creation. The name SHE WHO IS communicates the image of a God in whom all creation lives and dwells and has its being. Finally, it also conveys the faithful God of the covenant as Holy Wisdom, a compassionate God who identifies with suffering humanity and creation and who draws humanity to join her in the work of the liberation of all creation from suffering and evil. SHE WHO IS can thus be understood as being within all, encompassing all and being with all, ever at work to set all creation free. It is an evocative and transforming symbol of the God of Israel who is Creator, Savior, and Sanctifier of her people.

The Trinitarian God Who Suffers

Having conceded that the task of speaking about the Trinity as a whole is considerably more difficult than naming the three *hypostases*, Johnson proposes that one right way to speak about God is "to speak about the Trinity as a symbol of the mystery of salvation, in the midst of the world's suffering, using female images."[54] In this proposal Johnson is drawing attention to the fact that an overriding experience of the majority of persons alive in our times and indeed, as she comes to argue, of the very planet itself, is that of suffering.[55] She is pointing out that a question that therefore needs to be at the center of contemporary theological concern is how the living God revealed in the Scriptures as being always dynamically active to save can be understood in relation to this suffering world.

---

[53] Johnson, *SHE WHO IS*, 244–45.

[54] Ibid., 212–13.

[55] See Johnson, *Women, Earth and Creator Spirit* (New York: Paulist Press, 1993), and "Turn to the Heavens and the Earth: Retrieval of the Cosmos in Theology," *CTSA Proceedings* 51 (1996) 1–14.

Because of the strong evocation of the God of compassion and liberation in the story of the burning bush, referring to God as QUI EST immediately focuses the question of God's involvement in the suffering of the world. Within the metaphysical discourse of Scholasticism, however, suffering as a state of vulnerability was considered incompatible with divine nature, which, as being itself *(actus purus)*, was by definition unchangeable. There was also the central concern to preserve divine freedom from a dependency on creatures. The logic was that only a God who is independent of the world could be infinite, and therefore capable of acting to save the world. Such has been the sway of God understood as omnipotent, immutable, impassible, apathetic that this image prevailed even in the face of the consistent biblical witness of Jewish and Christian belief that has affirmed God's active care in the midst of pain.

As I have already observed, by the latter part of the millennium the collective awareness of the scope and intensity of suffering in the world has meant that a God understood to be simply a spectator to all this pain has come to be considered "morally intolerable."[56] In the twentieth century a strong strand within Jewish thought, Protestant theology, process theology, European Catholicism, and Latin American liberation theology emerged in which "divine capacity for suffering is a most characteristic expression of divine freedom active in the power of love."[57] It should be noted that this move to integrate suffering into the idea of God represents a huge shift in theological conviction. However, the fact that it has surfaced in these times from so many different theological sources and represents a range of theological views testifies to its credibility within contemporary thought.[58] Johnson's survey on the emergence of the notion of a suffering God from all the above sources leads her to conclude that "if ever there were a *kairos,* a critical moment, for the religious symbol of the suffering God, that moment would seem to be now."[59]

Divine Power

One of the criticisms of the symbol of the suffering God is that it is simply an anthropomorphic construction. In answer to this charge,

---

[56] Johnson, *SHE WHO IS,* 249.

[57] Ibid., 251. Those surveyed include Abraham Heschel, Hans Jonas, Jürgen Moltmann, Alfred North Whitehead, Sheila Greeve Delaney, Marjorie Suchocki, John Macquarrie, Hans Kung, Hans Urs von Balthasar, Jon Sobrino.

[58] See ibid. For examples of objections to this move, see Edward Schillebeeckx, *Christ: The Christian Experience in the Modern World* (London: SCM Press, 1980) 724–29; William J. Hill, *Search for the Absent God: Tradition and Modernity in Religious Understanding,* ed. Mary Catherine Hilkert (New York: Crossroad, 1992) 152–63.

[59] Ibid.

Johnson observes that from a feminist perspective, it is clear that the attribute of impassibility as traditionally interpreted is equally anthropomorphic:

> In the patriarchal system the nonrelational human male exercising unilateral power sits at the pinnacle of perfection. Relationality and the inevitable vulnerability that accompanies it are correspondingly devalued as imperfections. Being free from others and being incapable of suffering in one's own person because of them become the goal.[60]

This is a frightening picture. It depicts the image of an impassible, monarchical God that for centuries has held sway at the center of Christian theology and devotion, enshrining unilateral power as an ultimate goal and deriding vulnerability as weakness and imperfection. It evokes the violence and destruction wrought in the name of such a God, the scars of which both humanity and creation still bear today.[61] Feminist theology claims that such an anthropomorphic image is still dangerous for humanity and for the future of planet Earth.[62] By contrast, the image of a suffering God totally subverts this patriarchal image of perfection and this ideal of power. In claiming the image of a suffering God, feminist theology judges that self-containment and the absence of relationship do not represent the acme of perfection but rather signify imperfection.

In the discussion of God's power, Johnson is quick to note that any speech about the suffering of God should not convey that suffering is a value in itself. She points out that statements about "God's power that is weakness," with stress on the powerless suffering of God, can be dangerous, particularly for women:

> Structurally subordinated within patriarchy, women are maintained in this position, not liberated by the image of a God who suffers in utter powerlessness because of love. The ideal of the helpless divine victim serves only to strengthen women's dependency and potential for victimization . . . when what is needed is growth in relational autonomy and self-affirmation.[63]

Johnson rightly demonstrates that if weakness is so deified, the image of a powerless, suffering God becomes dangerous to women's genuine humanity and must be avoided. Women need to be freed from any

---

[60] Ibid., 252.

[61] See, for example, the stories of the destruction of peoples and cultures testified to within the literature published around 1992 to mark the five-hundredth anniversary of the bringing the gospel to the Americas.

[62] See, for example, McFague, *Models of God*, ix.

[63] Johnson, *SHE WHO IS*, 253–54.

rationale or mythology and any symbol system that confirms them in positions of being powerless victims who should "offer up" their pain and abuse for the "greater good" of maintaining peace. That has often meant keeping men as well as women held bound in the status quo of abusive power.

What is urgently needed instead is a redefinition of power. To explore the kind of power that provides an alternative to the unilateral power imaged by an impassible God, Johnson appeals to the experience of women who have found a way to exercise a power that liberates the disempowered rather than one that binds. Drawing from many feminist theologians who are seeking language to express the fruit of reflection on the exercise of that kind of power—Rita Brock, Sallie McFague, Sharon Welch, Wendy Farley, Anne Carr—she describes a power that is relational. "Neither power-over nor powerlessness, it is akin to power-with."[64] She elaborates: "Thinking of Holy Wisdom's 'almighty power' along these lines leads to a resymbolization of divine power not as dominative or controlling, nor as dialectical power in weakness, nor simply as persuasive power, but *as the liberating power of connectedness that is effective in compassionate love.*"[65]

This understanding of relational power is founded on a liberating strength that emanates from the free capacity to choose to become vulnerable in order to sustain a mutual loving relationship. It is a relational power that stands in contrast to the unilateral power communicated by the omnipotent God of classical theism. Bernard Loomer, whose classic essay "Two Kinds of Power" has been built upon by Rita Brock in her work on erotic power, defines relational power as "the ability to both produce and undergo an effect. It is the capacity both to influence others and be influenced by others."[66] In this understanding, the capacity to absorb an influence is as truly a mark of power as is the strength involved in exerting an influence. Reception of another indicates that a person is, or may become, large enough to make room for another within herself or himself. That notion is clearly congruent with a panentheistic understanding of God's kenotic relationship with the world described above. Moreover, "under the relational conception of power, what is truly for the good of any one or all of the relational partners is not a preconceived good. The true good is not a function of controlling influence. The true good is emergent from deeply mutual relationships."[67]

---

[64] Ibid., 270. See also 306, nn. 62–67.
[65] Ibid. (emphasis mine).
[66] Bernard Loomer, "Two Kinds of Power," *Criterion* 15, no. 1 (Winter, 1976) 20.
[67] Ibid., 21.

Johnson is referring to that kind of power when she describes "a vitality, an empowering vigor that reaches out and awakens freedom and strength in oneself and others. It is an energy that brings forth, stirs up and fosters life, enabling autonomy and friendship."[68] For the analogical imagination, this understanding of divine power does not diminish the autonomous power of the creature; rather, it signifies that "the glory of God is being manifest to the degree that creatures are most radically and fully themselves."[69] That is the power revealed by a Trinitarian God of mutual relations whose very being is communion. It is not a power that has to control. It is a power that emanates from persons who are free to love, to let new life come into being as it will, free to be vulnerable to the limits of the other. It is a power that is free enough to enter into suffering.

Female Metaphors for the Power of a Suffering God

In order to convey the truly liberating power of a suffering God, Johnson argues that it is necessary "to step decisively out of the androcentric system of power-over versus victimization and to think in other categories about power and pain and their interweaving in human experience."[70] She therefore turns again to women's interpreted experience as a source for symbols of pain that can evoke the mystery of God. She focuses first on the pain involved in birth and in the creative anger that leads to the pursuit of justice. Then she turns to the utter darkness of the experiences of grief and of degradation.

The symbol of birthing calls forth the twin experiences of intense pain and intense joy. When actively entered into, the experience of labor and delivery offers a vibrant metaphor of Sophia-God's struggle to bring a new heaven and a new earth to birth.[71]

> For a long time I have held my peace,
>   I have kept still and restrained myself;
> now I will cry out like a woman in labor,
>   I will gasp and pant. (Isa 42:14)

This image from the prophet Isaiah portrays God's intense active involvement in creation's coming to full term. Only in the *eschaton*—that which is already but not yet—will the delivery take place. God cries out in pain, longing for the completion of the birth.

---

[68] Johnson, *SHE WHO IS*, 269.
[69] Ibid., 229.
[70] Ibid., 254.
[71] Ibid., 255.

A second symbol that Johnson appeals to is the power of righteous anger. She refers to several stories of women moved by injustice to action and refers to the key essay of Beverley Wildung Harrison, "The Power of Anger and the Work of Love." Wildung Harrison argues that "anger is a mode of connectedness to others and it is always in a vivid form of caring."[72] Anger can surface the energy to act and to resist. It can, as Mary Daly observes, be "a transformative, focusing force."[73] It can be a "fury that is creative of life."[74] Johnson proposes that women ablaze with righteous anger is an excellent image of God's indignant wrath. She acknowledges that apart from fundamentalist preaching, the wrath of God is not frequently referred to in our day but suggests that it is an important image to retain. Like the image in the prophet Hosea of God as an angry mother bear (Hos 13:7-8), it "discloses God's outrage at the harm done to those she loves."[75] Thus imaging a suffering God through symbols of birth and just anger connects energy and strength with suffering. These symbols depict a relational power that is creative of new life.

Women's desolate experience of grief is often the consequence of their relational way of being in the world. Johnson suggests that this experience can provide another way of speaking about God who grieves over her beloved creation. She refers to many biblical examples of God's grief, for example, Jeremiah 31:15-20; 48:31, 36; Isaiah 16:9, where God laments over her beloved people who are crushed and broken and their land destroyed. Jewish rabbinic and kabbalistic traditions also develop the idea of divine sorrow, and the Jewish tradition of the Shekinah depicts God going with her people into exile. Because God is understood to be infinite, it can be argued that God's suffering also is infinite. The power of speaking about God in this way resides not just as a consolation for those who are suffering but also in the symbol's power to evoke hope—"if God grieves with them in the middle of disaster, then there may yet be a way forward."[76]

There is one further terrible symbol that Johnson brings forward as a way of entering into an understanding of God as one who suffers with us. It is women's experience of personal humiliation, fear, violation, and degradation that is also often associated with or accompanied by sexual abuse. Phyllis Trible's *Texts of Terror* focuses on biblical narra-

---

[72] Beverley Harrison, "The Power of Anger in the Work of Love," *Union Seminary Quarterly Review* 36 (1980–1981, Supplement) 49.

[73] Mary Daly, *Pure Lust: Elemental Feminist Philosophy* (Boston: Beacon Press, 1984) 375, quoted in Johnson, *SHE WHO IS*, 257.

[74] Johnson, *SHE WHO IS*, 258.

[75] Ibid.

[76] Ibid., 261.

tives of shocking abuse. Similarly, episodes often suppressed in Church history—women accused of being witches by the Inquisition, for example—reveal mass abuse and annihilation of women in the name of God. Johnson suggests that these and many more current stories provide profound symbols of the suffering God. She invites the reader to remember those hidden stories of degradation, to contemplate those female bodies and faces as one would contemplate an image of the bloodied Christ on the cross, recalling the words "Ecce homo" in recognition of the "unspeakable way they are images of the crucified."[77]

It should be noted in this context that there is a complexity in retrieving the cross as a symbol for women. Catherine Hilkert, in a survey of contemporary feminist theology, claims that "no symbol is more problematic for feminist theologians than the cross."[78] Countless women in violent and destructive marriages, for example, have been counseled to identify with the sacrifice of Jesus and to offer up their suffering in like manner. A central critique is that a preaching of the cross has encouraged women to accept the role of passive victim.[79] However, the experiences of Afro-American, African, and Asian women bring a different perspective. They claim the cross as a symbol of empowerment, since it has for generations enabled women to find a path of salvation within the stark oppression of their lives. The cross is for them a symbol of hope precisely because as womanist (Afro-American) theologian Jacquelyn Grant argues, "Jesus' suffering was not the suffering of a mere human [but of] God incarnate."[80] Johnson reflects this understanding of the cross in her address to the Catholic Theological Society of America entitled "Jesus and Salvation":

[77] Ibid., 263. See Johnson's reference to the theological insight expressed in the figure of *Christa*, Christ sculpted as a crucified woman by Edwina Sandys and displayed in 1984 at the Cathedral of St. John the Divine in New York City. 264. See also the powerful painting *Crucifixion, Shoalhaven*, 1979–1980, by the Australian artist Arthur Boyd, which also depicts a woman on the cross, in Rosemary Crumlin, *Images of Religion in Australian Art* (Kensington, N.S.W.: Bay Books, 1988). Boyd commented on his work in 1987: "I do not believe it is enough to say *he* represented all of us," 158–59.

[78] Elizabeth A. Johnson, Susan A. Ross, Mary Catherine Hilkert, "Feminist Theology: A Review of Literature," *Theological Studies* 56 (1995) 344. This article offers a brief but comprehensive discussion of this issue.

[79] For specific examples of this critique, see Mary Daly, *Beyond God the Father: Toward a Philosophy of Women's Liberation* (Boston: Beacon Press, 1973) 75–77, and Elisabeth Schüssler Fiorenza, *Jesus: Miriam's Child, Sophia's Prophet: Critical Issues in Feminist Theology* (New York: Continuum, 1994) 102. These are referred to in Johnson, Ross, Hilkert, "Feminist Theology," 344–45.

[80] Jacquelyn Grant, *White Women's Christ and Black Women's Jesus* (Atlanta: Scholars Press, 1989) 212.

> In Jesus the Holy One enters into solidarity with suffering people in order to release hope and bring new life. . . . The cross remains, but its symbolic nexus changes. It stands in history as a life-affirming protest against all torture and injustice, and as a pledge that the transforming power of God is with those who suffer to bring about life for others.[81]

Her emphasis is precisely on the overcoming from within, against all odds, by the power of love.[82] In this symbol she sees Holy Wisdom identifying with the pain and the violence that women suffer on whatever cross and keeping watch with them. And, conversely, she suggests that the raw degradation of those who suffer without any hope of justice points to the depths of the suffering God.[83]

Divine Suffering

In her exploration of the one God, Johnson has emphasized that the inconceivable power that gives life to the world and sustains it is relational. She names this power, this omnipotent God, Holy Wisdom— "pure, unbounded love, utterly set against evil, totally on the side of the good."[84] Drawing from women's experience rather than from classical definitions, she traces the contours of this love: "Love includes an openness to the ones loved, a vulnerability to their experience, a solidarity with their well-being, so that one rejoices with their joys and grieves with their sorrows. This is not a dispensable aspect of love but belongs to love's very essence." She concludes that "love does entail suffering in God," but hastens to add that "as a summation of compassionate love, the symbol of divine suffering appears not as an imperfection but as the highest excellence."[85] This is a redefinition of an omnipotent God. Omnipotence is understood as the free, unlimited capacity to make room within the self for the other. God's freedom in this act of self-limitation is central: "In the act of creating, therefore, divinity withdraws. God makes room for creation by constricting divine presence and power. . . . God's generous self-emptying is the condition for the possibility of finite existence in its own autonomy."[86]

---

[81] Elizabeth Johnson, "Jesus and Salvation," *CTSA Proceedings* 49 (1994) 1–18.

[82] See Johnson, *SHE WHO IS*, 263.

[83] See ibid., 264.

[84] Ibid., 265.

[85] Ibid., 266.

[86] Ibid., 233. See also 233–36. It is significant to recall that Johnson's redefinition of God as omnipotent here should be understood in the context of relational autonomy described above.

The symbol of the suffering God signals that the mystery of God is present in solidarity with those who suffer. It signals that God's compassionate love struggles against destructive forces at work in the world and so calls humanity into an alliance that leads to a praxis of resistance and healing. And then, when in spite of every effort, suffering still prevails, "the symbol of the suffering God can help by awakening hope that historical failure is not the last evidence of what the future holds."[87] Out of the deepest darkness, the living remembrance of the mystery of Holy Wisdom who came among us, who suffered and died and who rose, defeating death, can release the energy to resist despair and to choose life. The symbol of the suffering God empowers: "It signifies the power of suffering love to resist and to create anew."[88]

Johnson finally recalls that language of a suffering God is of course not a literal description of God. She warns that the rule of analogical speech must be applied here with full rigor. Nevertheless, she has demonstrated that one can speak of a suffering God by reentering the powerful biblical story of covenant and liberation and remembering the living God—SHE WHO IS—revealed as being dynamically present with her suffering people. She shows that the God who suffers is also revealed by the redemptive image of Jesus-Sophia, the crucified one, love poured out; of Spirit-Sophia, who, according to Scripture and rabbinic writing, is compassion poured out, forever "speaking, crying, admonishing, sorrowing, weeping, rejoicing, groaning, comforting";[89] of Mother-Sophia, the revelation of the fecundity of relational power and love who freely makes room within for creation to come to be. Johnson thus shows that to contemplate the mystery of the one Trinitarian God as a living mystery of personal relations at the heart of the universe is to come to know Holy Wisdom, the triune God who suffers with us.

[87] Ibid., 268.

[88] Ibid., 271.

[89] Ibid., 266. Johnson refers to Pope John Paul II, who describes the Spirit personifying the suffering God (albeit with a distinct theology of suffering) and entering "into human and cosmic suffering with a new outpouring of love, which will redeem the world."—*Lord and Giver of Life (Dominum et Vivificantem)* (Washington: United States Catholic Conference, 1986) 39.

CHAPTER 7

Reclaiming the Creator Spirit, Women, and Earth

The exploitation of the earth . . . is intimately linked to the marginalization of women, and both of these predicaments are intrinsically related to forgetting the Creator Spirit.[1]

A third significant contribution that Elizabeth Johnson makes to the contemporary retrieval of the Trinitarian God is the emphasis she gives to reclaiming the importance and place of the Holy Spirit within a Christian theology of God. In agreement with many other theologians, she assesses that the Holy Spirit has been neglected in Christian theology and practice, and she sets out to redress this neglect.[2] Instead of beginning her Trinitarian theology in the classic manner with the "first" person of the Trinity, she chooses an inductive approach, beginning "from below," from humankind's experience of the Spirit. In so doing, she claims methodological connections with "certain broad streams of existential, historical, religious, logical, theological and feminist wisdom."[3]

---

[1] Elizabeth Johnson, *Women, Earth and Creator Spirit* (New York: Paulist Press, 1993) 2.

[2] See ibid., 129–31, 294, nn. 14-17. Johnson refers specifically to the opinions of Yves Congar, Heribert Mühlen, Walter Kasper, John Macquarrie, Georgia Harkness, Norman Pittenger, Joseph Ratzinger, Kilian McDonnell, Wolfhart Pannenberg, J. R. Foster, Margaret Kohl, G. J. Sirks.

[3] Elizabeth Johnson, *SHE WHO IS: The Mystery of God in Feminist Theological Discourse* (New York: Crossroad, 1992) 123.

159

Then, in a further critical move, to which I have already referred, she links the neglect of the Spirit with the exploitation of the earth and the marginalization of women and argues that because these three relationships are so intrinsically interconnected, none of them can be addressed in any useful way in isolation from each other. Her analysis is that the Holy Spirit can only be effectively reclaimed within Trinitarian theology and be fully reinstated within the Christian life if the major issues of the ecology and sexism are simultaneously addressed.

In this chapter I focus on Johnson's theology of the Holy Spirit within the context of a retrieved symbol of the Trinity and on its consequences for women and the ecology. I examine her critique of the strict adherence to the traditional structure of the symbol, always ordered as "Father, Son, and Holy Spirit" and the effects of this phenomenon on the perceived importance of the Holy Spirit within Christian life. I explore the symbolic and practical significance of her choosing an inductive approach to Trinitarian theology and then investigate her constructive analysis of the connections between women, earth, and Holy Spirit.

The Structure of the Triune Symbol

One of the significant learnings of the modern era is that justice cannot be achieved for an individual person if the society or institution in which she or he lives and works is structured toward injustice. This awareness is expressed in the feminist axiom "The personal is the political." Specific efforts to redress a wrong have inevitably proved to be fruitless unless the whole system is brought under scrutiny and renewed according to just laws and provisions. Thus "structural injustice" has been identified as a crucial arena for action if there is to be any lasting and effective social justice within societies and among the peoples of the world. In turn, it has also been recognized that for structural injustice to be effectively eradicated, it must be addressed at the level of the powerful religious and cultural symbols that shape the mythological base of a particular society or system.[4]

---

[4] As Johnson often reminds the reader: "The symbol of God functions." See also Stephen Happel, "Symbol," in *The New Dictionary of Theology,* ed. J. Komonchak, Mary Collins, Dermot Lane (Dublin: Gill and Macmillan, 1987) 996–1002; Mircea Eliade, *Images and Symbols: Studies in Religious Symbolism,* trans. Philip Mairet (New York: Sheed & Ward, 1961); Bernard Lonergan, *Method in Theology* (New York: Crossroad, 1972); David Power, *Unsearchable Riches: The Symbolic Nature of the Liturgy* (New York: Pueblo, 1984); Karl Rahner, "The Theology of the Symbol," *Theological Investigations* 4 (Baltimore: Helicon Press, 1966) 221–52; Paul Tillich, "Theology and

Johnson argues that the central Christian symbol of the triune God has worked to hold in place a level of structural injustice for women. She maintains that it does this through "both its male imagery and the hierarchical pattern of divine relationships inherent in the structure of reigning models of the symbol itself."[5] That is, Johnson is proposing that if this symbol is to be fully retrieved, not only must the issue of imagery be addressed (as explored in Chapter 5), but the structural problem of the symbol must be identified and owned, and alternatives must be provided. She is arguing that the symbol of God holds such power that unless this problem of its structure is addressed, it will subtly continue to subvert the teaching on the equality of the divine persons and thereby subvert the equality of human persons, as it has done for the past two millennia.

Johnson begins the task of addressing the structure of the triune God by seeking to identify the historical source of the issue. Early Trinitarian debate about the triune God records a significant struggle to come to agreement on the equality of the three persons in the one God. Both the powerful legacy of monotheistic Judaism and the influence of Neo-Platonic philosophy led to early formulations enshrining the notion that the Word and the Spirit were only emanations of the one God, the unoriginate source of divinity. However, in the light of the Council of Nicea and in the expansion of the article on the Spirit in the Nicene-Constantinopolitan Creed, "the three *hypostases* were posited as equally related, one to another, while remaining distinct."[6]

In the period when this promulgation of the equality of persons was being hammered out, the classic presentation of the doctrine of the Trinity that claims the Father as the principle and source of the triune God was also formulated and has been so proclaimed virtually ever since. That has been a central tenet of Trinitarian teaching:

> Classical theology insists with great rigor on this pattern of proceeding, which is indeed reflective of the biblical narratives in which the Father sends the Son and, together with the Son or alone, also sends the Spirit (see Jn 20:21; 14:26). It is argued that in this order and its resulting relations lies the identity of the three persons. What keeps them distinct is the way they do or do not proceed from each other.[7]

Symbolism," in *Religious Symbolism*, ed. F. E. Johnson (New York: Institute for Religious and Social Studies, 1955); David Tracy, *The Analogical Imagination: Christian Theology and the Culture of Pluralism* (New York: Crossroad, 1981).

[5] Johnson, *SHE WHO IS*, 193. See also J.N.D. Kelly, *Early Christian Doctrines* (San Francisco: Harper & Row, 1978) 109–37, 223–79.

[6] Johnson, *SHE WHO IS*, 194.

[7] Ibid., 194–96.

That order has been applied in speech about both the immanent and the economic Trinity. Johnson identifies the relentless adherence to this set order as one source of the problem of the neglect of the Spirit. She argues that when this model of the Trinity, which "focuses on the procession of the first to second to third," is continually used, "a subtle hierarchy is set up and, like a drowned continent, bends all currents of Trinitarian thought to the shape of the model used."[8] She posits that despite the battle of subordinationalism being won in theory, the insistence on the right order of the processions led to ontological priority being given to the Father and then to the Son, with the Spirit coming an inevitable third. The exclusive use of this order of Trinitarian processions has meant that the Spirit is almost always considered last. Even though the Church's firm teaching on the radical equality of the three persons has remained constant, it has failed to counter this implicit Trinitarian hierarchy in the popular mind and imagination. A practical inequality followed from this asymmetry of Trinitarian relations, with the Son and the Spirit being perceived to have less authority than the Father, the "first person" and the apex of a divine pyramid.

Johnson thus points to the tension created between the Trinitarian doctrine of coequal persons and the analogy of procession used to interpret it. She argues for the need to apply the rule that all speech about God is necessarily incomplete and imperfect: "specifically, the tension between the confession that the Spirit is to be equally worshipped and glorified and the metaphor of proceeding with its connotation of possible subordination, heightens awareness that the model of love proceeding is only a partial one."[9]

Johnson draws attention to a further difficulty. She observes that because this model mirrors so well the existence of patriarchal structures in Church and society, it "both reproduces and supports such structures."[10] The symbol of the Trinity, always structured in a way that is suggestive of hierarchy, has been used to validate hierarchical structures. Johnson notes, along with other feminist theologians, that even the basic metaphor of "procession" used within the formula carries the weight of rank and order of precedence.[11] And, referring to predominant patriarchal understandings of law and order she suggests that:

[8] Ibid., 196.

[9] Ibid., 144.

[10] Ibid., 197.

[11] See ibid., 143, 197, 299, n. 12. Johnson refers here specifically to Virginia Woolf's oft-quoted caution about where the "procession of the sons of educated men" can lead. See Virginia Woolf, *Three Guineas* (New York: Harcourt, Brace, 1938) 36, and also Mary Daly, *Gyn/Ecology: the Metaethics of Radical Feminism* (Boston: Beacon Press, 1978) 37–42.

Argumentation in [this structure's] favor betrays a mindset which assumes that if a certain order of precedence is not kept, with a single ruler at the top and all proceeding from there, then chaos will break out, personal identity become indistinct, and harmony be destroyed. A different order of unity based on mutual personal relations and shared responsibility is not envisioned.[12]

Thus Johnson focuses on a foundational assumption of Trinitarian belief, namely, that the identifying uniqueness of each of the persons of the Trinity comes from their relation of origin. She shows how this fundamental teaching gave rise to a set order of processions that in turn has led to a set formulation of Trinitarian structure. She argues that the popular hierarchical perception of this set formula has undermined a second foundational belief regarding the triune God, namely, that each of the three persons of the Trinity is radically equal to each of the others. She points out that what has followed in practice is that the symbol of the Father at the top of this hierarchy came to be considered more important than the Son, who in turn came to be considered more important than the Spirit.

In order to address this dilemma, Johnson returns to biblical sources to examine whether it is always necessary to adhere to this strict order of the Trinitarian processions. Her research leads her to argue that "theology has been highly selective in its focus on the Father-Son-Spirit pattern."[13] An example of an alternative ordering is demonstrated in a key passage in Luke's Gospel (4:16-20), where it is not the Father but the Spirit who sends Jesus. Johnson appeals to Jürgen Moltmann, whose work with scriptural data reveals several orders of proceeding. She notes that in his *Trinity and the Kingdom*, Moltmann discerns a pattern of different orderings that unfolds through the Gospel narratives and the epistles:

> Before the resurrection the sequence reads Father-Spirit-Son. For the Spirit is so powerfully active in the birth, baptism, and passing over of Jesus' life in death and resurrection that Jesus can be said to live from the works of the creative Spirit. After the resurrection the order becomes Father-Son-Spirit, for Jesus is now made a life-giving spirit and

---

[12] Johnson, *SHE WHO IS*, 197. As a woman who has been involved for many years in institutional change within the Roman Catholic Church, my experience corroborates this observation. A hierarchical mindset is strongly resistant to establishing structures that are based on mutual collaboration and decision-making. There are always spoken or unspoken fears that chaos will result from such a way of proceeding.

[13] Johnson, *SHE WHO IS*, 195.

himself joins in the sending of the Spirit to the community of disciples. Finally when we consider the eschatological transformation of creation the sequence becomes the Spirit-Son-Father, for the Spirit is the power of the new creation and brings all to rebirth.[14]

Johnson points out that in this last sequence Moltmann is proposing that the Spirit is the active subject from whom the Father and the Son receive their glory and from whom they receive the world as their home. Moltmann himself expresses it in this way:

> The Spirit is the glorifying God. The Spirit is the unifying God. In this respect the Spirit is not an energy proceeding from the Father or from the Son; it is a subject from whose activity the Son and the Father receive their glory and their union, as well as their glorification through the whole creation, and their world as their eternal home.[15]

Such imagery depicts the Spirit in an intradivine authorizing role rather than in that of the solely receptive image evoked by the Father-Son-Spirit structure.

In her critique of this exclusive use of this set ordering of the Trinitarian symbol, Johnson is not disputing the uniqueness of the divine persons that derives from their relation of origin. She is arguing that this truth can and needs to be properly communicated by alternative orderings. With Moltmann, Johnson seeks to demonstrate that the biblical witness that lies at the heart of the Trinitarian doctrine can be a source for alternative expressions of the triune formula. Having identified that the strict adherence to the Father-Son-Spirit pattern is one significant reason why the Spirit became the "forgotten person" of the Trinity, and having linked this set structure to the legitimation of the patriarchal subordination of women, she points to the possibility of other patterns present in the scriptural testimony and pleads the case for their application in Trinitarian theology and liturgical use. In choosing the methodology of her own work on the Trinity, she then applies this principle. It is a basic plank in her attempt to provide a platform for the reclaiming of the importance and the place of the Holy Spirit.

A Theology of the Triune God "from Below"

In Western theology, speaking about the triune God in the order of Father-Son-Spirit was affirmed in a particularly powerful way through

---

[14] Ibid. See Jürgen Moltmann, *The Trinity and the Kingdom of God*, trans. Margaret Kohl (New York: Harper & Row, 1981) 89, 126.

[15] Moltmann, *The Trinity*, 89, 126.

the *Summa* of Thomas Aquinas. When this was adopted in the West as the preferred textbook in theology, it became customary to order a theology of God in two distinct treatises: *De Deo Uno*, which focuses on the divine nature, and *De Deo Trino*, which deals with the three divine persons in the sequence of Father to Son to Spirit. Johnson notes that this deductive approach led to great clarity of exposition but that, despite Aquinas's own belief and clear teaching on this matter, it also led to the one nature of God being perceived to be separate from the divine persons and from the historical experience of salvation in the lives of believers.[16]

Johnson owns that a significant moment in the evolution of her own Trinitarian theology occurred when it became clear that she needed to begin "not with the unity of the divine nature nor even with the 'first person' of the Trinity, but with the Spirit, God's livingness subtly and powerfully abroad in the world."[17] She notes that although many theologians emphasize that the arena of the Spirit's work is within the unfolding history of humanity and creation, such is the weight of tradition that theologians, for the most part, do not translate this into practice in their method.[18] Beginning with the experience of the Spirit means for Johnson beginning in particular with the experience of women. Because of millennia of neglect and, in many instances, complete denial of women's experience, one primary strand of her methodological commitment is to place the experience of women at the center of her theological discourse. The very unpredictability of women's responses (according to the normative male perception) is recognized to be an asset, because it more truly mirrors the way the Spirit moves and acts in her work of building communion. When Johnson asks which moments or events mediate God's Spirit, she acknowledges that "the answer can only be all experience, the whole world":

> There is no exclusive zone, no special realm, which alone may be called religious. Rather since the Spirit is creator and giver of life, life itself with all its complexities, abundance, threat, misery, and joy becomes a primary mediation of the dialectic of presence and absence of divine mystery. The historical world becomes a sacrament of divine presence and activity. . . . Wherever we encounter the world and ourselves as held by, open to, gifted by, mourning the absence of, or yearning for

[16] See Johnson, *SHE WHO IS*, 121.

[17] Ibid., 121–22.

[18] See Johnson, "Review Symposium: Author's Response," *Horizons* 20 (1993) 340. See also Johnson, *SHE WHO IS*, 293, n. 3, where she makes references to specific sections of the works of Karl Rahner, Jürgen Moltmann, James Mackey, and Walter Kasper.

something ineffably more than immediately appears, whether that "more" be measured by beauty and joy or in contrast to powers that crush, there the experience of the Spirit transpires.[19]

The realm of the Spirit is not focused and containable. Akin to the multiple and varied expressions of women's religious experience, the horizon of the Spirit is as wide as the world itself, and no human concept can capture it.

Johnson does, however, put forward three historical mediations for particular consideration. Focusing first on the natural world, she submits that until recently there has been little sustained theological reflection on what Johannes Baptist Metz has called "the Alps experience"—the experience of being caught up in the wonder of the immensity, complexity, and sheer beauty of the natural world. Neither has there been much articulation of what Johnson herself calls "the Chernobyl experience"—that now common experience of profound inner protest that occurs when a person is confronted either directly or through the media with evidence of the massive destruction of natural life-systems of the planet. She suggests that anyone who has entered into either of these sets of experiences—of amazed delight or despairing angst—"has potentially brushed up against an experience of the power of the mystery of God, Creator Spirit."[20] Johnson is suggesting that reflection on the Spirit present in both of these very different experiences of the natural world, of presence and of absence, provides an important entry point into the life of the triune mystery.[21]

Second, Johnson reflects on personal and interpersonal experience as an important arena that mediates to human life the Spirit's presence and absence. Like Zizioulas, she recognizes the power of relationships to create persons. She suggests that persons "seek and are found by the Spirit" in the very process of the multiple expressions of loving relationships.[22] Even the experience of broken relationships, she holds, mediates traces of divine absence and compassion for those able to receive them. Within utter darkness and devastating loss, new life and love can be discovered.[23] Johnson is drawing here on Schillebeeckx's

[19] *SHE WHO IS*, 124–25.

[20] Ibid., 125.

[21] See also Johnson, "Heaven and Earth Are Filled with Your Glory," in *Finding God in All Things*, ed. Michael Himes and Stephen Pope (New York: Crossroad, 1996) 86–87.

[22] Johnson, *SHE WHO IS*, 125.

[23] A powerful example of this was recorded in Australian newspapers describing the funeral of the wife of the sole survivor of a tragic landslide at the alpine resort Thredbo in 1997. They reported that Stuart Diver reflected on the terrible hours

notion of "negative contrast experience" to make the case that experiences of oppression, injustice, or absence can be revelatory of God, but not in a direct way.[24] Rather, the Spirit is operative in the resistance and defeat of evil or as sustaining a person in absence. Thus she is arguing that the whole spectrum of experiences that initiate a human being into genuine personhood—finding one's voice, tasting righteous anger, acting prophetically, accepting forgiveness, taking responsibility for one's life, acting according to one's conscience, making peace, entering into the acute pain of loss—all are moments that mediate the mystery of God's Spirit. Each such experience provides an invitation, through the action of the Spirit, into the mystery of divine communion.

Third, Johnson suggests that experience of the Spirit is also mediated at the level of the macro systems by which human beings are structured into groups. As in an individual person's life, so in a group's life there are moments and places of choice when the call to fullness of life can be collectively accepted or rejected. Wherever, for example, within the life of a particular people "diversity is sustained in *koinonia;* wherever justice and peace and freedom gain a transformative foothold—there the living presence of powerful, blessing mystery amid the brokenness of the world is mediated."[25] Wherever true life is discovered in the life of a family, an interest group, a nation, the Spirit of God is at work.[26]

Each of those historical mediations that Johnson explores points to a more fundamental acknowledgment that "whenever people speak in a generic way of God, of their experience of God or of God doing something in the world, more often than not they are referring to the Spirit."[27] Christian belief has held that even before God was incarnated in Christ, the life-giving Spirit was at work in the world enlivening and renewing all creatures. Starting with the Spirit, therefore, "coheres not

---

and days of being trapped in a freezing concrete tomb beside the body of his dead wife. He read these lines by cartoonist poet Michael Leunig to convey the heart of that profound experience of darkness for him: "Love is born With a dark and troubled face When hope is dead And in the most unlikely place Love is born: Love is always born."—Michael Leunig, *The Prayer Tree* (Melbourne: HarperCollins, 1990) 6.

[24] Johnson, *SHE WHO IS*, 63. See also 285, n. 4.

[25] Ibid., 126. As this is being written there is occurring within Australian society a particularly telling example of this phenomenon. The thirtieth anniversary of the 1967 constitutional referendum, which gave indigenous Australians the right to be included in the census count in their own country, has provided an opportunity for all Australians to work together toward a national process of reconciliation.

[26] See Walter Kasper, *The God of Jesus Christ*, trans. Matthew J. O'Connell (New York: Crossroad, 1991) 202.

[27] Johnson, *SHE WHO IS*, 127.

only with the existential but also with the historical pattern by which faith in the triune God arises."[28] The credibility of this approach is further confirmed by the fact that theology, and Trinitarian theology in particular, necessarily begins with the human experience of salvation, and it resonates with the ancient art of discernment of spirits, which has always relied on the fruits of the Spirit to confirm the authentic action of God. The "dialectic of the Spirit's presence and absence is known in its effects—new life and energy, peace and justice, resistance and liberation, hope against hope, wisdom and courage and all that goes with love."[29]

Finally, Johnson suggests that an inductive approach to speaking about the triune God can have the effect of making this symbol more accessible to contemporary persons. As noted above, discourse in many different disciplines—existential, historical, religious, logical, theological and feminist—argues for the validity of a methodology that begins from experience. Starting from experience is more likely to be attuned to and to nourish the religious sensibility that underlies the critical questions at the heart of many of the current issues that grip the imagination and concern of persons today. An inductive approach to Trinitarian theology suggests that being "awake" to the fullness of life's events, to the action of the Holy Spirit, is an important way into the triune life of God.

Beginning her Trinitarian theology with the Spirit opens up for Johnson "three key insights significant for a feminist theology of God, namely, the transcendent God's immanence, divine passion for liberation and the constitutive nature of relation."[30] Claiming that God's indwelling and nearness, named as immanence, were "greatly neglected by classical theism," she observes that reflection on the action of the Spirit which is in the world but not bound by it "directs language to do justice to divine immanence and transcendence simultaneously, showing that these two are not opposite poles but correlative concepts."[31]

Second, the ways in which the Spirit operates also show that God is not neutral toward the world. God's clear intent is to free captives and to let the oppressed go free. The Holy One is thus revealed as actively seeking liberation for all that is held bound.

Third, a fuller appreciation of both the Spirit's immanence, and her desire for the freedom of humanity and of all creation, lead to a recognition of the Spirit's role in relationships, in creating *koinōnia:* "What is

[28] Ibid., 123.
[29] Ibid., 122.
[30] Ibid., 147.
[31] Ibid.

immediately striking is that there is no possible aspect of the Spirit of God, either *ad intra* or *ad extra*, that can be spoken about without factoring in the idea of relation in an essential way. . . . Relationality is intrinsic to her very being."[32] At the same time the Spirit is essentially free: "While remaining in herself, she renews all things" (Wis 7:27). Freedom and relation are therefore shown to be essential to one another and to enhance one another mutually.

Johnson's final assessment is that perhaps the longest-reaching effect of considering the Spirit first and from a feminist perspective may well be that it subverts the dominance of the patriarchal image of God that has so limited human beings' access to the mystery of the triune God and, in turn, has limited the well-being of the whole of humanity.[33] If this proves to be so, as I believe it will, this approach will have contributed significantly to the retrieval of the triune symbol.

Women, Earth, and Creator Spirit

Since the shift to begin a Trinitarian theology from experience of the Spirit is not a simple, optional reversal but rather an intrinsic exigency of Johnson's feminist methodology, it is not surprising that starting with the Holy Spirit led her to pursue the connections between the marginalizing of the Spirit and the marginalizing of women. And since starting with experience in today's world inevitably leads to an awareness of the endangered state of the global ecology, it is also not surprising that it further led to an awareness of the explicit connections between the marginalization of the Spirit, women, and planet Earth. In this section I begin with Johnson's naming of the issue of ecocide and her analysis of its root cause. I then follow her searching of women's wisdom, her redescribing humanity's relationship to the earth and to the Spirit as steps towards a constructive theological vision that can contribute towards changing this global situation.

Ecocide and an Analysis of Its Roots

Johnson suggests that to say that the peoples of the earth have an environmental problem is to understate the issue. She judges that the situation should be described as ecocide:

> At the present moment the earth is still a community of living creatures endowed with powerful, responsive forces for life. But it is being

[32] Ibid., 148.
[33] Ibid., 149.

wasted, with great violence, by multiple acts that add up to nothing less than ecocide. Our blue planet as a habitat for life stands in jeopardy due to atmospheric damage, deforestation, pollution of the seas, disruption of the ecosystems, destruction of habitat, extinction of species, loss of biodiversity, overpopulation, resource exhaustion, and nuclear proliferation.[34]

It is gradually being recognized by many peoples of the earth, at least in moments of clarity, that unless there is a radical reversal of this situation very soon, the life of the entire earth is in jeopardy. In the language of the Canberra assembly of the World Council of Churches in 1991, "The stark sign of our times is a planet in peril at our hands."[35] Within the Christian community, biblical scholars and theologians have begun to search the traditions in the light of this huge crisis of the very survival of life in an effort to construct a creative environmental ethic and spirituality.[36] There is still, however, a failure on the part of the majority of Christians, along with a majority of the peoples of the planet, to appreciate the full gravity of the crisis. It has not yet been widely owned as ecocide.

[34] Johnson, *Women, Earth and Creator Spirit*, 7–8.

[35] "Giver of Life—Sustain Your Creation," in *Signs of the Spirit*, official report of the seventh assembly of the World Council of Churches, ed. Michael Kinnamon (Geneva: World Council of Churches, 1991) 55. Quoted in Johnson, "Turn to the Heavens and the Earth: Retrieval of the Cosmos in Theology," *CTSA Proceedings* 51 (1996) 1–14.

[36] See, for example, Carol Adams, ed., *Ecofeminism and the Sacred* (New York: Continuum, 1993); Ian Barbour, *Religion in an Age of Science*, 2 vols. (San Francisco: HarperSanFrancisco, 1990); Thomas Berry, *The Dream of the Earth* (San Francisco: Sierra Club Books, 1988); Leonardo Boff, *Ecology and Liberation: A New Paradigm* (Maryknoll, N.Y.: Orbis Books, 1995); Brendan Byrne, *Inheriting the Earth: The Pauline Basis of a Spirituality for Our Time* (Homebush, N.S.W.: St. Paul Publications, 1990); Denis Edwards, *Jesus the Wisdom of God: An Ecological Theology* (New York: Orbis Books, 1995); John Haught, *The Promise of Nature: Ecology and Cosmic Purpose* (New York: Paulist Press, 1993); Kevin Irwin, ed., *Preserving the Creation: Environmental Theology and Ethics* (Washington: Georgetown University Press, 1994); Anthony Kelly, *An Expanding Theology: Faith in a World of Connections* (Newtown, Australia: E. J. Dwyer, 1993); Sean McDonagh, *The Greening of the Church* (Scoresby, Vic.: Canterbury Press, 1990); Sallie McFague, *The Body of God: An Ecological Theology* (Minneapolis: Fortress Press, 1993); Mary Heather McKinnon and Moni McIntyre, eds., *Readings in Theology and Feminist Theology* (Kansas City: Sheed & Ward, 1995); Ted Peters, ed., *Cosmos as Creation: Theology and Science in Consonance* (Nashville: Abingdon Press, 1989); Rosemary Radford Ruether, *Gaia and God: An Ecofeminist Theology of Earth Healing* (San Francisco: HarperSanFrancisco, 1992); Rosemary Radford Ruether, ed., *Women Healing Earth: Third World Women on Ecology, Feminism, and Religion* (London: SCM Press, 1996).

Johnson's assessment agrees with ecofeminism's analysis that humankind will not "get to the heart of the matter until its sees the connection between exploitation of the earth and the sexist definition and treatment of women."[37] She therefore sets out to address what she calls "a major taproot of the crisis, namely the dominant form of western rationality called hierarchical dualism."[38] That is a system of thought and action that divides reality into two separate and opposing spheres, with one sphere ranked as more valuable than the other. That system separates humanity from nature, rating humanity as more important than nature; it separates man from woman, judging man to be more valuable than woman; God is separated from the world and deemed to be of infinitely greater significance. Hierarchical dualism sets up a view of reality in which the lesser partner of each dualism tends to be seen as existing only to be of use to the more important partner.

Johnson points out that adherence to this philosophical construct of reality has had significant social and political consequences:

> The hierarchy of mind over body in the individual is therefore not a neutral construction but has political consequences. It translates into social structures of domination/subordination undergirded by the belief that man should rule over woman, the quintessential "Other" whose reproductive power and survival skills he needs and gets but whom he is also free to disparage.[39]

Along with women, non-ruling men and men from other classes and races also lose out in this system. They are also considered to be irrational and weak, not fit to hold authority and power. This dualism did not just affect the human community. Because the earth is matter, the opposite of spirit, it was the ruling male's responsibility to tame and control the earth along with women and slaves. Thus both women and the natural world were separated out against men. They were considered of little if any intrinsic worth. Their value resided primarily in their usefulness to men: "Women whose bodies mediate physical existence to humanity thus become symbolically the oldest archetype of the connection between social domination and the domination of nature."[40]

---

[37] Johnson, *Women, Earth and Creator Spirit*, 10. This is a central tenet of ecofeminism. See also Catharina Halkes, "The Rape of Mother Earth: Ecology and Patriarchy," in *Motherhood: Experience, Institution, Theology*, Concilium 206, ed. Anne Carr and Elisabeth Schüssler Fiorenza (Edinburgh: T&T Clark, 1989) 91–100.

[38] Johnson, *Women, Earth and Creator Spirit*, 10.

[39] Ibid., 12.

[40] Ibid., 13.

The history of Western anthropology reveals that at the dawn of the modern era this deeply embedded hierarchical dualism was further strengthened. At the time of the Enlightenment, Descartes's famous dictum "Cogito ergo sum" came to epitomize the philosophy of the time. It taught that the rational mind is "the essential self," while matter, nature, and the universe are objects to be overcome and mastered. This form of hierarchical dualism also separated the privileged male from other, "different" persons as well as from nature and from his own body. Within the philosophy of science that emerged during this era, nature was quantified as a thing that could be properly "probed, subjugated, manipulated."[41] Within this worldview, nature was considered to be "not a great teacher but man's servant, and man not nature's child but her master in accord with patriarchal rule."[42] Women came to be identified literally as well as symbolically with the natural world.

To illustrate the connection that was made between the subordination of women and the conquering of nature, Johnson refers to the imagery used by Francis Bacon, the founder of modern scientific method:

> [Francis Bacon] speaks of wresting new knowledge from nature's womb; of seizing her by the hair of her head and molding her into something new by technology; of penetrating her mysteries; of having the power to conquer and subdue her. . . . He writes: "Neither ought a man to make scruple of entering and penetrating into these holes and corners, when the inquisition of truth is his whole object. . . ."[43]

There remains still today a legacy of this language of man's domination of women and man's domination of the earth. Phrases such as "untouched virgin forests" and "the rape of the earth" continue to connect the exploitation of nature with abusive sexual exploitation of women. Johnson's assessment is that the two "are inextricably fused in theory and practice." She therefore concludes that the commonly held view that the ecological crisis springs from an anthropocentric view of the world is not accurate. With other feminist theologians, she suggests that it is more accurate to say that the problem lies in an *androcentric* world view. "Historically, not the superior identity of humanity in general but of man, understood as ruling class males in a patriarchal system, mandates the domination of nature."[44] Johnson thus concludes

---

[41] Ibid., 14.

[42] Ibid., 15.

[43] Ibid., Cited in Carolyn Merchant, *The Death of Nature: Women, Ecology, and the Scientific Revolution* (San Francisco: Harper & Row, 1980) 168.

[44] Johnson, *Women, Earth and Creator Spirit*, 16.

that hierarchical dualism is what she calls "the critical taproot of the ecological crisis."[45]

Johnson's analysis, however, does not end with tracing the connections between the exploitation of women and the earth. Johnson holds that hierarchical dualism also shapes the classical Christian doctrine of God. As described above, this form of the doctrine depicts God as "essentially separated from and over against the world, which is created to serve 'Him.'"[46] The doctrine of the incarnation and the teaching on the indwelling of the Spirit notwithstanding, that vision of God had the effect of separating women and all matter, including the body and sexuality, from the realm of the sacred. Man alone came to be understood as bearing the fullness of the image of God, while women were considered to bear the image of God only in connection with man, and nature not at all. That focus also led to the neglect of "the indwelling, sustaining presence of God within the fragility of matter and the historical process"—the Holy Spirit.[47] Because the work of the Spirit includes bringing forth and nurturing life, keeping all things connected, and renewing what the ravages of time and sin break down, Johnson also suggests that the work of the Spirit can be perceived to be "analogous to traditional 'women's work.'"[48] She argues that neglect of the Spirit thus has a symbolic connection with the devaluing of women and of nature.

In summarizing the profound influence of hierarchical dualism on humankind's appreciation of the earth, women, and the Holy Spirit, Johnson argues that those effects endured well into the twentieth century. She observes that we have been prevented from recognizing "the sacredness of the earth, which is linked to the exclusion of women from the sphere of the sacred, which is tied to [a] focus on a monarchical, patriarchal idea of God and a consequent forgetting of the Creator spirit, the Life-giver who is intimately related to the earth."[49] Her contention is that the state of ecocide which we are witnessing on our earth and which, however unwittingly, we are contributing to cannot be fully addressed until those interlocking oppressions are correctly identified and owned. Having thus diagnosed a root cause of the ecological crisis, Johnson proposes that theology now needs to reclaim "a unifying vision that does not stratify what is distinct into superior-inferior layers but reconciles them in relationships of mutuality."[50]

[45] Ibid., 17.
[46] Ibid., 18.
[47] Ibid., 19.
[48] Ibid., 20.
[49] Ibid., 21.
[50] Ibid., 22.

Women's Experience, Humanity's Kinship to the Earth and the Holy Spirit

Christian feminist thinking seeks a vision of wholeness that is not possible within a world picture shaped by hierarchical dualism. It seeks a new community that is built upon the mutuality of equals. Johnson claims that women's experience is an untapped source of wisdom that can reveal insights necessary for a constructive reclaiming of an ethos needed for an ecologically sustainable world. She therefore focuses on women's experience for the purpose of finding ways to address the problem of ecocide. She notes: "One of the clearest insights emerging to date is that women tend to experience themselves as a self in fundamental embodied connection with others. . . . Women as a group at this moment of time articulate their self-understanding with a strong accent on relationality."[51]

Reflecting on this phenomenon, Johnson observes that studies in the United States in personality formation point out that young boys have needed to differentiate themselves from their mothers by some measure of separation. By contrast, women establish their identity, not in separation from their mothers, but in a form of relational autonomy. They become distinct persons through interconnection.[52] She notes that building from this primal experience of childhood, "women's experience bears out again and again that the most life-giving exchange occurs when bonds are reciprocal or mutual."[53] This experience of interconnectedness therefore serves "to deconstruct the pyramid of hierarchical dualism and constructs in its place a circle of mutual unfettered interconnectedness." This has implications for understanding humanity's connection to the earth and implications for understandings of God. Johnson is thus suggesting that there is a well of women's experience and wisdom that reveals that relationships do not have to be "'over against' and 'superior to' but 'together with' moving in an interactive circle of mutual kinship."[54]

---

[51] Ibid. For an elaboration of this position, which describes women's experience as being distinctive from men's as well as being culturally constructed and socially mediated, see Tiina Allik, "Human Finitude and the Concept of Women's Experience," *Modern Theology* 9, no. 1 (January 1993) 67–85.

[52] See Johnson, *Women, Earth and Creator Spirit*, 75, n. 19. Johnson refers to Nancy Chorodow, *The Reproduction of Mothering* (Berkeley: University of California Press, 1978), and to Catherine Keller, *From a Broken Web: Separation, Sexism and Self* (Boston: Beacon Press, 1986).

[53] Johnson, *Women, Earth and Creator Spirit*, 27.

[54] Ibid., 28.

The issue of how humanity should understand its relation with the earth emerges as a critical question in this era threatened with ecocide. Johnson identifies three possible positions, which she describes as "the absolute kingship, the stewardship and the kinship models."[55] The kingship model is the position that arises from a world picture based on hierarchical dualism. It is a "top-down domination of nature by man."[56] The stewardship model she describes is also based on hierarchical dualism but requires human beings to be responsible stewards of the earth and of all creation. However, when, according to women's collective experience, interconnection and relational valuing of diversity are recognized as creative principles of sustained life, a model of kinship emerges as a preferable option. Johnson describes this model thus:

> It sees human beings and the earth with all its creatures intrinsically related as companions in a community of life. Because we are all mutually interconnected, the flourishing or damaging of one ultimately affects all. The kinship attitude does not measure difference on a scale of higher or lower ontological dignity but appreciates them as integral elements in the robust thriving of the whole . . . the kinship stance knows that we humans are interrelated parts and products of a world that is continually being made and nurtured by the Creator Spirit.[57]

From a religious perspective, the kinship model recognizes that the pull within human beings toward respect for the earth and all living creatures, including humanity, is itself a manifestation of the creative energy of the Holy Spirit.

The kinship paradigm gives emphasis to the intrinsic value of each species, with the enormous diversity of species revealing something of the complex immensity of the Creator, the Source of all life, whose very being they express. Johnson's option for the kinship model inevitably leads to a rethinking of our idea of God and God's relationship to the world. She suggests that it leads to a reclaiming of the "third" person of the Trinity: "What must the Creator be like, in whose image this astounding universe is created? Realization of its energy, diversity, relationality, fecundity, spontaneity, and ever-surprising mix of law and chance makes the time ripe for a rediscovery of the neglected tradition of the Creator Spirit."[58]

[55] Ibid., 29.
[56] Ibid.
[57] Ibid., 30–31.
[58] Ibid., 40.

How, then, can this "person" of the Trinity who as the giver of life renews, indwells, empowers be imaged? Calling upon the advice of Basil of Cappadocia, who in his great work on the Spirit encourages extravagance in speaking about the Spirit on the grounds that our thoughts always fall short of the reality, Johnson searches the Scriptures.[59] As I have set out in Chapter 5, an important and rich biblical source that she taps is the wisdom tradition. Calling on all the complex nuances of the female symbol, Johnson names the Holy Spirit, Spirit-Sophia, portraying her as the one who is very near in her work of vivifying, renewing, and gracing.[60] She also notes that the biblical writers draw from women's experience of mothering to symbolize the work of the Spirit:

> . . . she knits together the new life in a mother's womb (Ps 139:13); like a woman in childbirth she labors and pants to bring about the birth of justice (Is 42:14); like a midwife she works deftly with a woman in pain to deliver the new creation (Ps 22:9-10); like a washerwoman she scrubs away at bloody stains till the people be like new (Is 4:4; Ps 52:7).[61]

Searching biblical sources further, Johnson finds several cosmic symbols that are used to convey the primordial power of the Creator Spirit.[62] She shows how the biblical images of wind, fire, and water are used by many post-biblical writers to image the experience of the power and presence of the Spirit at work in people's lives. She refers, for example, to Cyril, bishop of Jerusalem, who when reflecting on the dialogue between Jesus and the Samaritan woman, describes the power of the Spirit enabling vibrant differences to blossom from a common source:

> Why did Christ call the grace of the Spirit water? Because by water all things subsist. Because water brings forth grass and living things. Because the water of the showers comes down from heaven. Because it comes down in one form but works in many forms: it becomes white in the lily, red in the rose, purple in violets and hyacinths, different and varied in each species. It is one thing in the palm tree, yet another in the vine, and yet in all things the same Spirit.[63]

---

[59] Ibid., 51. See Basil of Caesarea, *De Spiritu Santo,* ch. 19.49.

[60] See Chapter 5.

[61] Johnson, *Women, Earth and Creator Spirit,* 55–56.

[62] See ibid., 45–50, for many examples drawn from biblical sources.

[63] Johnson, "God Poured Out: Recovering the Holy Spirit," *Praying* 60 (May–June 1994) 5. See also Johnson, "Heaven and Earth Are Filled with Your Glory," *Finding God in All Things,* ed. Michael Himes and Stephen Pope (New York: Crossroad, 1996) 86–87; Johnson, *Women, Earth and Creator Spirit,* 50.

Johnson further appeals to one particularly gifted woman's visionary work on Christian doctrine for other vivid examples that are spun from these biblical images. Drawing directly from the rich imagery of Hildegarde of Bingen, medieval artist, musician, scientist, theologian, and advocate for justice, Johnson describes the Spirit as:

> the life of the life of all creatures; the way everything is penetrated with connectedness and relatedness; a burning fire who sparks, ignites, inflames, kindles hearts; a guide in the fog; a balm for wounds; a shining serenity; an overflowing fountain that spreads to all sides. The Spirit is life, movement, color, radiance, restorative stillness in the din. She pours out the juice of contrition into hardened hearts. Her power makes dry twigs and withered souls green again with the juice of life. She plays music in the soul, being herself the melody of praise and joy. She awakens mighty hope, blowing everywhere the winds of renewal in creation.[64]

Following the work of Augustine and Thomas Aquinas, Johnson focuses on two other images from the tradition which have been significant in describing the action and presence of the Spirit and which can still hold a powerful currency today. She names the Spirit "mutual love," the love of reciprocal relation, and "gift"—"God's *love* has been poured forth into our hearts through the *Holy Spirit* that has been *given* to us" (Rom 5:5).[65] Johnson reflects that this speaking of the Spirit as gift and the power of mutual love points toward "reciprocity in community as the highest good" and if taken seriously, would subvert the legitimization of patriarchal structures.[66] She further suggests that an alternative for those more abstract names of love and gift is "friend," and she takes up Sallie McFague's analysis of the model of the Holy Spirit as friend:

> What is relevant in speaking about the Spirit in this model is that friendship entails a reciprocity of relationship that exists independently of one's place in the social order, making it possible to cross boundaries of race, sex, class and even natures. Since the Spirit not only makes human beings friends of God but herself befriends the world, she can rightly be named friend par excellence.[67]

Other relational terms, such as "sister," "mother," "grandmother," are also suggested as possible names for the Spirit. In all these proposals

---

[64] Johnson, *Women, Earth and Creator Spirit,* 51.
[65] Johnson, *SHE WHO IS,* 142. Emphasis added.
[66] Ibid., 143.
[67] Ibid., 145.

Johnson has a liberating inclusive praxis in mind. She argues that speaking of the Spirit in all these ways "indicates an agenda for human life: we are loved in order to love; gifted in order to gift; and befriended in order to turn to the world as sisters and brothers in redeeming, liberating friendship."[68]

By calling upon all these sources for appropriate ways of naming the action of the Spirit, Johnson is suggesting that both the female and cosmic symbols in the Scriptures and the tradition can contribute toward healing the divided consciousness created by hierarchical dualism and can contribute to a much richer appreciation of the role of the Holy Spirit. She shows in particular that use of female symbols communicates that "being women and being fertile is not a dangerous polluted state but a participation in the fecundity of the Creator Spirit and, conversely, a sign of her presence."[69] By drawing on women's experience of life and kinship as a preferred model of humanity's relationship to nature, she shows how a vibrant theology of the Creator Spirit can overcome the dualism of spirit and matter and underscore the sacredness of the earth, the sacredness of bodies, the sacredness of women and men.

In summary, one can see that Johnson's addressing the power of the structure of the triune symbol is a significant component of her fundamental task of renaming the symbol of the triune God. Insights from this task contribute to her approaching Trinitarian theology from humanity's experience, and particularly from the neglected source of women's experience of Spirit-Sophia, God at work in the world. This work of reclaiming the Holy Spirit, so essential to a restored Trinitarian theology, connects the reclaiming of women and earth as intrinsic to a renewed pneumatology. In all this, Johnson's theological endeavor, which includes her articulation of an ecological spirituality, is directed toward praxis, toward transformative action that responds compassionately and with resilient hope to injustices to humanity and to the whole of creation.

Conclusion

Elizabeth Johnson's constructive feminist theology on the symbol of God, like Zizioulas's theological work toward a neopatristic synthesis, journeys to the very heart of the Christian tradition. Her choice to do this gives witness to her belief that the Holy Spirit, Giver of Life, was indeed the creative impulse that prompted the human struggles to

---

[68] Ibid., 146.
[69] Johnson, *Women, Earth and Creator Spirit*, 57.

describe experiences of God revealed in Jesus Christ that led to the formulation of the doctrine of the Trinity. She makes it very clear, however, that the attempts to articulate eternal truths about the mystery of God were seriously limited by dominant patriarchal cultures that ensured that only male members of the Christian communities contributed to their formulation. Johnson's work, drawing as it does on a wealth of feminist theology and women's experience, makes a significant contribution toward remedying this neglect of two thousand years. The female imaging of the triune symbol that she proposes is firmly based in the Scriptures and tradition and provides a powerful alternative vision of the living God. It is a vision that both motivates and sustains transforming action toward creating a world in which the whole of humanity lives in kinship with its own multiple diversities and with all creation. It constitutes a major contribution toward the contemporary theological quest to retrieve the triune symbol of God.

Johnson's Trinitarian theology begins from experience. Zizioulas's begins from the revealed truths of a living faith. In Part Three I will explore what a mutually critical correlation of their respective theologies yields for a contemporary retrieval of the triune symbol.

Toward a Retrieval of the Symbol of the Triune God

CHAPTER 8

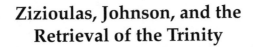

Zizioulas, Johnson, and the
Retrieval of the Trinity

The real face of our period, as Emmanuel Levinas saw with such clarity, is the face of the other: the face that commands, "Do not kill me." The face insists: do not reduce me or anyone else to your narrative. . . . God's shattering otherness, the neighbor's irreducible otherness, the othering reality of "revelation" (not the consoling modern notion of "religion"): all these expressions of genuine otherness demand the serious attention of all thoughtful persons.[1]

Theologian David Tracy acknowledges that the modern "turn to the subject" has been replaced in much contemporary thought by the postmodern "turn to the other." The presence of massive global suffering, he suggests, has brought to center stage "the reality of the others and the different." These are the realities "that destroy any teleological version of modern history [that inevitably leads to Western modernity] even as they allow a return of the eschatological God who disrupts all continuity and confidence."[2] As outlined in Chapter 1, my purpose is to contribute to the contemporary retrieval of the symbol of the triune God. I have focused on the Trinitarian theologies of Elizabeth Johnson and John Zizioulas because I believe they both demonstrate that this

---

[1] David Tracy, "The Hidden God: The Divine Other of Liberation," *Cross Currents* 46, no. 1 (1996) 5–6.

[2] Ibid., 7.

183

ancient symbol of the eschatological God who is at the center of Christian faith can speak powerfully to the disruptive postmodern global realities that Tracy so tellingly names. I am arguing that when these Trinitarian theologies are brought together in mutually critical correlation, they offer a further contribution to the retrieval of the Trinitarian symbol.

This chapter will briefly describe what these two theologies hold in common and then will begin with a mutually critical correlation of their different methodologies. Chapter 9 will correlate their distinctive contributions to pneumatology and christology as foundational elements within their Trinitarian theologies. Chapter 10 will focus on the primary ways in which both theologians image the triune symbol, and Chapter 11 will explore what emerges when their Trinitarian theologies are brought into dialogue with two of the great existential realities of our times—the issues of suffering and the ecological crisis. In this correlation I will be drawing from material that has already been presented and discussed within the contexts of the preceding chapters. There is one exception to this: in the section on pneumatology, I will refer to an article by Zizioulas entitled "Ecclesiological Implications of Two Types of Pneumatology," precisely because it focuses on the essential differences between the pneumatologies of Zizioulas and Johnson and thus assists in the specific task of this chapter.

Factors in Common

Despite many fundamental differences, the theologies of Johnson and Zizioulas hold a great deal in common. The most obvious factor is that both are absolutely convinced of the practical significance of the symbol of God for humanity and the world. Zizioulas claims that "Trinitarian theology has profound existential consequences,"[3] and Johnson argues that "the symbol of God functions as the primary symbol of the whole religious system, the ultimate point of reference for understanding experience, life, and the world."[4]

More specifically, both theologians argue that the doctrine of the Trinity has profound and particular contributions to make toward contemporary understanding of personhood, humanity, and the whole of creation. Zizioulas focuses on what the Trinitarian mystery reveals about the nature of personhood. Johnson explores how the triune sym-

[3] John D. Zizioulas, "The Doctrine of God the Trinity Today," in *The Forgotten Trinity*, ed. Alasdair I. C. Heron (London: BCC/CCBI, 1991) 19.

[4] Johnson, *SHE WHO IS: The Mystery of God in Feminist Theological Discourse* (New York: Crossroad, 1992) 4.

bol provides a powerful challenge for Church and society with respect to what full humanity can mean for women as well as for men. Both argue strongly that theology needs to come to grips with the serious implications of the ecological crisis. Through their teaching, writing, and lectures in the public forum, they have both sought to bring to bear the wisdom of the theological tradition on humanity's struggle to work toward solutions for this massive global dilemma. Each communicates a passionate care for the future of the planet and its peoples and a belief that God's "good news" revealed by Jesus the Christ is of immense saving significance for a future of hope. Both are confident that God's truth can be communicated in ways that hold enduring value for succeeding generations.

Both theologians acknowledge the need to situate Trinitarian theology within the story of salvation. For Zizioulas, whose work is firmly located within the Eastern tradition, pneumatology holds a place of prime importance. He explicitly seeks to redress an imbalance within Trinitarian theology and within the tradition of the West by restoring appropriate emphasis to the Holy Spirit. Johnson identifies a similar serious neglect and responds to this by beginning her Trinitarian theology with the Holy Spirit. Both also focus on the place of christology within a contemporary theology of the doctrine of God. They both explore what the symbol of Christ can mean for understanding true personhood, power, and freedom and emphasize the cosmic and eschatological significance of the whole Christ.

In their unambiguous valuing of the tradition, both Johnson and Zizioulas acknowledge that all doctrines of the Church can become fossilized and irrelevant unless they are brought into constant dialogue with contemporary realities. In their ongoing approach to this task of reading the signs of the times and drawing from an evolving body of knowledge of humanity and the universe, they explicitly choose to return to the historical sources and contexts of the dogmas in order to tap directly into the full liberating intent of these teachings. Zizioulas is acutely aware of the gulf between the Eastern and Western theological traditions, and he addresses some of his work specifically "to the Western Christian who feels as it were, 'amputated,' since East and West followed their different and autonomous paths." He describes his work as a contribution to a neopatristic synthesis that he believes is "capable of leading the West and the East nearer to their common roots, in the context of the existential quest of modern man."[5]

---

[5] John D. Zizioulas, *Being as Communion: Studies in Personhood and the Church* (New York: St. Vladimir's Press, 1985) 26.

Johnson is acutely aware of the neglected experience of women in the formulation of the Church's tradition and in its leadership, life, and liturgy: "Inherited Christian speech about God," she writes, "has developed within a framework that does not prize the unique and equal humanity of women, and bears the marks of this partiality and dominance."[6] She believes, however, that there is a wisdom enshrined in the classical doctrines of Christianity that might be retrieved. Johnson is thus concerned that women's voice and experience of God are recognized, valued, and brought into dialogue with the dominant male expressions of the tradition. Zizioulas is concerned to ensure that the wisdom of East and West are brought into a creative dialogue that will lead to unity within the Christian Church.

In summary it may be said that both theologians understand their task to be to recover the inherent wisdom of the tradition in order to engage it with the questions and issues of today's world. Zizioulas focuses on the true nature of personhood while Johnson's focus is on the full humanity of every person. Both are convinced that difference flourishes in communion.

Different Methodologies

Zizioulas's Trinitarian Theology "from above"

Zizioulas's theological method is based upon his conviction that doctrines of the Church need to address the contemporary questions of humanity and so be "received" by succeeding generations and by different cultures.[7] His theological research, founded on the Church's life during the first three centuries,[8] leads him to conclude that "an interpretation without an historical base, or an historic description without an interpretation of what is discussed in the framework of the current times, would suggest an unauthentic theology."[9] He is thus explicit that theology needs to be both situated within an accurate historical context and subject to ongoing interpretation in the light of the emerging questions of humanity. He argues that the truths enshrined in dogmas need to be made accessible to succeeding generations through the language and symbol systems of their times and cultures.[10] Basic to his theologi-

---

[6] Johnson, *SHE WHO IS*, 15.

[7] See Chapter 4.

[8] See de Jean Pergame, *L'Eucharistie, l'evêque et l'église durant les trois permiers siècles*, trans. Jean-Louis Parlierne (Paris: Theophanie, Desclée de Brouwer, 1994).

[9] Pergamon, "To einai tou Theou kai einai tou anthropou," *Synaxis* 37 (1991) 14.

[10] See, for example, Zizioulas, "The Church as Communion," *St. Vladimir's Theological Quarterly* 38 (1994) 12–13.

cal method is his strong conviction of the value that the Christian theological tradition holds for humanity. He believes that the truths of faith
expressed in the dogmas have a "connection to the essence of our
lives."[11] He holds that they need to be reinterpreted for each new epoch
precisely because they have something very valuable to offer different
times and different cultures.[12]

In an article published in 1991 to respond to Orthodox critics who
were accusing him of devaluing the mysteries of the faith by bringing
them into the dialogue with contemporary philosophies of person and
existence, Zizioulas defended his position:

> A transference of the tradition from one generation to another cannot
> happen . . . without addressing the questions of humanity. It is a bad
> conservatism to deny every transference of something old to a new
> shape. Such conservatism was not evidenced by the Holy Fathers when
> they introduced "homoousios" into the Nicene creed, nor in their
> speaking of the difference between "ousia" and "energies." Nor would
> the complex philosophy of Maximus the Confessor be able to find sup-
> port from the spirit of conservatism which is shown by those today
> who reject every use of contemporary philosophical expression in the-
> ology. Interpretation of dogma must include an analysis of the original
> meaning and be expressed in contemporary terms, exactly as the Holy
> Fathers of the Church did.[13]

Zizioulas begins his Trinitarian theology from above from what
God has revealed about Godself through encounters with the Chosen
People. He focuses on the fact that the doctrine of the Trinity was formulated from the early Christian communities' experiences of the God
of Jesus Christ and that it developed as an articulation of their coming
to know God as a Trinity of persons through initiation into the Christian community by baptism, confirmation, and Eucharist.[14] He emphasizes that doctrine was expressed in the religious and philosophical

---

[11] Ibid., 13.

[12] It is interesting to note strong similarities between Zizioulas's position on this
and that of his teacher Georges Florovsky. The latter taught that "dogma is in no
way a new revelation. Dogma is merely witness. . . . With the formulation of dogmas the church gave expression to revelation in the language of Greek philosophy.
Or, if you prefer, the church translated revelation out of the poetic, prophetic
Hebrew speech into Greek."—Georges Florovsky, "Offenbarung, Philosophie und
Theologie," *Zwischen den Zeiten* 9 (1931) 470, 472, quoted in Duncan Reid, *Energies of
the Spirit: Trinitarian Models in Eastern Orthodox and Western Theology* (Atlanta: Georgia Scholars Press, 1997) 45.

[13] Pergamon, "To einai tou Theou kai einai tou anthropou," *Synaxis* 37 (1991) 14.

[14] See Zizioulas, *Being as Communion*, 16–17.

concepts available to the early Church and needs to be passed on by being brought into dialogue with the questions that emerge in each contemporary period. He holds, however, that the center and starting point of the theological process is *Theologia*, Godself.

This conviction is reflected in Zizioulas's preference for the Cappadocians' doxological theology. While careful about respecting the various historical contexts within which revelation took place, he claims:

> The safest theology is that which draws not only from the Economy, but also, and perhaps mainly, from the vision of God as He appears in worship. The Cappadocian way of thinking is thus strongly behind the Eastern preference for a meta-historical or eschatological approach to the mystery of God as contrasted with the Western concern with God's acts in history.[15]

Zizioulas believes that the doctrine of the Trinity has something important to offer, not because it proposes "a theoretical proposition about God," but because of the possibility of "relating one's existence to this faith; Baptism in the Trinity means entering into a certain way of being which is that of the Trinitarian God."[16] This reveals a critical dimension of Zizioulas's theological method and of his Orthodox understanding of Trinitarian doctrine, namely, that its significance does not reside in its value as an intellectual truth but in its capacity to open up a way of living and being. His theology is drawn from and leads to the liturgical and devotional life of the Church and needs to be understood from within the context of a lived, existential communion.

It is out of such convictions that Zizioulas argues for the importance of including the whole Christian tradition within contemporary theology. In 1993 he challenged the Eighth Orthodox Congress in Western Europe to recognize the presence of the Orthodox Church in Western Europe as "one of the most important signs of Divine Providence in our time":

> It is not for her own sake that the Orthodox Church is given this blessing, but for the sake of the entire humanity, indeed for the sake of the entire cosmos. . . . The Orthodox Church is called . . . to relate tradition to the problems of modern Western man, which are rapidly becoming the problems of humanity in its global dimension.[17]

---

[15] John D. Zizioulas, "The Teaching of the 2nd Ecumenical Council on the Holy Spirit in Historical and Ecumenical Perspective," in *Credo in Spiritum Sanctum*, vol. 1, ed. J. S. Martins (Vatican City: Libreria Editrice Vaticana, 1983) 40.

[16] Zizioulas, "The Doctrine of God the Trinity Today," 19.

[17] Pergamon, "Communion and Otherness," *St. Vladimir's Theological Quarterly* 38, no. 4 (1994) 347–48.

He is arguing that the tradition must be related to the critical questions of humanity because it holds the key to their meaning. More specifically, on this occasion Zizioulas also identified the West as an important entry point for any real influence on global realities because of the power and dominance flowing from its political and economic dominance. He therefore believes that there is some urgency for the theological tradition to engage creatively with Western humanity's quest for ultimate meaning. His method is to identify specific critical issues that he believes the theological tradition can enlighten by its wisdom and to bring them into dialogue with the tradition. As developed above, the two major issues that he pursues at depth are the search for the full meaning of the human person and the ecological crisis.

Another important strand in Zizioulas's method has been shaped by the fact that his life's work has been situated so centrally within the ecumenical movement of this century. As Chapter 4 above has demonstrated, critical issues in the area of ecclesiology have focused his theological questions. For example, he argues that many of the problems of unity within the Church can be traced to the place assigned to pneumatology in Christians' understanding of the Church and its structures and ministries.[18] He recognizes that the issues that keep Christians apart often have profound theological roots and argues that until these are addressed, all other surface attempts at unity will be frustrated. His exploration of "The Church as Communion" provides another telling example of this—he argues that an understanding of the Christian concept of *koinōnia* is crucial if unity is to be achieved within Christianity.[19]

In many ways John Zizioulas's method of doing theology "from above," beginning from Godself as revealed in the tradition, mirrors his own position within the Church. Having inherited a rich theological tradition, Zizioulas's work as a theologian has flourished at its center. Within his own tradition and sometimes in conflict with his Orthodox brethren, he has been a powerful advocate for the importance of the Christian tradition to engage actively with the contemporary questions of the wider Church and humanity.[20] As a teacher of theology and a Church leader, he has sought to make the riches of the tradition

---

[18] See Zizioulas, "The Doctrine of God the Trinity Today," 21–22.

[19] See Chapter 4.

[20] In his introduction to Zizioulas's keynote address at the Halki summer seminar in 1997 on "Justice and Environment," Dr. Nickolas Constas from Holy Cross Greek Orthodox School of Theology, Boston, described the Metropolitan as "*the* most important contemporary theologian [whose] creative synthesis of systematic theology and patristics has irrevocably altered the focus and direction of Orthodox Theology."

accessible for the lives of his fellow believers and for the world. His theological method is consistent with his life experience.

Johnson's Trinitarian Theology "from below"

Elizabeth Johnson begins her Trinitarian theology "from below," from the world. She describes her work as "a theology of God starting out from below, beginning with the vivifying and renewing Spirit as God's presence in the world and then exploring in succession speech about each of the 'persons' of God's Trinity."[21] In starting from the experience of the world rather than the doctrines of the Church, she draws from a source that has been almost totally neglected by traditional theology—the experience of women, especially poor women.

Because Johnson is not proceeding in the classic mode, she is more explicit than Zizioulas about the methodology she intends to use. She announces that she will "draw on the new language of Christian feminist theology as well as on the traditional language of Scripture and classical theology."[22] She elaborates:

> By Christian feminist theology I mean a reflection on God and all things in the light of God that stands consciously in the company of all the world's women, explicitly prizing their genuine humanity while uncovering and criticizing its persistent violation in sexism, itself an omnipresent paradigm of unjust relationships.[23]

Justice for women suffering from the multiple oppressions of classism, racism, sexism, and poverty therefore become the touchstone of her work as a Christian feminist theologian.[24] She recognizes that there is a glaring contradiction between the identity of women as *imago Dei* and the historical condition of women in church and society. She focuses this most explicitly when she states:

> This leads to the clear judgement that sexism is sinful, that it is contrary to God's intent, that it is a precise and pervasive breaking of the basic commandment "Thou shalt love thy neighbour as thyself" (Lv 19:18; Mt 22:39). It affronts God by the defacing of the beloved creature created in the image of God.[25]

---

[21] Johnson, *SHE WHO IS*, 13.
[22] Ibid., 8.
[23] Ibid., 13.
[24] See ibid., 11.
[25] Ibid., 9.

Johnson notes that theology's classical tradition "has aided and abetted the exclusion and subordination of women." She also notes, however, that despite the oppression that has been endorsed by the sexist interpretations of the Christian message, the tradition has in fact served to sustain "generations of foremothers and foresisters in the faith."[26] Johnson therefore argues that it is necessary to give the Christian tradition a hearing while also calling it to account. She seeks to interpret the tradition with a feminist hermeneutic in order to discover if there is "anything in the classical tradition in all its vastness that could serve a discourse about divine mystery that would further the emancipation of women."[27]

Having been thoroughly initiated into the classical theological tradition of the West, Johnson has found that when read within a feminist hermeneutic, Church teaching on the Spirit, on the incarnation, on creation, and on the Trinity is in fact capable of releasing "fragments of wisdom and fruitful possibilities." She therefore seeks "to accomplish a critical retrieval [of the tradition] in the light of women's coequal humanity."[28] As stated in Chapter 1, her method comprises three interrelated tasks that have become the basic method of feminist theology: (1) a critical analysis of inherited oppressions, (2) the search for alternative wisdom and suppressed history within the tradition, and (3) the work of constructive new interpretations of the tradition in tandem with the experience of women's lives. This method, which begins with critical reflection on existential realities, is directed toward transforming action that will build a new community.[29]

In describing this methodological position, Johnson notes that her appeal to women's experience has been a source rarely considered in the history of theology and acknowledges, with many other feminist theologians, the difficulties in specifying precisely what comprises women's experience.[30] As indicated in Chapter 1, this theological method, with its focus on the multiple oppressions of poor women, led her to identify with the oppression and suffering of all the poor of the world. It ensured that she would later need to confront another major form of contemporary global injustice—the ecological crisis.

As a citizen of the United States of America, Johnson has benefited from living in one of the most affluent nations on the earth. However, motivated by her own experience of injustice as a woman in society

[26] Ibid.
[27] Ibid.
[28] Ibid., 10.
[29] See ibid., 29–31.
[30] See Chapter 1.

and Church, she has consciously sought to reach outside the world of her inherited domain and to situate her theological work within a context of global suffering. Johnson's method in pursuing a theology of God is that of feminist liberation theology. She observes that this method is only one way of speaking about this core religious symbol, and she is aware that feminist theology, with its task of drawing on the experiences of women, is still in its early stages of evolution. She does not want the established systems of theology to restrict its vigorous growth and development. However, aware that many women have already abandoned the tradition because it had become for them "a land of famine instead of a land of plenty," she proceeds with the hope that her work will be able to demonstrate that justice toward women and right speaking about God are essentially inseparable.[31]

A Correlation of Methodologies

Zizioulas begins his Trinitarian theology from the formulation of the dogma and is confident that this doctrine holds enormous existential significance for humanity because it can open up the way to freedom and life. The concern of his method is therefore essentially to interpret and communicate. Johnson's method is very different. It is one of critical analysis, retrieval, and reconstruction. While Zizioulas presumes that the doctrines of the Church, despite the limits of their expression, are inherently salvific, Johnson is acutely aware that the theological tradition and the Church have often been a source of oppression rather than liberation for many of the poorest of the earth. Nevertheless, Johnson approaches the tradition with a profound but critical hope that theological sources can be retrieved in ways that are liberating for all of humanity and creation.

Johnson deliberately sets out to situate her methodology within the large, global realities of a suffering world. More specifically, she searches the truths of faith through the neglected lens of women's experience. Both these factors pose a significant challenge to the way Zizioulas has applied his method. While clearly acknowledging the need for the truths of faith to be in dialogue with the questions of humanity, he gives no evidence that he recognizes that the question of the full humanity of half the human race is of significance for any authentic theology of the doctrine of God. Similarly, the obscene and ever-present reality (courtesy of modern media) of suffering in the world is not an issue that seems to have explicitly shaped his questions about how the triune God can be interpreted by the peoples of this age, most

---

[31] Johnson, *SHE WHO IS*, 12.

of whom are poor and suffering. Nor has the related issue of the growing inequalities between the rich and the poor of the earth.

Theoretically, there is no reason why Zizioulas's method "from
above" could not engage with these critical questions or at least take
them into account. In fact, his addressing the quest for the meaning of
personhood and the ecological crisis illustrates that a true engagement
with critical questions of the age is intrinsic to his method. Johnson and
Zizioulas demonstrate that both a theology "from below" and a theology "from above" can engage creatively with the existential questions
of our times.

A great strength of Zizioulas's method is its coherence with the
theological vision that shapes it. His method reflects his theological
belief that the dynamic life of God's very self and all that has been created by God in love are in creative communion. That is the underlying
premise behind his insistence that the truths of faith need to be re-
received in each new period. It also undergirds his emphasis that it is
the work of the Spirit to create events of communion rather than merely
to reveal set truths. His method therefore conveys the message that
God is continually at work in the present to create new life and that this
God is a God of "persons in communion."

Johnson's method conveys a similarly powerful dynamism. It
conveys the view that there is a strong personal source impelling this
work, one that can renew and restore what is broken. This is the God of
Compassion, SHE WHO IS, who sees our suffering and who invites
humanity to collaborate in her work of liberation.

Thus both theologians apply their respective methodologies in
ways that engage creatively with the tradition as a living entity and
powerfully illustrate an important truth about the very nature of Trinitarian theology. Catherine LaCugna expresses it thus:

> Perhaps in no other area of theology is it more important to keep in
> mind than in Trinitarian theology that the "object" upon which we re-
> flect is another "subject" or "self," namely, the God who relentlessly
> pursues us to become partners in communion. God who is Love
> chooses to be known by love, thus theological knowledge is personal
> knowledge.[32]

It is my judgment that a theology "from below" is more likely to ensure
that the profoundly disturbing and difficult questions of each age are
recognized to be an arena of God's action and can be brought into dialogue with the living tradition. However, the methodology "from

---

[32] Catherine Mowry LaCugna, *God for Us: The Trinity and Christian Life* (New
York: HarperSanFrancisco, 1991) 332.

above" applied by Zizioulas also invites the one engaging with it into a personal encounter with the triune God who is also actively present at the heart of the search.

The next chapter will pursue a mutually critical correlation of two primary symbols within the Trinitarian theologies of Johnson and Zizioulas. It will focus on pneumatology and christology and the significance of their relation with each other within the triune symbol.

CHAPTER 9

Pneumatology and Christology
in Mutual Relation

Christology itself cannot be treated as an autonomous subject:
it is conditioned constantly by Pneumatology, and as such it is
to be organically related to Ecclesiology. This brings Trinitarian
Theology itself into Ecclesiology.[1]

One of the factors that continues to emerge in an analysis of Zizioulas's theology is its synthetic nature. He insists that the big picture must always be held in view if the component parts are to be properly understood. More specifically, he is adamant that christology and pneumatology exist in dynamic relation to each other and that both always need to be interpreted in the context of this relationship and within the fullness of a theological vision of the triune God, of creation, salvation, Church, the sacraments, the eschaton.[2] Zizioulas's Trinitarian theology has convinced me of the significance of this claim, and I have adopted it as an underlying premise in this chapter.[3]

The Trinitarian theologies of Zizioulas and Johnson both reclaim the importance and place of the Holy Spirit within a Christian theology of the triune God. In company with a number of contemporary theologians,

---

[1] John Zizioulas, "Ordination—A Sacrament? An Orthodox Reply," *Concilium* 4 (1972) 34.

[2] See ibid.

[3] Yves Congar also argues that a balanced theology of Church requires a balance between our understanding of the role of the Spirit and the role of Christ. See Yves Congar, *I Believe in the Holy Spirit* (New York: Seabury Press, 1983) 2:3–64.

195

they assess that the Holy Spirit has been neglected in Christian theology and practice.[4] I begin this chapter with Johnson's contribution to a recovery of pneumatology and its relevance for a retrieval of the triune symbol. That will be followed by a description of Zizioulas's analysis of the legacy of two types of pneumatology from the early Church,[5] his elaboration of the one adopted by the East, and his proposed synthesis of those two strands as needed for these times. The second part of this chapter will examine Zizioulas's christology and then focus on the constructive feminist proposal that is at the center of Johnson's christology before examining what a correlation of their christologies suggests.

The Retrieval of Pneumatology and the Triune Symbol

Johnson's Pneumatology

Johnson states that the relevance of beginning with experience when speaking about the triune God is based on the fact that it "coheres not only with the existential but also with the historical pattern by which faith in the triune God arises."[6] That approach also corresponds to the *modus operandi* of many fields of contemporary discourse. However, unlike a number of theologians, including Zizioulas, whose work gives great emphasis to the priority of Spirit, Johnson translates that into a particular methodological option.[7] She makes a choice to begin her theology of the triune God from the experience of the Spirit.[8]

Johnson describes the struggle to arrive at this decision as the most intellectually difficult moment in writing *SHE WHO IS*.[9] It was a struggle that was born of a central concern in her whole work, which she describes as the effort "to reconcile the two halves of my own mind, rooted and educated as I am in the classical Catholic tradition and converted as I have become to the feminist paradigm in theology and life."[10] Her initial instinct in writing a theology of the Trinity was to begin in the classic mode with the "first person," the unoriginate origin of all

---

[4] See Elizabeth Johnson, *SHE WHO IS: The Mystery of God in Feminist Theological Discourse* (New York: Crossroad, 1992) 129–31, 294, nn. 14–17.

[5] See John Zizioulas, "Implications ecclésiologiques de deux types de pneumatologie," *Communio Sanctorum: Mélanges offerts à Jean-Jacques von Allmen* (Geneva: Labor et Fides, 1981) 141–54.

[6] Johnson, *SHE WHO IS*, 123.

[7] See Johnson, "Review Symposium: Author's Response," *Horizons* 20 (1993) 340, and *SHE WHO IS*, 293, n. 3.

[8] See Johnson, *SHE WHO IS*, 121–22.

[9] Johnson, "Review Symposium," 340.

[10] Ibid., 339.

things, and to use feminist analysis to interpret God as Mother-Sophia. However, when she started in this way, with what she describes as the "most unexperienced" of the "three persons," it created such a deep dissonance with feminist method that she was impelled to rethink her outline. Feminist consciousness finally required her to subvert the traditional order. She was drawn to begin with "the historical experience of the triune God in the economy of salvation and therefore from the actual life of believing persons."[11] That meant that by taking close account of the neglected experience of women, she could center her theology of the Holy Spirit and of the triune God in the place where "the dialectic of God's presence and absence shapes life in all its struggle."[12]

That was a significant move. The very structure of Johnson's Trinitarian theology communicates her understanding of the Spirit's identity and function. She acknowledges that the widest possible horizon of experience is the arena of the Spirit's domain. As I noted in Chapter 7, when Johnson poses the question about which times or events mediate the Holy Spirit, she argues that "the answer can only be all experience, the whole world."[13] She observes that if it is owned that the whole created order is sacred ground, the dualisms of Neo-Platonism so endemic to Western perceptions of reality are dealt a serious blow. The divine may be associated with the material world as well as with the spiritual world, with the body as well as with the soul, with female as well as with male, with black as well as with white. By actively claiming the presence and power of the Holy Spirit at work in all of creation and seeking to bring this into Christian praxis, not only is the "neglected person" of the Trinity brought strongly into the foreground but women and the earth are also reclaimed as the domain of the holy.

Johnson suggests that this inductive approach to pneumatology can also nourish religious sensibility. Nature, social systems, and relationships are all arenas of the Spirit's action, whether they be the joy of the experience of presence or the pain of loss in absence. She emphasizes that the tradition teaches that the Spirit is profoundly present in both positive and negative experiences, and she draws on a series of classic images from the tradition that reinforce this understanding of the Spirit's identity.[14] The primary name that Johnson adopts for the

---

[11] Johnson, *SHE WHO IS*, 121.

[12] Ibid.

[13] Ibid., 124. See Chapter 7.

[14] See Johnson, "God Poured Out: Recovering the Holy Spirit," *Praying* 60 (May–June, 1994) 5; "Heaven and Earth Are Filled with Your Glory," in *Finding God in All Things*, ed. Michael Himes and Stephen Pope (New York: Crossroad, 1996) 86–87; *SHE WHO IS*, 125–27.

Holy Spirit is Spirit-Sophia. She notes that "the most extended biblical instance of female imagery of the Spirit occurs in the wisdom literature."[15] She shows how the many images used for wisdom symbolize God's transcendent power pervading and ordering the world, interacting with both nature and humanity to draw them onto the path of life.[16] Spirit-Sophia's presence fills the universe and is ever present as a renewing, reconciling power rejoicing in the world and "delighting in the human race" (Prov 8:31).

Johnson draws from many other vibrant images from the tradition to illustrate that the consistent experience of the early Christians showed the Holy Spirit to be not only the cause of differentiation by being the source of many varied charisms but also "the principle of unity in the church, indeed in the whole cosmos."[17] By referring to examples of this in the contemporary world,[18] she encourages the believer to recognize that it is the work of the Spirit to enable relationships or bonds of kinship among creatures. In her Madeleva lecture, she argues that "fellowship, community, *koinonia* is the primordial design of existence, as all creatures are connected through the indwelling, renewing, moving Creator Spirit."[19] This emphasis on the twin role of the Spirit as the one who enables the diffuse and different entities of the universe to flourish in all their uniqueness, while at the same time being the source of relationship and communion, is a teaching from the tradition that Zizioulas also spells out with great vigor.

In summary, one may say that Johnson's contribution to the retrieval of pneumatology constitutes a significant element in her theology of the triune God. She shows that when biblical and classical teaching are brought into dialogue with insights from feminist theology, and when the Spirit's deeds are pictured as the work of a female acting subject, ways for speaking about God that were previously closed to the imagination are opened up.[20] Her own assessment is that the most significant contribution that her pneumatology brings to a retrieval of the triune symbol is her decision to begin a theology of the Trinity with the Spirit. I agree with this and with her judgment that there is a great deal more in this approach to the Trinity that is worth investigating by theologians.[21]

---

[15] Johnson, *Women, Earth and Creator Spirit* (New York: Paulist Press, 1993) 51.
[16] Ibid., 53.
[17] Ibid., 8. See also Chapter 7.
[18] See Chapters 5 and 7 for multiple examples.
[19] Johnson, *Women, Earth and Creator Spirit*, 44.
[20] See Johnson, *SHE WHO IS*, 148.
[21] See ibid., 149, and Johnson, "Review Symposium," 340.

Zizioulas's Pneumatology

A strong emphasis on the Holy Spirit is also central to Zizioulas's Trinitarian theology. In an article written in 1981, he distinguishes between two early biblical and patristic sources that are expressed as two different types of pneumatology. Both are connected to the mystery of the Church.[22] According to the first type, the Spirit is given to the Church in order to empower it to accomplish its work of mission to the world. That idea is found in the Gospels, but particularly in the Acts of the Apostles, where the miraculous expansion of the Church within the Greco-Roman world is described as a manifestation of the Spirit in history. That type of pneumatology, Zizioulas suggests, is accompanied by a particular type of christology and ecclesiology. The Spirit is given through Christ, appears as an agent of Christ, and is called the "Spirit of Christ." The Spirit's work is to accomplish the mission of Christ and to give Christ glory. The Church is understood as a missionary Church in dispersion and becomes the Body of Christ. In that line of thought, history is linear and the Church extends between the Ascension of Christ and the Second Coming. Zizioulas observes that this is clearly the type of pneumatology that was adopted by the West.

A second type of pneumatology that occupies an important place in the Christian Testament is eschatological. While in the first type of pneumatology the Spirit is given by the risen Christ, in the second the Spirit enables the resurrection to take place. In the Gospels of Matthew and Luke, the Spirit is shown to be responsible not only for the resurrection but also for the birth of Christ. In Mark's Gospel, Christ is "constituted by his baptism . . . in and through the Spirit."[23] All these accounts of the life and death of Jesus provide a perspective from the eschaton with the Spirit as an active agent throughout. Consequently, it is possible to say, in contrast to the first type, that pneumatology is the source of christology and that it gives the Church more of an eschatological rather than a mission focus. The Church in this perspective is depicted not as scattered but as a gathered community.[24] This is the pneumatology adopted by the East.

Zizioulas himself clearly identifies most with the second type of pneumatology. The Holy Spirit is primarily understood as a communion *(koinōnia)* who builds community rather than as a power *(dynamis)* who helps certain individuals to accomplish a particular mission.

---

[22] See Zizioulas, "Implications ecclésiologiques de deux types de pneumatologie," 141–54.

[23] Ibid., 142.

[24] See ibid., 143.

Community is understood to be the means in and through which persons come to true identity. The Spirit realizes the event of Christ in history, and the community that expresses the communion of the Spirit is inseparable from the presence of Christ. That, in turn, emphasizes the holiness of the Church and provides a vision of how all the baptized are drawn through the process of divinization *(theōsis)* into the very communion of God.[25] This type of pneumatology is powerfully expressed in the great communal act of the Eucharist, which is understood as an eschatological event. Zizioulas draws a connection between this understanding of pneumatology and developments that have taken place in Western philosophy toward an ontology of relation. Referring to the work of E. Levinas and M. Buber, he recalls that in theology a relational ontology is only possible through a christology that is conditioned by pneumatology.[26] As I have explored in Chapter 4, this type of pneumatology implies an ontology in which communion is a requisite for individuality: "Everything in the Church and the Church itself *are* because *they exist in relation.* The Church *is* only because it is the Body *of* Christ (this relation gives to the Church its identity)."[27]

Zizioulas observes that in the New Testament, in Luke-Acts for example, the two types of pneumatology coexist in the same text without apparent difficulty. He notes, however, that this synthesis was lost later in the Church's development and argues that the greatest theological differences between East and West can be traced to a divergence in these two pneumatologies.[28] He believes that it is essential to work toward a new synthesis if there are to be any durable solutions to ecumenical issues. Furthermore, he acknowledges that there is both a historical imperative for the Church as the people of God to be fully engaged in the issues of the world and an eschatological imperative to provide a dynamic vision of hope for the world that depicts the coming of the kingdom fully realized in Christ.

As discussed at some length in Chapter 4, a crucial dimension of Zizioulas's theology is his emphasis on the importance of a theological understanding that developed in the early Church, namely, that pneumatology and christology have to "exist simultaneously and not as separate or successive phases of God's relation to the world."[29] He

---

[25] See ibid., 143–44.

[26] See ibid., 151.

[27] Zizioulas, "Implications ecclésiologiques de deux types de pneumatologie," 151.

[28] See ibid., 146. Zizioulas compares the two types adopted by West and East that are epitomized in the writings of Clement of Rome and Ignatius of Antioch.

[29] Zizioulas, "The Pneumatological Dimension of the Church," *Communio* 1 (1974) 143.

stresses that "it is the Spirit that opens reality to become relational." In that sense he, like Johnson, argues that an understanding of the role of the Spirit is crucial in addressing the ecological crisis. He also stresses that "the mystery of the church is born out of this christological-pneumatological event in its integrity."[30] Zizioulas seeks to correct the notion that the Church is merely inspired or animated or led by the Spirit. He emphasizes that the Spirit constitutes the Church as the Body of Christ. He states that "the proper and specific function of the Spirit" is "to create life in an event of communion by rendering the life of God a reality here and now."[31]

Zizioulas draws attention to a fact which Johnson also emphasizes but which is often overlooked, namely, that the Holy Spirit is not only a power that unites but also a power that divides. It is the Spirit who distributes different gifts, charisms, and ministries within the various local communities. It is the Spirit who renders each entity particular and unique. Moreover, in his emphasis on a central facet of Orthodox teaching that it is the Spirit who brings the eschaton into history (Acts 2:17), he stresses that the Spirit does not merely bring life to a preexisting structure but in fact re-creates it. The Spirit "confronts history with its consummation, with its transformation and transfiguration," and "changes linear historicity into a *presence.*"[32] According to this understanding, the Spirit, as we have seen, comes again and again as an *event,* active to create relationship and communion. In the Eucharist, at the epiclesis, the Church asks for "an event of communion, a pentecostal event in which the world enters into the realm of personal freedom and lives eternally . . . through being drawn into the life of God."[33]

In summary, Zizioulas's pneumatology emphasizes that being in the Spirit brings humanity and all of creation into Christ and into the very communion of Godself. He stresses that the Holy Spirit is the person of the Trinity who actually realizes in history that which we call Christ. Through the work of the Spirit the Church is gathered and incorporated into the eternal filial relationship between the Father and the Son. The "many" become "one" in Christ and are thus drawn into God's life of communion. What emerges clearly in Zizioulas's pneumatology, and therefore in his Trinitarian theology, is the strong primary role of the Spirit.

---

[30] Ibid., 146.

[31] Ibid., 148.

[32] Zizioulas, *Being as Communion: Studies in Personhood and the Church* (New York: St. Vladimir's Press, 1985) 180.

[33] Zizioulas, "The Eucharistic Prayer and Life," *Emmanuel* 85 (1979) 195.

A Correlation of Pneumatologies

There are some clear similarities between Zizioulas's focus on the significance of the person of the Spirit's ever-creative and life-giving relationship with all creation and Johnson's efforts to retrieve the significance of the Spirit as the first person of the triune God that humanity encounters. Johnson is in agreement with Zizioulas when she states that according to the witness of Scripture, Jesus is "a genuine Spirit-phenomenon, conceived, inspired, sent, hovered over, guided and risen from the dead by her power."[34] Zizioulas argues that there is nothing more unbiblical than starting to consider the Holy Spirit only after the figure of Christ has been completed, since the biblical accounts show Christ being constituted by the Holy Spirit. He holds that the Spirit should be seen not just as an assistant to each individual in reaching Christ but as the means by which the person participates in Christ. Being in the Spirit brings humanity *into* Christ.[35]

Both theologians emphasize that a primary role of the Spirit is to build communion and that this enables the differences and particularities of each created entity to flourish in its uniqueness. Zizioulas begins from a meta-historical vision of the future and stresses the significance of the action of the Holy Spirit as the person of the Trinity who draws the many into the one Christ and so into God's triune life. He emphasizes the significance of the Spirit creating "events" of communion from which flow many different and varied charisms for the Church and the world.

Johnson describes that same action in terms of the Spirit's capacity to enable relationships of mutuality and friendship, which in turn enable differences of all kinds to flourish and to be transcended through genuine communion. She begins with humanity's experience of God in the world and pictures the Spirit as a female acting subject who "passes into holy souls and makes them friends of God, and prophets" (Wis 7:27). Johnson's focus is on the Spirit at work in the world, while Zizioulas's emphasis is on the Spirit and the Church.

One clear difference in the approaches of the two theologians is that Johnson places great significance on the praxis that needs to flow from the communion that the Spirit creates. She emphasizes the action needed to reshape the contemporary world according to the justice and peace of God's good news proclaimed in Jesus. In this she reflects the "mission" type of pneumatology of the West, which Zizioulas identi-

---

[34] Johnson, *SHE WHO IS*, 150.

[35] See Zizioulas, "Human Capacity and Human Incapacity: A Theological Exploration of Personhood," *Scottish Journal of Theology* (1975) 441–42.

fies as being present in the witness of the early Church. Zizioulas's focus of the same powerful action of the Spirit is through the lens of the second type of pneumatology, also present in the Christian testament. This is through an eschatological vision, preserved in the liturgy of the Eastern Church, in which the full communion of the final reconciliation of all things in Christ is brought momentarily into present realities through the Eucharist. It is obvious, as Zizioulas himself argues, that the presence of both of these pneumatologies need to be acknowledged and valued if the full impact of the work of the Spirit is to be received by the Christian Churches.

Both these important emphases also need to be included in a retrieval of the triune symbol. Western theology is still one-sidedly centered on the symbol of Christ, and this imbalance continues to distort the Christian Churches' structures and praxis.[36] The dynamic vision of these pneumatologies reaches back into powerful biblical images and communicates the Spirit persistently prompting initiatives that stretch across the divide of difference and truly foster events of difference in communion. It also communicates the Spirit luring believers into communion with the one Christ, into the source of God's very self and so to become partners with Divine *Koinōnia*, three-personed God. It is my experience that exposure to this vision invites a person of faith into new ways of relationship with God, the Church and the world and opens up a path of liberation.

The Significance of Christology in Retrieving the Triune Symbol

Zizioulas's Christology

In Zizioulas's christology, Christ is portrayed as a Spirit phenomenon. He emphasizes that the Spirit constitutes Christ in history, and describes the action of the Spirit breaking into history and forming the "corporate personality" of Christ.[37] Christ's very identity is thus understood to be conditioned by the existence of the "many." The Church is therefore part of the definition of Christ, and christology includes ecclesiology.[38] In fact, Zizioulas claims that without the Church, the eternal Son is not Christ.[39]

[36] See Chapter 4.

[37] See Zizioulas, *Being as Communion*, 110–11. This is explored in Chapter 4.

[38] See Zizioulas, "The Ecclesiological Presuppositions of the Holy Eucharistic," *Nicolaus* 10 (1982) 342.

[39] See Zizioulas, "The Mystery of the Church in the Orthodox Tradition," in *One in Christ* 24, no. 4 (1988) 300.

That emphasis on the identity between Christ and the Church can lead to the accusation, as noted in Chapter 4, that there remains no distinction between the Christ of glory and the sinful, imperfect Church on earth.[40] However, Zizioulas argues that it is only in the Eucharist that this momentary identification occurs.[41] He holds that the eucharistic community is the Body of Christ par excellence "simply because it incarnates and realises our communion with the very life and communion of the Trinity."[42] Further, Zizioulas recalls that christology was very early recognized to be "cosmic" and that the whole creation must be included in the Church's vision of Christ. Referring to the letters of Paul to the Ephesians and the Colossians, he notes that the person of Christ is not only the "first born among many brethren" but also the one in whom "all things *(ta panta)*" are brought into existence (Col 1:16-17). The mystery of Christ as the "head" of the new humanity is thus extended to include the entire cosmos (Col 1:18).[43] Zizioulas argues that "we must teach ourselves and our children that we are members of a community which regards creation as Christ's body."[44] "All things" are thus understood to be incorporated into Christ and brought into communion with God's triune self. Zizioulas's vision of the Christ is as an all-inclusive being, a corporate personality, and an eschatological reality. He makes it very clear that Christ is by definition a relational being and is "inconceivable as an individual."[45]

A second factor in Zizioulas's christology that contributes to his theology of the triune God is his emphasis that Jesus Christ realizes, in history, the very reality of the person. Zizioulas seeks to show that christology can give the assurance to humankind that the pull toward freedom that he identifies as an impulse toward personhood is not illusory. He argues that the historical reality of Jesus the Christ both opens the door for human beings to become persons and reveals what the fullness of personhood can be. He points out that in the East, the starting point of christology is the *hypostasis*, the person, of Christ. The Church's most explicit formulation of the ontology of Christ is the definition of Chalcedon—the teaching that the divine and human natures

---

[40] See Chapter 4.

[41] See Zizioulas, "The Ecclesiological Presuppositions of the Holy Eucharistic," 342.

[42] Zizioulas, *Being as Communion*, 114.

[43] Zizioulas, "The Mystery of the Church in the Orthodox Tradition," 301.

[44] Pergamon, "Orthodoxy and Ecological Problems: A Theological Approach," in *The Environment and Religious Education: Presentations and Reports, Summer Session on Halki 1994*, ed. Deuteron Tarasios (Militos Editions, 1997) 30.

[45] See Zizioulas, "The Mystery of the Church in the Orthodox Tradition," 299.

are unified without confusion or change, without division or separation, in the one *hypostasis*, or person, of Christ. Christology is therefore understood as the assurance to the human person that her or his nature can be "assumed" and hypostasized in a way that is free from ontological necessity. The unity of the human and the divine that was effected in Christ means that the human person is now capable of the freedom and love that exist within the communion of the triune God.[46] Christ is thus a powerful symbol of the dialectical unity of created and uncreated in a way that retains the integrity and identity of each.

A related insight developed by Zizioulas is that "being in Christ" means that difference no longer predicates destructive divisions.[47] Difference can instead be recognized as a necessary component of communion. Zizioulas rightly recognizes that fear of the "other" is pathologically inherent in our existence as contemporary persons and that it results not only in the fear of the other but of *all otherness*.[48] Difference is itself, therefore, a threat and is feared as a cause of division. By contrast, the personhood revealed by patristic theology includes an understanding of difference as a vital element for any true communion. The mystery of Christ as person reveals that otherness and communion are not in contradiction but coincide. Within Christ the integrity of the humanity and the divinity is not obliterated by the unity of the person. The union of the human and the divine in one person does not lead to the dissolving of differences but to the affirmation of otherness in and through love. Zizioulas thus claims that a significant manifestation of the move from individuality to personhood in Christ through the Spirit is the shift in human beings from seeing *difference* as a source of division to recognizing it as an intrinsic value and a means of communion.

The significance of Zizioulas's christology and its place within his theology of the triune God is revealed most clearly within the movement of the eucharistic liturgy. Within the action of the liturgy he focuses on the gathering of the many different persons who make up the pilgrim people of God. He emphasizes that they are gathered by the impulse of the Spirit. It is within the one Christ that all the different entities of creation are offered to the Father, the unoriginate source of all life, and so are brought into God's dynamic life of eternal communion. Through this action they attain the promise of the freedom of full personhood. Within the Eucharist, the eschatological vision of the whole Christ momentarily connects with the journey of history and offers a powerful witness and impetus toward a future of hope.

[46] See Zizioulas, *Being as Communion*, 54–56.

[47] See Chapter 2.

[48] See Pergamon, "Communion and Otherness," *St. Vladimir's Theological Quarterly* 38, no. 4 (1994) 349–50.

Johnson's Christology

Consistent with her feminist method, Johnson's christology begins with history and the world. Her analysis reveals that christology's narrative, symbol, and doctrine have been thoroughly assimilated into a patriarchal view of the world. She shows that instead of being a source of liberation, the Christ symbol has been used as a justification for domination. By the time of Constantine, Christ was portrayed as the King of glory, the Pantocrator, the principle of headship and cosmic order. His heavenly reign became the cornerstone upon which a patriarchal order of family, empire, and Church was set up and sustained. "Thus co-opted," argues Johnson, "the powerful symbol of the liberating Christ lost its subversive, redemptive significance." In the first instance, therefore, christology provides a problem for Johnson in her quest to retrieve the symbol of the triune God. Her primary concern is encapsulated in the claim of some feminists that of all doctrines of the Church, "Christology is the one most used to suppress and exclude women."[49] In her analysis, however, the root of the problem does not have to do with the fact that Jesus was male; it has to do with the way Jesus' maleness is construed in official androcentric theology and ecclesial praxis resulting in a christological view that effectively diminishes women.[50]

Johnson argues that christology was central in shaping the doctrine of God and today is again revolutionizing the theology of God. She therefore returns to the original sources of the christological doctrine and searches current christological scholarship for the basis of a reclaimed symbol of Christ that can be liberating for women.[51] Drawing from contemporary sources, Johnson shows that the story of Jesus reveals a God who is intrinsically relational within Godself and with the world in ways that are personal and life-giving. The death-resurrection event that has been recovered by the application of critical methodology to the Scriptures reveals a God of victorious love relating in solidarity with suffering humanity: "Christ Crucified and risen . . . manifests the truth that divine justice and renewing power leavens [sic] the world in a way different from the techniques of dominating violence."[52] The conclusions of contemporary christological research also radically revise the emphasis in the classical tradition on the impassibility of God, and contemporary liberation and feminist theologies em-

---

[49] Johnson, *SHE WHO IS*, 151. See also Chapter 5.
[50] See ibid., 152.
[51] See Chapter 5.
[52] Johnson, *SHE WHO IS*, 159.

phasize an "evercoming, liberating" God who seeks liberation and wholeness for all humanity and creation.[53]

In returning to the sources of christology, Johnson appeals to the inclusive intent of the doctrinal teachings of Nicea and Chalcedon. Those teachings make it unambiguously clear that Christ became one with humanity, thus saving women as well as men; that Jesus is one person in whom the divine and human are neither mixed nor confused, so that his human characteristics, specifically his maleness, do not flow into the divine identity of the Christ. Those conciliar texts in their historical context do not emphasize Jesus' maleness as being doctrinally significant but rather his humanity in solidarity with all creation.

In a particular way, Johnson's work of retrieval of the Christ symbol focuses on the identification of Jesus with the biblical personification of *Sophia*. She points to the fact that wisdom literature was one of the primary sources of the doctrines of the incarnation and the Trinity. Her research reveals how wisdom christology not only reflects the depths of the mystery of God but also "points the way to an inclusive christology in female symbols."[54] That identification of Jesus with *Sophia* is the centerpiece of Johnson's constructive contribution to a restored christology. It is also central to her primary project—the need to address that question of "unsurpassed importance," namely, the right way to speak about God. She demonstrates that the name Jesus-Sophia for Christ is faithful to the insights of the tradition's christological doctrine and that at the same time enables it to be freed from its androcentric images and expressions. That name functions to stem the "leakage" of Jesus' male identity as a human being onto the divine preexistent One who was with God in the beginning.

The very gender dissonance created by the name Jesus-Sophia is liberating. As a name for the second person of the Trinity, it signals that God is incomprehensible, and the initial discomfort created by the name invites the believer into the mode of the apophatic, of "not-knowing" in the face of divine mystery. And yet at the same time, paradoxically, it functions in a kataphatic mode. The name Jesus-Sophia taps into the rich imagery of the wisdom tradition that draws from the whole of life, even the stuff of everyday life, and depicts this as sacred and the very arena of God's action.

Naming the "second person" of the Trinity as Jesus-Sophia also enables a retelling of the Gospel story of Jesus of Nazareth through the wisdom tradition. *Sophia's* characteristics of graciousness, creativity, and passion for justice become keys for interpreting the mission of

---

[53] See ibid., 154–58.
[54] Ibid., 99. See Chapter 5.

Jesus. Because of the cosmic dimensions of the wisdom tradition, the name Jesus-Sophia draws attention to the fact that as the embodiment of *Sophia,* Jesus the Christ's redeeming care is portrayed as extending to all creatures and to the whole earth itself. The explicit connection with wisdom discourse opens faith to a global perspective that is able to be inclusive of other religious paths. Thus feminist theological speech about Jesus the Wisdom of God serves to shift the focus of reflection off maleness and onto the intrinsic significance of the whole Christ.[55]

A Correlation of Christologies

It is in their emphasis on the whole Christ that the christologies of Johnson and Zizioulas meet. Like Zizioulas, Johnson affirms that christology is a pneumatological phenomenon, "a creation of the Spirit who is not limited by whether one is Jew or Greek, slave or free, male or female . . . the body of the risen Christ becomes the body of the community; all are one in Christ Jesus (1 Cor 12; Gal 3:28)."[56] Johnson does not place as much emphasis as Zizioulas does on Christ as an eschatological reality, but she is clear about the importance of the eschatological character of the risen Christ. Both focus on the many different entities being gathered into the whole Christ by the action of the Spirit in word, sacrament, and assembly. This common strand of their christological vision, however, leads each of them to different emphases and conclusions. Johnson's leads her to contemplate the whole suffering Body of Christ reflected in the life of the community of Church and world:

> The focus is not on Jesus alone in a sort of Jesus-ology, but on looking with him in the same direction toward the inclusive well-being of the body of Christ, that is, all suffering and questing people: "just as you did it to one of the least of these who are members of my family, you did it to me" (Mt 25:40). Moreover, the liturgical place of encounter is not only word and sacrament but the assembly of the community itself.[57]

Zizioulas's contemplation of the whole Christ, celebrated most fully in the Eucharist, leads him to conclude that the significance of christology resides in the fact that Christ constitutes the ontological ground of every person. His conclusions are essentially symbolic and metaphysical. Johnson's lead to the need for action. Whereas Zizioulas's

---

[55] See Chapter 5.
[56] Johnson, *SHE WHO IS,* 162.
[57] Ibid.

emphasis is that in Christ each person can come to freedom and love, Johnson's emphasis recognizes that Christ is constituted by the power of the Spirit when the hungry are fed. Her christological vision intrinsically includes "looking with [Jesus] in the same direction toward the inclusive well-being of the body of Christ, that is, all suffering and questing people." That way of seeing prompts the assembly toward a praxis in which the least are brought to the center and found to be in Christ.

The christologies of Zizioulas and Johnson both, therefore, present a strong vision of an inclusive, eschatological, cosmic Christ. Johnson notes, moreover, that "with the inclusive and eschatological character of Christ kept firmly in view, the maleness of Jesus can be reprised in the whole Christ and interpreted without distortion."[58] Her methodological choice to begin a theology of God with the Holy Spirit also means that her christology does not neatly fit the pattern described by Zizioulas as typical of the West. She emphasizes the need for action to relieve the suffering of the poor after the manner of Jesus, but like Zizioulas, she also emphasizes the dynamic action of the Spirit in bringing about the one Christ as an event of communion. Both theologians rely on the Christic formulations of the early Church to validate the importance they place on the whole Christ, and they engage this vision with critical questions from contemporary questions and scholarship.

The differences between the christologies of Johnson and Zizioulas are significant and mirror the differences of their perceptions of Church and world. Johnson's profound concern to engage the question of God with the need to recognize the full humanity of women is not an expressed concern of Zizioulas at all. Her research into Jesus as the Wisdom of God and her naming Christ as Jesus-Sophia are of central significance for the retrieval of the symbol of the triune God. Zizioulas's christology, like his pneumatology, is essentially meta-historical and eschatological and, unlike Johnson's, functions most powerfully within a liturgical framework. What he describes is an ideal that is far from realized as a norm in a sinful, patriarchal, and ecumenically divided Church. Nevertheless, it does provide a vision that can enormously enrich the very different emphases within Western theology and spirituality. And his christological focus on the reality of the person realized in history functions to provide a liberating and practical vision of how the human person can coexist with creation within the divine in freedom and love.

Johnson's christology, encoded in the name Jesus-Sophia, constitutes, I believe, a breakthrough in the task of retrieving the triune symbol.

---

[58] Ibid.

It cuts the Gordian knot of "Christ-He" and enables a female naming of the triune God that is based on a firm biblical foundation and is totally congruent with Trinitarian doctrine. In a very different way, Zizioulas's christology opens up the possibility of personhood whereby "the distance of individuals is turned to the communion of persons."[59] A vision that incorporates both could significantly affect how human persons understand themselves and all creation and how they can envision the future together. It can, therefore, generate practical possibilities for life in the world.

The next chapter focuses on those two critical aspects of the triune symbol as well as on the issue of the pattern of relationships communicated by the symbol. It explores persons, naming, and structure as foundations for a renewed Trinitarian theology.

[59] Ibid., 442.

CHAPTER 10

Foundations of Trinitarian Theology:
Persons, Naming, Structure

The triune symbol safeguards the idea that the distinctiveness or self-transcending uniqueness of each person is essential, belonging to the very being of God. At this point classical doctrine and feminist insight again vigorously coalesce.[1]

The Christian doctrine of the Trinity confesses that the God revealed by Jesus is one God of three coequal, coeternal persons. John Zizioulas places the concept of person at the heart of his Trinitarian theology, and "persons in communion" is the primary image he uses for the Trinity. The Trinitarian symbol of a community of equal persons is completely compatible with the feminist vision that personal uniqueness can flourish through profound companionship that respects differences and values them equally.[2] This chapter will focus on Zizioulas's naming the triune God as persons in communion and correlate Johnson's response to the use of "person" for the three in God. It will then bring Johnson's alternative constructive proposal for the naming and the structure of the triune God into dialogue with Zizioulas's theology.

---

[1] Elizabeth Johnson, *SHE WHO IS: The Mystery of God in Feminist Theological Discourse* (New York: Crossroad, 1992) 219.

[2] See ibid.

The Significance of Person in Trinitarian Theology

Zizioulas's Vision of the Triune God as "Persons in Communion"

Zizioulas retrieves the Cappadocian description of God as "persons in communion" and claims that this doctrine has existential consequences. He believes that living out of this theology can contribute to humanity's quest for "personhood, freedom, community and the world's survival."[3] His research of the patristic sources for the doctrine of the Trinity reveals that it was the struggle to develop language to speak about the Christian experience of the triune God of love that generated a breakthrough in the ontology of person. He asserts that the being of the triune God is the communion between the three persons and that "person" can be conceived, not as an adjunct to being, but as being itself. To be a person means to be in relation. He understands being as communion and that there is no true being without communion. Relation, therefore, can be understood as an ontological category. Zizioulas argues that in God it is possible for the particular to be ontologically ultimate because of the unbreakable and living communion between Father, Son, and Spirit. He emphasizes that God's love, which came to be identified with ontological freedom, resides not in God's nature but in God's personal existence.[4]

The ecstatic and hypostatic understandings of person that emerge from Zizioulas's probing of the origins of Trinitarian doctrine throw new light on what it means for a human being to live out her or his potential as a person created in the image of God. Those insights also contribute to humanity's continuing search to understand what it means to be a fully free human person. They reaffirm what studies in other disciplines also suggest, namely, that to live fully as a unique person in relation means breaking through the confining and dehumanizing limits of individualism and living a life of inclusive communion with other persons and other created entities. This provides a vision much needed in today's world: that persons can flourish in communion. Conversely, Zizioulas also argues that it is essential for theology to take into account all other disciplines that are pursuing this question of personhood: "We must actually begin from the point where these non-theological concerns emerge in our time."[5] He is one of many theologians who argue con-

---

[3] John Zizioulas, "The Doctrine of God the Trinity Today: Suggestions for an Ecumenical Study," in *The Forgotten Trinity*, ed. Alasdair I. C. Heron (London: BCC/CCBI, 1991) 29. See Chapter 1.

[4] See Chapter 2.

[5] Zizioulas, "The Doctrine of God the Trinity Today," 27.

vincingly that contemporary understandings of person can help uncover important dimensions of the mystery of the triune God.[6]

It is in the liturgy that Zizioulas's imaging of God as persons in
communion particularly comes to life. It is the Holy Spirit, the Life-
giver, source of many charisms in the community, who gathers the diverse members into an assembly. As they assemble, they bring with
them the gifts of creation. At the one table of the eucharistic liturgy the
many are constituted into the one person of Christ. It is as the Body of
Christ that the many-become-one are offered to the Father and are
drawn into the communion of the triune God. Entering into the liturgical action thus provides a way for the believer to relate to each of the
three persons in God, Father, Son, and Spirit, and to participate in the
dynamic relationality and love of the three persons in communion.
Zizioulas describes this when he states that "the existence of God is revealed to us in the Liturgy as an event of communion."[7]

A Correlation with Johnson's Trinitarian Theology

In an address given in Rome in 1981 to mark the anniversary of the
Second Ecumenical Council, Zizioulas argues that it is important for
both the East and the West to appropriate the Cappadocian theology
that lay behind this council. His analysis is that in the course of history,
Cappadocian and Western thought were never given the opportunity
to really meet except in the context of a polemic. He maintains that this
has meant that the history of the reception of this defining council was
interrupted and never came to full maturity. He refers in particular to
"its most important and existentially decisive intention to give ontological priority to the Person in God and in existence in general."[8]

When the central image of this Orthodox theologian's Trinitarian
theology—persons in communion—is brought into critical correlation
with that of Elizabeth Johnson, it becomes obvious that this analysis
could provide a key to a fundamental difference in their work. Johnson
certainly subscribes to God as personal and to the importance of relationality in the doctrine of God, but she does not subscribe to the centrality of an ontology of person as Zizioulas does. In fact, as I have
described in Chapter 2, she finds it highly problematic to put emphasis
on the three "persons" in God.[9]

[6] See Chapter 2.
[7] John Zizioulas, "The Teaching of the 2nd Ecumenical Council on the Holy
Spirit in Historical and Ecumenical Perspective," in *Credo in Spiritum Sanctum*, ed.
J. S. Martins (Vatican City: Libreria Editrice Vaticana, 1983) 39.
[8] Ibid., 49. See also 45–48 for a further elaboration of this.
[9] See Chapter 2.

Johnson's critique of the use of person comes under the rubric of language about the Trinity being used in ways that are descriptive and literal. She claims:

> Applying the word [person] in its contemporary usage to the triune God inevitably yields the notion of three distinct somebodies. When Christians are not being their usual aTrinitarian, monotheistic selves, we are tritheists.[10]

This comment is consistent with her stated understanding of person as "a social being with a distinct center of consciousness." It seems that this definition of person is very similar to that of Rahner and Barth, who have been criticized for subscribing to a limited, individualistic notion of person. By contrast, much twentieth-century study of the nature of personhood places emphasis on person as a relational category.[11] That emphasis is congruent with Zizioulas's definition—that to be a person is to be in relation.[12] It connects with what Walter Kasper describes as a "revolution in the understanding of being" in which "the highest category is not substance but relation."[13]

It is important to note that in subscribing to a limited definition of person, Johnson does not undervalue the significance of relationality in Trinitarian theology. Quite to the contrary, she entitles one chapter of her work on the Trinity "Triune God: Mystery of Relation."[14] She acknowledges that Trinitarian theology, based as it is in the biblical story of salvation, has consistently taught that what constitutes the three divine persons is their relationality, that is to say, relationship both constitutes each Trinitarian person as unique and distinguishes one from the other. It is on the basis of this teaching that she describes the Trinity as "a mystery of real, mutual relations" and can state that "at the heart of holy mystery is not monarchy but community; not an absolute ruler, but a threefold *koinonia*."[15] Moreover, she notes that this points to a sense of ultimate reality that is very congruent with the feminist values of mutuality, relation, equality, and community in diversity.[16]

---

[10] Elizabeth Johnson, "Trinity: To Let the Symbol Sing Again," *Theology Today* 34, no. 3 (1997) 304.

[11] See Walter Kasper, *The God of Jesus Christ*, trans. Matthew J. O'Connell (New York: Crossroad, 1991) 289. See also Catherine Mowry LaCugna, *God for Us* (New York: HarperSanFrancisco, 1991) 255.

[12] See Chapter 2.

[13] Kasper, *The God of Jesus Christ*, 156.

[14] See Johnson, *SHE WHO IS*, 191–223.

[15] Ibid., 216.

[16] See ibid., 211.

As discussed in Chapter 6, Johnson further explores the meaning of relation in the Trinity through the metaphor of mutuality experienced in friendship and through the ancient concept of Eastern theology, *perichoresis*. She reflects on women's experience to elaborate the notion of freedom in personal relation, which she argues must be retained from the classical teaching on God. That leads her to examine the connection between the freedom of the relational self and what she describes as a "new construal of the notion of person." She writes:

> Women seek to articulate an extensively relational self grounded in a community of free reciprocity. What is slowly coming to light is a new construal of the notion of person, neither as a self-encapsulated ego nor a diffuse self denied, but self-hood on the model of relational autonomy. Discourse about God from the perspective of women's experience, therefore, names toward a relational God who loves in freedom.[17]

Given this elaboration of the evolving nature of person, it is surprising that Johnson does not revise her opinion about the value of person for the naming of God. She does not draw the connection between the centrality of relationship (communion) in Trinitarian theology and the centrality of person that is so pivotal in Zizioulas's theology, and indeed in the work of many other contemporary theologians.[18] One reason for that could be that Johnson does not draw from the Cappadocian source that is so central in Zizioulas's theology. She gives no evidence of being aware of Zizioulas's claim that a semantic shift occurred in the concept of person when fourth-century pastor-theologians brought the worldview of the Bible into conjunction with Greek thought. For Zizioulas, that was an event of enormous significance both for the theology of the triune God and for humanity's capacity to grasp what it means to come to full freedom as a person. For Johnson, as for most theologians of the West, it is as if this move did not happen. She writes:

> In the original Greek, the word used to describe the three divine persons, hypostasis, did not connote "person" as we mean it today, a social being with a distinct center of consciousness and freedom, but something in philosophy to [sic] a distinct manner of subsistence. The word has drifted semantically in a wide arc over the course of the centuries.[19]

Johnson's reflections on "person" thus do not take into account that the Greek philosophical meaning of *hypostasis* was radically conditioned

---

[17] Johnson, *SHE WHO IS*, 226.
[18] See Chapter 2.
[19] Johnson, "Trinity: To Let the Symbol Sing Again," 304.

by biblical perceptions of the God of Jesus, the personal, passionate God of Israel. That fact seems to give credence to Zizioulas's analysis that Cappadocian thought has not really "met" Western theology. As outlined in Chapter 2, Zizioulas argues that in Western thought the historical evolution of a concept of person was derived from a combination of two basic components: rational individuality (Boethius) and psychological experience and consciousness (Augustine). He holds that "person" thus came to be understood in the West as an individual: "a unit endowed with intellectual, psychological and moral qualities centred on the axis of consciousness . . . an autonomous self who intends, thinks, decides, acts and produces results."[20] It certainly seems that Johnson's Western theological heritage through Augustine, Aquinas, and Rahner is more consistent with this concept of person than that of the Cappadocians. She refers to the concept of person as simply one image among many that are needed to talk about God. Having referred to the writings of Augustine and Anselm, for example, she comments: "The great minds of classical theology were aware of the poetic nature of 'person' when we speak of Trinity, of its symbolic nature, and did not at all intend that it be taken literally."[21]

It goes without saying that Zizioulas does not intend that "persons in communion" or any other concept should be taken as a literal description of God. However, drawing from patristic sources in dialogue with current studies of personhood, he does make a very strong case for the significance of "person" (understood as one who is in relation, in communion) for plumbing the mystery of both humanity and divinity and of their relationship with the whole of creation in time and eternity. The image "persons in communion" coheres powerfully with the feminist agenda,[22] and I am convinced that it is an essential concept within a restored symbol of the triune God.

The Power of Naming and the Triune God

Like Zizioulas, Johnson is profoundly aware of the existential power of the symbol of God. That awareness shapes her theology, however, in ways that are very different from Zizioulas's. Johnson's theology is based on a recognition that language for God has functioned for millennia to "support an imaginative and structural world that excludes or subordinates women" and that this, in turn, "undermines women's

---

[20] John Zizioulas, "Human Capacity and Human Incapacity: A Theological Exploration of Personhood," *Scottish Journal of Theology* (1975) 405–6.

[21] Johnson, "Trinity: To Let the Symbol Sing Again," 305.

[22] See Chapter 6.

human dignity as equally created in the image of God."[23] For Johnson, as for many other contemporary theologians, that presents a very serious issue for theology, and especially for a theology of God.[24] The centerpiece of Johnson's Trinitarian theology is her constructive response to that critical issue.

SHE WHO IS—Spirit-Sophia, Jesus-Sophia, Mother-Sophia

Johnson's concern "to speak rightly of God" leads her to question the exclusive naming of the Trinity as Father, Son, and Spirit. Her commitment to a feminist retrieval of the tradition prompts her to undertake a critical analysis of this exclusive naming of God, to search for alternative wisdom and suppressed history, and to propose constructive new interpretations of the tradition that are congruent with the experience of women's lives.

When Johnson describes her agenda for retrieving the symbol of the triune God, she suggests that one right way to speak about God is "to speak about the Trinity as a symbol of the mystery of salvation, in the midst of the world's suffering, using female images."[25] She searches the tradition for female alternatives that faithfully announce the God of Jesus Christ revealed by the Spirit. She also deliberately situates this theological task within the context of the all-pervading presence of suffering in the world. Her proposal therefore gives emphasis to the triune God as Compassion poured out in solidarity with a suffering world. Her proposal to name God as SHE WHO IS and as Spirit-Sophia, Jesus-Sophia, Mother-Sophia offers a major contribution to the task of redressing the idolatrous use of exclusive male language for naming the triune God.

The name SHE WHO IS points to the God of Israel (YHWH) who is revealed in the narrative of the burning bush as the personal, compassionate, faithful God who is dynamically active to save humanity and all creation. Johnson intends this name to be understood as an abbreviation of the saving story of Exodus. Given her reluctance to use "person" in the naming of the triune God, it is important to recall that one of the major reasons Johnson chooses to name God SHE WHO IS is to call attention to the nature of the being of God. It is founded on her understanding that "God's being is identical with an act of communion . . . and so is inherently relational."[26]

---

[23] Johnson, *SHE WHO IS*, 3.
[24] See Chapter 5.
[25] Johnson, *SHE WHO IS*, 212–13.
[26] Ibid., 238.

The name Spirit-Sophia, as outlined in the section on pneumatology, focuses on humanity's experience of God in the world and pictures the Spirit as a female-acting subject. The linking of *Sophia* with Spirit communicates an immediate personal dimension to the Spirit's all-pervasive presence as well as the rich nuances of God understood in Wisdom categories. It communicates something of "the gracious, furious mystery of God engaged in a dialectic of presence and absence throughout the world, creating, indwelling, sustaining, resisting, recreating, challenging, guiding, liberating, completing."[27] As Johnson suggests, starting the name of the Trinity with Spirit-Sophia instead of God the Father subverts "at the outset the dominance of the patriarchal image of God."[28]

The name Jesus-Sophia has, I believe, great significance for the retrieval of the symbol of the triune God. In ways that are based in, and congruent with, the scriptural and doctrinal tradition, this name enables the believer to think about, and relate to, the second person of Trinity as a female as well as a male subject. It enables the believer to relate to the male historical Jesus as Savior and Liberator, and to the female Sophia as the preexistent One who was with God in the beginning. The name Jesus-Sophia provides a key that can unlock the hegemony of an exclusive male imaging of the Trinitarian persons, without unraveling the relational identity and communion of the three persons that are at the heart of the Christian expression of the mystery of the triune God. It therefore breaks through what had hitherto seemed an impenetrable boundary in Trinitarian theology.

The name Mother-Sophia plumbs the rich imagery of Holy Wisdom as the unoriginate origin and goal of the universe. The mother image also evokes the paradigm of panentheism that Johnson employs to communicate God's freedom in relationship to the world.[29] This female image conveys something of the concept of God's kenotic self-limitation in creation while reclaiming the female person as a worthy image of the divine:

> This symbol lifts up precisely those aspects of women's reality so abhorred in classical Christian anthropology—the female body and its procreative functions—and affirms them as suitable metaphors for the divine. More than suitable, in fact, for they wonderfully evoke the mystery of creative, generative love that encircles the struggling world. . . . As some of our poets now say, "in her we live and move and have our being."[30]

[27] Ibid., 133.
[28] Ibid., 149.
[29] See ibid., 231.
[30] Ibid., 235.

Thus, besides communicating the tender and the tough love of a mother for a child, the name Mother-Sophia depicts a God who makes room for creation by constricting divine presence and power. It leads to a redefinition of God as omnipotent.

Naming the triune God as Spirit-Sophia, Jesus-Sophia, and Mother-Sophia literally turns the traditional naming upside down. While retaining the distinctions of Trinitarian relations, it provides a valid alternative to the exclusive male naming and structure of Father, Son, and Holy Spirit. By proposing an alternative naming of the triune symbol that has a sound basis in the Bible and tradition, it offers a key contribution to a retrieval of the symbol of the triune God.

A Correlation with Zizioulas's Theology

Just as Johnson gives no evidence of being aware of the significance of the move in fourth-century theology that led to a breakthrough in the understanding of person as an ontological category, so Zizioulas's theology does not acknowledge the seismic shift which is occurring now through feminist theology and which is affecting "the very nature of theology itself." David Tracy notes that "the realities of sexism have been exposed in every major symbol of the tradition."[31] Rebecca Chopp observes further that feminist theology is not just providing a mere corrective, but women's experience, which has been almost totally neglected for millennia, is now also contributing to a reformulation of Christianity.[32]

Zizioulas is clear that Trinitarian theology has existential consequences. However, such is the culture of the Orthodox tradition and the utter centrality of worshiping God as Father, Son, and Spirit within it that his theology gives no indication of any recognition of the distorting effects of sexism within Christian symbols, and in particular, of the serious limits that it has placed on a theology of God. The significance of the concepts of relation and person in Zizioulas's theology also means that his theology has much that is highly congruent with feminist theology. However, he makes no connections between right speech about God and the "pervasive exclusion of women from the realm of public symbol formation and decision-making."[33] Feminist theology and all that it brings to the development of theology as a whole are con-

---

[31] David Tracy, *Journal of Feminist Studies in Religion* 7, no. 1 (Spring, 1991) 124. See also Chapter 5.

[32] See Rebecca Chopp, *The Power to Speak: Feminism, Language, God* (New York: Crossroad, 1991) 21. Emphasis mine.

[33] Johnson, *SHE WHO IS*, 4.

gruent with much that is fundamental to Zizioulas's work and can contribute significantly to his theological vision. Similarly, it is my conviction that his theological method and vision can contribute creatively to many of the insights that feminist theology offers in these times.

The Structure of the Triune Symbol

Johnson's Proposal

Johnson maintains that the triune symbol of God has contributed to structural injustice for women and their patriarchal subordination, not only by its male imagery but also by "the hierarchical pattern of divine relationships inherent in the structure of reigning models of the symbol itself."[34] As discussed in Chapter 7, Johnson argues that unless the problem of the structure of the Trinity is addressed, it will subtly continue to subvert the teaching on the equality of the divine persons. It will also thereby continue to subvert the equality of human persons, as it has done for the past two millennia.

Johnson's analysis is that the classic presentation of the Trinity that acknowledges the Father as the principle and source of the triune God has led to ontological priority being given to the Father.[35] She is not disputing the distinctiveness of the Trinitarian persons that is based upon their relations of origin. Her work *SHE WHO IS* provides vivid testimony to the uniqueness of each of the Trinitarian persons. Rather, she is arguing that the exclusive use of a set order in the naming of the Trinity as Father, Son, and Holy Spirit has meant that belief in the radical equality of the three persons has failed to counter an implicit Trinitarian hierarchy. The teaching of the monarchy of the Father has tended to mean that the Spirit and the Son have been perceived as being less significant than the Father. Johnson draws attention to significant social and political consequences of a hierarchical understanding of the Trinity that has been used to validate hierarchical structures in Church and society in ways that have favored the ruling male elite but have disempowered everyone else. The hierarchical imaging of the triune God has effectively neutralized any social and political significance of the consistent doctrinal teaching on the mutual and equal relations of the three persons of the Trinity.

In order to address this problem, which is at the heart of feminist critique of the triune symbol, Johnson returns again to the traditional sources of the doctrine. With Jürgen Moltmann, she argues that the

[34] Ibid., 193.
[35] See ibid., 196.

Christian scriptures reveal different orderings that can and should be used as alternative expressions of the triune formula:

> In Luke's gospel, it is the Spirit who sends and commissions the Son. In John's gospel it is the Son who glorifies the Father and sends the Spirit. The Father also sends and glorifies. There is no one pattern set in stone, in literal fashion, but all these texts attempt to give expression to the one mystery of self-communicating love approaching the world to heal, redeem and liberate.[36]

Johnson's argument here is consistent with her appeal for the necessity to adhere to the classic "rules" for speaking about God (see Chapter 5). Any exclusive name for the incomprehensible God by definition becomes idolatrous. That also applies to an exclusive sequence of names. All speech about God must be recognized to be analogous. The specific focus of Johnson's proposal is concerned with the tension and ambiguity generated by the hierarchical connotations of the exclusive use of the sequence Father-Son-Spirit. She argues that all the various patterns of Trinitarian order need to be harnessed if the Holy Mystery of the triune God is to be expressed in ways that do not distort a central truth of the doctrine. Spirit-Son-Father and Father-Spirit-Son are other orderings that have a scriptural base. Johnson's concern is that the names used for the Trinity should not impede the prophetic teaching on the equal and mutual relationships within the *koinōnia* of the triune God. They should communicate that truth with clarity. Her hope is that instead of being a symbol that reinforces and validates structural injustice, the Trinity could be what, according to classical teaching, it truly is—a symbol that "summons the church to be a community of sisters and brothers in kinship with the earth, equal partners in mutual relationship sent to bring the world into this dance of life."[37]

The Structure of the Trinity: A Correlation with Zizioulas's Theology

Zizioulas's theology offers a "response" to such a proposal from Cappadocian sources. It comes from a consideration of doxological theology and the contrast between *Theologia* and *Oikonomia* in a major address he gave in Rome on the occasion of the anniversary of the Second Ecumenical Council. Drawing directly from his theological mentor Basil, Zizioulas observes:

[36] Johnson, "Trinity: To Let the Symbol Sing Again," 308.
[37] Ibid., 309.

> If one looks at the Economy in order to arrive at Theologia one begins with the Holy Spirit, then passes through the Son and finally reaches the Father. The movement is reversed when we speak of God's coming to us; the initiative starts with the Father, passes through the Son and reaches us in the Holy Spirit. In the latter case the Spirit can be said to come third in order but Basil does not seem to insist on that. The main point, when referring to the Economy, seems to be that the Spirit is a forerunner of Christ; there is no phase or act of the Economy which is not announced and preceded by the Spirit.[38]

Zizioulas is here acknowledging that different patterns for naming the Trinity are possible and that starting to speak of the triune God with the Holy Spirit from the economy is a valid option. He is thus upholding Johnson's proposal to use alternative patterns for the Father-Son-Spirit sequence and supporting an inductive approach to Trinitarian theology that would speak of the Trinity as Spirit-Son-Father.

In the same address Zizioulas describes the significance of the two different doxologies used in the early Church, one probably of Alexandrian origin: "Glory be to the Father through *(dia)* the Son in *(en)* the Holy Spirit," and the other preferred by Basil: "Glory be to the Father with *(syn)* the Son, with *(syn)* the Holy Spirit":

> If . . . one speaks of God in terms of liturgical and especially eucharistic experience, then, Basil argues, the proper doxology is that of *syn* and this makes the inter-Trinitarian relations look entirely different. The three persons of the Trinity appear to be equal in honour and placed next to one another without hierarchical distinction, almost as if the Monarchy of the Father itself were an irrelevant matter.[39]

Zizioulas goes on to explain that this preferred doxology of Basil supports "his favourite idea that the oneness of God is to be found in the *Koinonia* of the three persons."[40] These reflections suggest that there was a fluidity in Trinitarian expression and perception in the early Church and that Basil, at least, placed primary value on the significance of the equality of the Trinitarian persons and on their mutual life in communion rather than on any set formula for naming the Trinity. Those are, in fact, the very values that Johnson's proposal is seeking to reinstate.

A related issue in Zizioulas's Trinitarian theology is the significance he places on the symbol of the monarchy of Father. For him, all

---

[38] Zizioulas, "The Teaching of the 2nd Ecumenical Council on the Holy Spirit," 38.
[39] Ibid., 39.
[40] Ibid.

speech about the Father being the cause of the Trinity resides in the fact that it gives clear emphasis to the centrality of God as person.[41] It also emphasizes the divinity and uniqueness of each of the Trinitarian persons deriving from their relation of origin, and it illustrates God's personal freedom. Johnson's proposal concerning the importance of using more than one formulation of the Trinitarian mystery can accommodate the importance of each of these truths. It is clear, however, that Zizioulas's emphasis on the Father as "cause" does more than this—it has the effect of reinforcing the hierarchical distinctions within the triune symbol. That is specifically at odds with the primary intention of Johnson's proposal.

It is relevant to recall in this context that Zizioulas's understanding of hierarchy is different from that of the hierarchy exercised in the Church of the West. He describes it as a "notion in the idea of personhood" and has to do with *specificity of relationship*.[42] He states that within the Church the exercise of hierarchical authority should be congruent with "a dynamic *perichoresis* in and through the whole body."[43] However, despite this more inclusive interpretation of hierarchy, it is clear that naming of the Trinity exclusively as Father, Son, and Holy Spirit inevitably contributes to maintaining the status quo of existing patriarchal structures in Church and society.[44] At a symbolic level, stress on the monarchy of the Father communicates a vision of a hierarchic "power over" rather than a mutual "power with." As Johnson recalls again and again, "The symbol of God functions."

---

[41] It is relevant to note here, as Catherine LaCugna points out, that Gregory Nazianzen taught that monarchy is not limited to a single person. See *Orationes* 29.2; 31. Quoted in LaCugna, *God for Us*, 390. See also Thomas Torrance, *The Christian Doctrine of God: One Being, Three Persons* (Edinburgh: T&T Clark, 1996) 184–85.

[42] Zizioulas, "The Pneumatological Dimension of the Church," *Communio* 1 (1974) 151–52. See also Chapter 4.

[43] Ibid., 154. See also Chapter 4.

[44] In a study of the Church as an image of the Trinity, Miroslav Volf, a theologian of the Free Church tradition, comments: "By emphasizing that the Father is the personal αιτα of the Son and Spirit, Zizioulas has underscored the asymmetry within the trinitarian communion." Volf later traces the implications of this within Zizioulas's ecclesiology: "One encounters in the relation between the bishop and congregation the same asymmetrical structure of communality that according to Zizioulas attaches to inner-trinitarian relationships. . . . It is thus doubtful whether Zizioulas's understandings of the relation between the one and the many genuinely has excluded 'all pyramidal notions' from his ecclesiology as he asserts." Miroslav Volf, *After Our Likeness: The Church as the Image of the Trinity* (Grand Rapids/Cambridge: Wm. B. Eerdmans, 1998) 79, 112.

Zizioulas's central radical vision of "persons in communion" offers a very significant contribution to a retrieval of the triune symbol in our times. However, if the power of this vision is to be fully released, it is essential that the naming and the structure of the reigning models of the Trinitarian symbol as addressed by Johnson be seriously taken into account.

CHAPTER 11

Trinitarian Theology in Practice:
The Issues of Suffering and the Ecological Crisis

The power of God's compassionate love enters the pain of the world to transform it from within.[1]

In this final chapter of mutually critical correlation, Zizioulas's and Johnson's different theologies of the triune God are put to work. I explore what happens when they are brought into dialogue with the issue of suffering in the world and with the global ecological crisis.

Suffering and the Triune God

The Trinitarian theologies of Zizioulas and Johnson diverge in their approaches to suffering and the Trinity. For Johnson, it becomes essential to grapple with the coexistence of a triune God, whose very being is relational, and the stark phenomenon of the suffering of the world. For Zizioulas, the consideration of a God who suffers becomes a point of concern because he judges that it inevitably leads to the loss of divine freedom and transcendence.

Zizioulas's Rejection of the Concept of a Triune God Who Suffers

For Zizioulas, the issue of speaking of a triune God who suffers is intrinsically related to an understanding of the relationship between

[1] Elizabeth Johnson, *SHE WHO IS: The Mystery of God in Feminist Theological Discourse* (New York: Crossroad, 1992) 270.

the economic and the immanent Trinity. He makes his position on this very clear. While fully supporting the need to base a theology of the Trinity in the economy, he believes that Trinitarian theology must show that God is clearly transcendent to the world and that the immanent Trinity is *more than* the economic Trinity.[2] "Otherwise," he argues, "the Incarnation is projected into God's eternal being; he becomes suffering by nature."[3] Zizioulas rejects the concept of a suffering God because he holds that it subverts the intention of the doctrine of *creatio ex nihilo*— "that God existed *before* and *regardless* of the world."[4]

Zizioulas is concerned that the concept of the suffering God in contemporary Trinitarian theology is "nothing but a return to the classical monistic view of existence according to which the being of God and the being of the world are inseparably linked up in some kind of affinity."[5] He argues that this endangers the absolute ontological freedom of God. Ever since the Enlightenment, he suggests, humanity has not been ready to operate with the notion of transcendence and has therefore sought to explain everything in terms of immanence. His analysis is that contemporary Trinitarian theologians, in their zeal to make this central doctrine of God relevant, try to show its importance by "making it an indispensable part of human experience."[6] He refers in particular to Jürgen Moltmann's historical theology, *The Trinity and the Kingdom of God,* and to James P. Mackey's personal approach in *The Christian Experience of God.* Ever the ecumenist, Zizioulas is concerned that the direction within contemporary Trinitarian theology that speaks of a suffering God will have deleterious effects for Christian dialogue with other world religions. He argues that "neither a Jew nor a Mohammedan would ever be able to grasp this kind of God."[7]

The central point for Zizioulas is that what we can say about God from God's acts in history is different from what we can say about how God is eternally. He believes that the symbol of a suffering God offers no real hope for a suffering humanity, because such a God "is in constant need of historical reality (involving suffering) in order to be what he will be, true God."[8]

---

[2] See Chapter 1.

[3] John Zizioulas, "The Doctrine of God the Trinity Today: Suggestions for an Ecumenical Study," in *The Forgotten Trinity,* ed. Alasdair I. C. Heron (London: BCC/CCBI, 1991) 24.

[4] Ibid., 23.

[5] Ibid.

[6] Ibid.

[7] Ibid.

[8] Ibid.

Johnson's Speaking of a God Who Suffers

Johnson's approach to this issue is consistent with her overall methodology and is very different from that of Zizioulas. She begins from the existential reality of the suffering world. She asks what is the right way to speak about God in the face of the weight of all this suffering: "Are human beings the only ones who weep and groan, or can this also be predicated of the holy mystery of God who cherishes the beloved world?" In response to this question, she suggests that "the classical attribute of impassibility becomes a test case for reinterpretation" and that "feminist theology has its own reconstructive contribution to make"[9] to this issue. She argues that because true relationality includes a capacity for compassionate identification with suffering, honoring the triune God as a "Mystery of Relation" points to the need to consider the symbol of a God who suffers.

Johnson's exploration of divine being from women's experience yields an alternative description of "perfection." She judges that compassionate connectedness more truly represents God's perfection and relationship with the world than an impervious completeness.[10] She agrees with the analysis of other feminist theologians that attributes of self-containment and the absence of relationship enshrined in the classic images of God do not represent ultimate divine perfection. She seeks a redefinition of power as essentially relational. Such an understanding of power means that a powerful person would have the capacity to choose to become vulnerable in order to sustain a mutual loving relationship. That in turn leads to a re-imaging of the omnipotent God as one who is "powerful" enough to be free to enter into the suffering of another. In order to describe God's relationship with the world, she opts for the position of panentheism, describing this as "a model of free reciprocal relation: God in the world and the world in God while each remains radically distinct. The relation is mutual while the differences remain and are respected."[11] In adopting this position, Johnson is firm in her acknowledgment that God's freedom to be God's divine self can and must remain at the center of any reinterpretation of God's relationship with the world.[12]

By naming God SHE WHO IS, Johnson evokes the mystery of the omnipotent God of the Bible, who is in solidarity with all those who suffer and are oppressed and who draws humanity to join her in the work of the liberation of all creation. Johnson sees the cross as "the

[9] Johnson, *SHE WHO IS*, 246.
[10] See ibid., 225. See also Chapter 6.
[11] See Johnson, *SHE WHO IS*, 231.
[12] See Chapter 6.

paradigmatic locus of divine involvement in the pain of the world."[13] Divine Wisdom enters into the suffering of the world and overcomes it from within through the power of love. She owns that in this symbol "something of the mystery of God is darkly manifest: Christ crucified, the wisdom and power of God" (1 Cor 1:22-23).[14] In Christ crucified, divine suffering is revealed as true power and strength. Johnson therefore concludes that "love does entail suffering in God" and that as "a summation of compassionate love, the symbol of divine suffering appears not as an imperfection but as the highest excellence."[15]

In speaking about the suffering God, Johnson is careful to note that there is a "dark side to such language in its potential to play into women's [or any oppressed person's] victimization by glorifying suffering."[16] Her response to this issue is a reinterpretation of the significance of the attribute of impassibility and a redefinition of omnipotence from a biblical base. Johnson sees the symbol of the suffering God as a symbol of hope for a suffering world. In contrast to Zizioulas's position, she argues, along with many others,[17] that such a proposal does not take from God's freedom but rather that the "divine capacity for suffering is a most characteristic expression of divine freedom active in the power of love."[18]

A Correlation of These Two Positions on the Symbol of a Suffering God

Zizioulas's fundamental position concerning theological doctrines is that they must be received and re-received, that they must be brought into dialogue with the critical issues of every age. On this count he would support the necessity of engaging the doctrine of the Trinity with this central issue of our age—the vast and pervasive presence of suffering around the globe. In so doing, however, he will not tolerate what he perceives to be any limiting of the transcendence of God. In this case, he clearly believes that to image the triune God as suffering binds God to human and historical categories, and he therefore judges that speaking of a God who suffers is mistaken and unhelpful for recovering the full import of the Trinitarian God for today.

Johnson's passionate concern "to speak rightly about God" leads her to argue consistently that theology has seriously distorted both the

---

[13] See Johnson, *SHE WHO IS*, 263. See also Chapter 6.
[14] Ibid.
[15] Ibid., 266. See also Chapter 6.
[16] Johnson, *SHE WHO IS*, 271.
[17] See Chapter 6.
[18] Johnson, *SHE WHO IS*, 251.

divine and the human by confining God-talk within narrow, "man-made" boundaries. In so doing, she is as committed as Zizioulas is to preserving the proper distinctions between uncreated and created and to preserving God's freedom to be as God is in Godself. In choosing to speak of a suffering God, she recalls that theological speech is not a literal description of God. "The rule of analogical speech," she insists, "applies here in full strength."[19] She would thus agree with Zizioulas that God is *not* a suffering God but that God is *more than* a suffering God. She would concur that fidelity to true speech about the incomprehensible God leads one to the apophatic, to the realm of "not-knowing," to the place where only praise is finally possible. However, she does not conclude from this that it should prevent the kataphatic use of images suggestive of key characteristics of God that have been revealed in the economy.

On the contrary, Johnson is clear about the necessity for many images for God. She is clear that, for centuries, the limited speech about God as impassible and omnipotent has conveyed very destructive messages about power and has worked against women being able to understand themselves as formed in the image of God. It is within such a theological context that she proposes the religious symbol of the suffering God as an important contribution to a recovery of the Trinity in these times. Her proposal to name God as SHE WHO IS seeks to evoke "the power of God's compassionate love [which] enters the pain of the world to transform it from within."[20] She insists on God's transcendent power, but it is understood as a power to love, a power to enter freely into relationships with all the vulnerability that this entails.

I believe that Zizioulas's primary concerns for preserving God's utter transcendence and freedom are taken into account within Johnson's proposal and that her combining the naming of God as suffering with a redefinition of divine power makes an essential contribution to any retrieval of the triune symbol of God.

The Trinity and the Ecological Crisis: An Ethic and an Ethos

Zizioulas's Theological Response to the Ecological Crisis

Central to Zizioulas's theology is his emphasis on the teachings of Chalcedon—on the significance of Christ becoming one with humanity,

---

[19] Ibid., 271. See also 204, where Johnson is explicit that "the symbol of the Trinity is not a blueprint of the inner workings of the godhead. . . . In no sense is it a literal description of God's being *in se*."

[20] Ibid., 270.

of uncreated becoming truly one with created while retaining absolutely the uniqueness of both divinity and humanity. When Zizioulas reflects on the ecological crisis, he focuses on the mystery of the incarnation opening up an eternal destiny for all that is created. Because of the union effected in Christ between human and divine, humanity and the natural world are destined to be drawn by a process of divinization *(theōsis)* into God's triune life. Zizioulas's engagement of theology with ecology leads inexorably to the heart of all that is—to a God revealed as a communion of three divine persons into whom humanity and all creation are drawn. He therefore concludes that if the ecological crisis is to be addressed, the human person must be able to recognize his or her origin and destiny in the dynamic life of the triune God.[21]

Zizioulas addresses the ecological problem through the lens of an eschatological future in which all creation is, in some way, already sharing the life of dynamic eternal communion of the divine persons of the Trinity. The "place" where this future meets the present is in the Eucharist, and it is through participation in the Eucharist that Zizioulas believes both humanity and the whole creation are renewed and transfigured in Christ through the power of the Spirit. The ecclesial community of the Church is therefore of critical importance if the ecological crisis is to be dealt with in a way that will endure. Christians are called by virtue of their baptism into Christ to be "priests of creation," which means that they are to relate to creation in such a respectful way that nature is enabled to develop its full potential. Zizioulas holds that when this happens, the material world, through this communion, is elevated to the level of humanity's existence and acquires a personal dimension.

Zizioulas's analysis is that the ecological crisis is fundamentally a crisis of culture and that placing hope in rational and ethical solutions alone, as Western societies have appeared to do, is doomed to ultimate failure. He suggests that there is a prior need for a new culture in which the *liturgical dimension* has central place and determines the ethical principle. He proposes "education through worship": "By this I mean the acquaintance of a human being from childhood with a holistic approach to reality involving all of creation."[22] His vision is that a child is initiated into a rich sacramental life within the ecclesial community and, over a lifetime, grows into a full relational life as a person who learns how to create communion with other human beings and with all creation.

[21] See Chapter 3.

[22] Pergamon, "Orthodoxy and Ecological Problems: A Theological Approach," in *The Environment and Religious Education: Presentation and Reports, Summer Session on Halki 1994,* ed. Deuteron Tarasios (Militos Editions, 1997) 30.

Zizioulas believes that it is through the symbolic offering of the bread and wine at the anaphora of the Eucharist that creation is opened up to infinite existence and the fragmentation and decomposition that lead to death are overcome: "When the church lifts up the gifts of creation, all created existence opens up to the infinite and the hands of the human person become the instruments of eternal life for the entire cosmos."[23] Moreover, Zizioulas also believes that what is enacted symbolically in the liturgy so forms a person's vision of reality that this spills over into how that person acts in the world. He argues that a religious culture that explicitly values creation and pictures it included in an eternal future provides a firm basis for the necessary change in behavior that humanity needs to make in relation to the environment. Within his perspective, the role of the eucharistic liturgy and the role of the Church are utterly crucial. The Church needs to provide a viable community wherein a person is initiated into a way of being in the universe, into living an ethos that will shape and sustain ethical behavior and decisions that will affect the environment.

Zizioulas's approach has shifted from an anthropocentric view of the world to an acknowledgment of the need to shift to a cosmic perspective: "Human beings are part of the natural cosmos and thus their salvation is as part of the cosmos."[24] He argues: "We do not have bodies, we are bodies. We should relate to nature not as individuals standing separately but as partakers of nature."[25] His theological and liturgical vision of humanity as "priest of creation," however, still holds that humanity has a key role to play in the salvation of the universe.

Johnson's Theological Response to the Ecological Crisis

Johnson describes the task of addressing this crisis of ecocide as "the most serious moral and religious challenge facing our generation."[26] She endorses the insight from ecofeminism that there is an intrinsic connection between the exploitation of the earth and of women and pursues the conviction that "the distortion found in those two instances also influences the Christian experience and doctrine of the mystery of God."[27]

---

[23] John Zizioulas, "The Eucharistic Prayer and Life," *Emmanuel* 85 (1979) 195.

[24] Pergamon, "Ethics Versus Ethos: An Orthodox Approach to the Relation Between Ecology and Ethics," in *The Environment and Ethics: Presentations and reports, Summer Session on Halki '95,* ed. Deuteron Tarasios (Militos Editions, 1997) 26.

[25] Pergamon, "Orthodoxy and Ecological Problems," 28.

[26] Elizabeth Johnson, *Women, Earth and Creator Spirit* (New York: Paulist Press, 1993) 10.

[27] Ibid.

Johnson provides a convincing argument that hierarchical dualism is the root cause of an interconnected set of oppressions.[28] To counter this, she identifies the task of developing an ecological ethic and spirituality that are based on "a unifying vision that does not stratify what is distinct into superior-inferior layers but reconciles them into relationships of mutuality."[29] Her constructive contributions toward this task are drawn from women's experience, from an understanding of relationship to the earth that is based on a kinship model, and from a restored theology of the Holy Spirit, of God active and present in the world. The twin elements that she considers essential for an ecological spirituality that can be taught and nourished by accessing the "Book of Nature" are contemplation—"a way of seeing that leads to communion"[30]—and a prophetic stance that "names new sins against God's gracious will: biocide, ecocide, geocide" and takes action to remedy those destructive systems of injustice.[31] Of all those strands, her contribution toward a vibrant pneumatology is of particular significance because it links her response to the ecological crisis directly with her Trinitarian theology.

Johnson is convinced that a new ethical horizon is needed to support hard choices in political, social, and economic arenas if justice for the whole earth is to be achieved. She believes that Christian theology has a critical role in developing this by providing a unifying vision that will help "disrupt human dominance and promote the whole community of life."[32] In her presidential address to the Catholic Theological Association of America in 1996, she made an impassioned plea to her fellow theologians to interpret the whole of reality in the light of faith and to turn their theological focus to "the entire interconnected community of life and the network of life-systems in which the human race is embedded."[33] She believes that a compelling and unifying theological vision can best provide a basis for the collective will necessary to address the ecological crisis besetting the contemporary world.

Given her passion and concern for the issue, it is surprising that Johnson does not explicitly harness what I believe is her most signifi-

---

[28] See Chapter 7.

[29] Johnson, *Women, Earth and Creator Spirit,* 22.

[30] Ibid., 63.

[31] Ibid., 65. See also Johnson, "Heaven and Earth Are Filled with Your Glory," in *Finding God in All Things,* ed. Michael Himes and Stephen Pope (New York: Crossroad, 1996), for a more developed exposition of contemplation and prophecy as requisite elements for an ecological spirituality.

[32] Johnson, "Heaven and Earth," 96.

[33] Elizabeth Johnson, "Turn to the Heavens and the Earth: Retrieval of the Cosmos in Theology," CTSA *Proceedings* 51 (1996) 1.

cant contribution to the kind of unifying theological vision needed to counter the ecological crisis, namely, her own theology of the triune God. What is immediately obvious to anyone who has been exposed to this theologian's Trinitarian vision is that the very theological synthesis she proposes provides a most powerful contribution toward healing the divided consciousness created by hierarchical dualism. The essential elements of her Trinitarian theology address this root cause by offering a constructive alternative that is firmly founded on the tradition. All the elements of this synthesis, separately and together, work to deconstruct hierarchical dualism and to build a new life-sustaining vision that is firmly based on the doctrines of the triune mystery. As Johnson states and restates, the symbol of God does indeed function. I am suggesting that her retrieval of the triune symbol is her most significant contribution to the ecological crisis, because it provides a strong unifying vision that is capable of sustaining a transforming ecological ethic and praxis.[34]

Correlation of the Theological Responses to the Ecological Crisis

The conviction of both John Zizioulas and Elizabeth Johnson that the symbol of God has existential consequences is illustrated in specific ways when each engages theologically with the issue of the ecological crisis. Their approaches to this massive contemporary problem are entirely consistent with their respective theological methods. Zizioulas's is essentially ecclesial, while Johnson's is more obviously from the world and able to appeal to non-believers. Both engage in a historical analysis of Christianity's involvement with the crisis, but Zizioulas's theological contribution to its solution is primarily drawn from the Eastern tradition and is meta-historical and liturgical, while Johnson's is from a Western feminist liberation theology that is based on women's experience and is directed to a just praxis. Johnson's focus is an ethical vision that is sustained by a contemplative, prophetic spirituality. Zizioulas's focus is on initiation into a eucharistic vision within the ecclesial community which creates an ethos that shapes and sustains a whole way of living and being.

Both theologians' historical analyses identify the emergence of a destructive dualism as the heart of the problem.[35] Zizioulas's emphasis

---

[34] This is also argued by Michele Anne Grimbaldeston, "Sophia Renewing the Earth: An Ecological Re-Reading of Elizabeth Johnson's Feminist Trinitarian Reconstruction of the God Symbol" (Honours thesis, School of Theology, The Flinders University of South Australia, 1997).

[35] For Johnson's analysis, see Chapter 7; For Zizioulas's, see Chapter 3.

is on the dualism between humanity and nature that came to permeate all aspects of the Church's life, worship, and ministry. He notes that physical matter ceased to be celebrated as God's gift and was rejected as either insignificant or a source of evil. Matter thus became considered dangerous for those pursuing a genuinely spiritual life. The sacraments, and especially the Eucharist, instead of giving ritual expression to the sacredness of matter, became focused on the spiritual. Meanwhile, in the secular realm, humanity and humanity's rational powers became the measure of all things. Johnson specifies that dualism as "hierarchical dualism," whereby one sphere (male) is ranked as more valuable than the other (female). Thus, although a recognition of the destructive force of dualism informs their respective analyses of the root of the problem, their different readings of it and their particular theological perspectives lead to different theological responses.

A major difference is that Johnson's Trinitarian theology is not expressed in either ecclesial or liturgical terms, whereas Zizioulas's theology can only be fully grasped through the ecclesial and liturgical. The latter's vision of fullness of life in God is profoundly ecclesial and is realized within a worshiping Christian community.[36] As a feminist liberation theologian, Johnson agrees with Zizioulas that the bodily as well as the symbolic and the artistic is critically important. However, the ecclesial and the liturgical sources so powerfully invoked in Zizioulas's Trinitarian theology are not specifically harnessed to contribute to Johnson's retrieval of the triune symbol. A vital path of entry into the Trinitarian mystery is through doxology and through the experience of communion within the Christian community. I believe that Johnson's important work would be significantly strengthened if she were to draw more explicitly from these sources.

Conclusion

Having been exposed to the strengths of both these theological approaches, it seems obvious that together they offer a powerful and comprehensive entry into a living Christian perspective that has much to offer the world in this new millennium. Johnson's profound feminist re-reading of the tradition provides a vision of God and the world that is literally transformative. It speaks to women and men of all cultures, and especially the poorest, presenting a dynamic picture of a compassionate God who draws each person into the work of liberation for all. It exudes hope and inspires ethical action. Zizioulas's primary picture

---

[36] See Zizioulas, "The Eucharistic Prayer and Life," 195–96; Pergamon, "Orthodoxy and Ecological Problems," 29.

of a person being drawn into an experiential knowing of God as persons-in-communion through being initiated into the life of an inclusive Christian community is likewise significant for these times. It offers a means of initiation into an ethos through its powerful ritual and symbolic world that stretches into eternity but is rooted in a dynamic present. This offers a way of grounding the theological vision of *koinōnia* that both theologians share.

I have noted many times that the strength of Zizioulas's theology is precisely his holistic theological vision. The power of his whole theological system is able to be brought to bear on every issue. Johnson, however, as I observed with respect to her ecological theology, does not always seem to draw on the full potential of her whole theological vision.[37] Johnson's strength, by contrast, is her holistic view of the world. She situates her theology within a much more rigorous and complete view of contemporary realities than Zizioulas does. She acknowledges, for instance, the links between the ecological crises and other major contemporary crises. She connects the blight of injustice toward the earth with all injustices and endemic suffering in the world. Both these approaches are vitally important.

These two contrasting observations concerning the broad contours of these two theologians' work lead to an obvious third observation, which is that regardless of each one's significant personal gifts and insights as a theologian, it is abundantly clear that the theological vision of both have been radically shaped by the strengths and weaknesses of the traditions within which they have been formed and educated. One is grounded primarily, but not exclusively, in history and the *Economia*, the other primarily, but not exclusively, in the eschaton and *Theologia*. This research has demonstrated the necessity of drawing from the wisdom of both these major traditions if the fullness of the Christian tradition is to be received and re-received by the whole Church for the world.

In the final chapter I will draw from the strengths of these two Trinitarian theologies, from East and West, from female and male perspectives, to propose some directions for a constructive contribution toward a retrieval of the triune symbol.

---

[37] See also my reference to Johnson's work on mariology providing a possible fruitful source for the use of female images of God in Chapter 5.

CHAPTER 12

Toward a Constructive Retrieval
of the Symbol of the Triune God

Here is a teaching that is new . . . (Mark 1:27).

*Desire and reason work in unison once you've caught some
glimpse of the Reality that is seeing you. And this is wisdom.*[1]

The revelation of the God proclaimed by Jesus of Nazareth was
indeed "a teaching that is new." Former categories for understanding
divinity were exploded by the God revealed to those initiated into the
life of the early Christian communities. Here it was claimed that the
great, personal, and saving God of Israel had become irrevocably joined
with humanity in the person of Jesus and continues to be present in the
risen Christ through the power of the Spirit. It was believed that in
Christ all creation is destined for eternity by being drawn into the communion of God's own life.

It took four centuries for Christians to formulate this new teaching
about God into doctrinal language that was congruent with the philosophy of the Greco-Roman cultures within which Christianity first
developed. Christian theology today is seeking to return to this ancient
and ever-new teaching of the triune God. It is seeking to discover what
this central Christian symbol can mean for humanity and creation in

---

[1] Robert Dessaix, *Night Letters: A Journey through Switzerland and Italy,* ed. Igor
Miazmov (Sydney: Picador, Pan Macmillan, 1997) 263. Dessaix is here "translating"
from Dante's *Paradiso.*

this era. It is seeking to retrieve and communicate the "otherness" of the triune God that still shatters the idolatrous boundaries of humanity's limited constructs about who God is. Christians today inherit new understandings about the nature of "relation" and "person" and a new, thrilling and still-unfolding story of the origins and nature of the cosmos. Dialogue with those new insights ensures that the triune symbol functions in fresh ways to reveal truths about the God of Jesus Christ and that the reception of Trinitarian doctrine of God continues to occur in these times.

In this final chapter I bring together some key elements that emerge from this mutually critical correlation of the work of two contemporary Trinitarian theologians. I begin by identifying elements that I believe must be taken into account within a method for the retrieval of the symbol of the triune God. I then identify six theological strands that also need to be taken into account if the power of this symbol is to be able to be tapped in all its fullness.

Key Elements of a Method for a Retrieval of the Symbol of the Trinity

The mutually critical correlation of the Trinitarian theologies of Elizabeth Johnson and John Zizioulas has confirmed that any authentic future Christian theology of God must include in its methodology explicit efforts to bridge the divide between the living traditions of the East and the West. The preceding chapters illustrate very clearly that if this does not occur, only part of the revelatory wisdom of the Christian symbol of God can be accessed. When both traditions are brought into dialogue, theology can begin to communicate more of the fullness and the depth of the God revealed within the Christian story and of the ways that humanity and all of creation are drawn into relation with this God.

A second essential element is that such a methodology must ensure that women's voices are heard along with men's. In this book I have argued that the methodology of feminist theology needs to be taken into account for any authentic retrieval of the triune symbol of God to occur in these times. That claim is based on a now commonly owned awareness that the Christian theology of God has been dominated for centuries by exclusively male images of an all-powerful, almighty God and that this idolatrous limitation in thought and worship about God has been damaging for all humanity and especially for women. As Karl Rahner has observed, "The true radicalism in the doctrine of God can only be a continual destruction of an idol, an idol in the place of God, the idol of a theory about God."[2] Feminist theological methods of critique, historical retrieval and theological construction insist that new interpretations of symbols for God must be forged in relationship with the experience of women and other excluded groups. They must be tested to ensure that they lead to transformation and not oppression. I am proposing that fidelity to the full divinity of God, to the full humanity of all peoples, and to the integrity of creation requires adherence to the basic components of this method.

More recently another constituent has been offered as an important addition to feminist method. That is the call to harness difference explicitly as an ally rather than to treat it as a threat.[3] That factor has proved an important component of this work of retrieval. Specifically, the challenge to me as a woman formed within the Western tradition has been "to engage difference in the work towards authentic solidarity in word and deed."[4] In my work of a feminist retrieval of the Trinity, that challenge has found expression in my engaging not only with the feminist theology of Elizabeth Johnson but also with the work of a male Orthodox theologian. That quest has involved a preparedness to honor John Zizioulas's theological vision while challenging its failure to acknowledge or address many of the central concerns of feminist theology. It has required a preparedness to be challenged in turn by a rich and vibrant Christian religious vision that is radically different from that of the West. Zizioulas himself, whether unwittingly or not, is in strong agreement with this methodological option when he identifies "fear of the other" and "fear of otherness" as a critical issue of our times. It is his Orthodox Trinitarian vision that makes him a powerful advocate of the need to espouse the redemptive ethic of "difference in communion."[5] His work demonstrates the need for this component to be included in a theological method for retrieving the doctrine of the Trinity.

---

[2] Karl Rahner, "Observations on the Doctrine of God in Catholic Dogmatics," *Theological Investigations* 9, trans. Graham Harrison (New York: Herder and Herder, 1972) 127. Quoted in Anne Carr, *Transforming Grace: Christian Tradition and Women's Experience* (San Francisco: Harper & Row, 1988) 141.

[3] See Chapter 1, where I refer to the contribution of womanist theologian Shawn Copeland. It should be noted, however, that other women theologians—Mujeristas, Asian women, African women, Latinas, lesbian feminists, Jewish feminists—have also sought to harness difference as an ally in their contributions toward an inclusive theological vision wherein all persons can find a home.

[4] M. Shawn Copeland, "Towards a Critical Feminist Theology of Solidarity," in *Women and Theology,* ed. Mary Ann Hinsdale and Phyllis H. Kaminski (Maryknoll, N.Y.: Orbis Books, 1995) 11.

[5] See Pergamon, "Communion and Otherness," *St. Vladimir's Theological Quarterly* 38, no. 4 (1994).

Finally, besides ensuring that a methodology for Trinitarian theology seeks to draw from the wisdom of the whole Christian tradition and from the voices of the whole of humanity in a way that embraces and celebrates difference, the correlation of Johnson's and Zizioulas's methodologies illustrates that both theology "from above" (a theology that begins with the tradition) and theology "from below" (a theology that begins with critical issues of humanity and creation) offer perspectives that are essential for a recovery of the triune symbol of God. Clearly, a particular theologian will choose to begin from one or the other place, and my own preference is to begin from experience. I am arguing, however, that both perspectives need to be taken into account.

Strands for a Reweaving of the Symbol of the Triune God

A mutually critical correlation of the Trinitarian theologies of Elizabeth Johnson and John Zizioulas suggests some essential components for a constructive retrieval of the symbol of the triune God. In this section I identify six strands that I believe need to be taken into account within a constructive theology of the Trinity.

1. *Divine* Koinōnia:
The Trinitarian God as Persons in Communion

The current pursuit of the meanings and implications of other related concepts such as "relationality," "difference," and "otherness" is part of the quest that Zizioulas identifies as an "existential preoccupation" on the part of contemporary humanity with the concept of person.[6] The current focus on the concept of person provides a significant entry point for a theology of the triune symbol to be brought into dialogue with contemporary quests for meaning.

The origins of Trinitarian formulation of God as three persons in mutual and equal relation recovers a key understanding that the being of God is communion. That is a foundational insight that needs to be at the center of any reclaiming of the Trinity. It addresses the problematic of Western theology which speaks of God's being as a "substance" and which has served over the centuries to communicate that God is remote from the concerns of humanity. Contemplating God's *being as*

---

[6] See, for example, David Tracy, "The Hidden God: The Divine Other of Liberation," *Cross Currents* 46, no. 1 (1996) and the whole edition of *Feminist Theology* 14 (January 1997). For an extensive bibliography on this issue, see Elaine Graham, *Making the Difference: Gender, Personhood and Theology* (Minneapolis: Fortress Press, 1996) 232–54.

communion opens up understandings of the ecstatic and hypostatic dimensions of the concept of person and anchors those dimensions of person in God's very self. This wisdom from the tradition that the being of God is a communion of persons reinforces and deepens the contemporary "discovery" that to live fully as a unique person in relation means living a life of inclusive communion with other persons and with all created entities.

In a complementary way, contemporary understandings of personhood serve to unlock aspects of traditional teaching of the Trinitarian mystery that have not been available to earlier generations. New construals of the meaning of "person" as essentially relational and interpersonal release powerful new dimensions of the triune symbol. The pedagogical principle that one can receive only according to one's capacity for reception comes into play here. Humanity has come to grasp through experience and research, and through listening to women's voices as well as men's, that to be a person is to be in relation and that the uniqueness of individual persons can best come to fruition through creative collaboration and communion with persons who are different from oneself. Because of those insights, the immensity of the mystery of God as a trinity of persons has begun to be revelatory in new and liberating ways. Contemporary studies and understandings of the nature of personhood enable a more complete and nuanced "reception" of this doctrine of God than has ever been possible before.

The symbol of God as "persons in communion" communicates not only the strong biblical teaching that God is personal but also that to be a person is to be in dynamic mutual relation with other persons and entities. By providing an image of different persons in communion, it gives witness to the fact that uniqueness flourishes within a true community of mutual relationships. When God is imaged as "persons in communion," the teaching that women and men are made in the image of God acquires new depths that can nurture the full dignity and humanity of all persons. God imaged as "persons in communion" thus has the potential to function as a powerful symbol of hope for human beings who struggle to understand what it means to be a person and to find ways to live together in this global village. It is a vital element for a retrieval of the triune symbol for our times.

2. *The Names and Ordering of the Trinitarian Symbol*

God's absolute otherness ensures that any name used for God has, by necessity, only a limited currency. If idolatry is to be avoided and if human persons are to be open to the full revelation of who God can be for humanity and the whole of creation, many names are essential. I began this research with the conviction that any serious retrieval of the triune God can properly occur only when the male imagery that has been used exclusively of the triune God for nearly two thousand years is acknowledged as problematic and is addressed. Elizabeth Johnson's work and that of other feminist theologians have confirmed this premise and have pointed to the related necessity of addressing the problem of the fixed hierarchical expression of the ordering of the symbol.[7] Given the nature of the triune symbol, both of these need to be addressed together.

A central and much-valued teaching about God from within the Judeo-Christian tradition is that God relates to all that is created in a personal way. Even though a plethora of images from all kinds of genres of discourse have been used to convey something of the truth about God, personal images have always been particularly prized. It is for that reason that feminist theology points to equivalent use of female and male images as an ideal for speech about God. However, as Johnson points out, because of the stronghold of exclusive male imagery within Christian theology and worship, there needs to be an extended time for using predominantly female images even to begin to restore the balance.[8] This work of initiating and enabling the use of female images of God is a work not only for theologians but also for liturgists, poets, musicians, songwriters, visual artists, architects, preachers, teachers, journalists, bishops, priests, ministers of every kind. The task of ensuring that female imagery for God can be used creatively to nurture faith in a God who is communion is a delicate and complex one. Therefore, if the triune symbol is to be restored, every source that nourishes and shapes the Christian imagination and popular devotion will have to be fully harnessed to bring about the transformation needed.

Because naming the three persons must be congruent with the biblical witness and communicate their relation of origin with each other, the further task of using many names for the Trinity poses particular difficulties. Johnson's feminist theology of the Trinity tackles this challenge very directly. Her renaming of God as SHE WHO IS and her renaming and reordering of the divine persons as Spirit-Sophia, Jesus-Sophia, and Mother-Sophia contribute an innovative and constructive proposal based on an authentic re-reading of the tradition. Her work in reclaiming christology and pneumatology provides a firm theological basis for this enterprise. I believe that Johnson's proposal of the name Jesus-Sophia constitutes a particularly important breakthrough in Trinitarian theology. That name frees the Christ figure from its male

---

[7] See Chapter 7.
[8] See Chapter 5.

loading while opening up the rich lode of female and wisdom sources. The implications of that image have scarcely begun to be tapped. Its theological bases need to be explored further while it is introduced into liturgical and devotional practice.

The problem of the ordering of the Trinity is related to the issue of an exclusive male naming of the symbol and has served to enshrine an implicit Trinitarian hierarchy. Johnson's remedy is that all the various Scriptural patterns of Trinitarian order need to be harnessed along with the classic ordering if the Holy Mystery of the triune God is to be expressed in ways that do not distort a central truth of the doctrine. An ordering that begins with the Spirit and an ordering that places the Spirit after the unoriginate Origin but before the Christs also needs to be used. Not only does this begin to restore significance to the Holy Spirit, it also ensures that the structure used for naming the Trinity does not impede the prophetic teaching on the equal and mutual relationships within the *koinōnia* of the triune God. As we have seen, Johnson herself translated this insight into the method she adopted for her Trinitarian theology. In the constructive work of retrieving the triune symbol, there is a great deal more in this approach that needs to be explored.[9]

While serious and sustained theological work needs to continue in this arena of renaming and reordering the symbol of the Trinity, there is opportunity now to begin to apply many names for God in liturgical and devotional practice. The stranglehold usage of exclusive God-He images has partly been broken. People with many different gifts are beginning to speak, sing, and image God as God-She and God-Three. The restoration of the power of the Trinity as a symbol of inclusive communion between persons has begun.

3. A Redefinition of Divine Omnipotence: A Triune God Who Suffers

Instant and global communication has brought to light one of the major challenges to theology in this century: the massive and acute presence of suffering in the world. The task of revisioning religious symbols must take this into account. For many, the all-powerful, monarchical God who for centuries has dominated Christian theology and devotion is "dead." The image of God as a spectator to suffering simply does not ring true with the God of compassionate love revealed in the Hebrew Scriptures nor with the God revealed by the life, death, and resurrection of Jesus of Nazareth. The image of an impassible God

---

[9] See Elizabeth Johnson, "Review Symposium: Author's Response," *Horizons* 20 (1993) 344.

that enshrines unilateral power as an ultimate goal and derides vulnerability as weakness and imperfection has begun to be replaced by images of a God of relational power that are congruent with scriptural and doctrinal witness. A restored contemporary Trinitarian theology holds that the touchstone against which to test every image is the dynamic *koinōnia* of love between the divine persons at the heart of the triune symbol. That in turn has led to the need for a resymbolization of divine power as relational power.

Relational power stands in direct contrast to the unilateral power communicated by the omnipotent God of classical theism. It is founded on the liberating strength that emanates from the free capacity to choose to become vulnerable in order to sustain a mutual loving relationship—"the liberating power of connectedness that is effective in compassionate love."[10] That is the power revealed by a Trinitarian God of mutual relations whose very being is communion. It is not a power that has to control; it is a power that emanates from persons who are free to love. It is free to be vulnerable to the limits of the other and to let new life come into being as it will. It is a power that is free enough to enter into suffering. Since love entails suffering, a retrieval of the symbol of the triune God who is Love must include images of a God who suffers.

To speak of a suffering God totally subverts the patriarchal image of perfection and the consequent ideal of unilateral power. It communicates that self-containment and the absence of relationship do not represent an ideal but rather signify imperfection. Omnipotence can thus be redefined as the free, unlimited capacity to make room within the self for the other. This evocative image of making room within oneself for another is one of the reasons that Elizabeth Johnson proposes that the name Mother-Sophia provides an appropriate alternative to the exclusive naming of Father for one of the Trinitarian persons. This redefinition of omnipotence also leads her to propose that the Trinitarian God be called "Suffering God: Compassion Poured Out." All the above insights toward a redefinition of power are congruent with the scriptural revelation of God. They need to be pressed into service if the energy of the triune symbol of God is to be fully released in this era.

4. *The Trinity as a Unifying Symbol Within a Whole Theological System*

The pneumatologies of both Johnson and Zizioulas uncover what can happen when the Holy Spirit is restored to her rightful place in theology and praxis. When a vibrant theology of the Holy Spirit is in

---

[10] Johnson, *SHE WHO IS*, 270.

place, the symbol of God is transformed for believers: the "neglected" person of the Trinity is acknowledged as God experienced both as presence and absence in all of life and is recognized to be not only the strength that assists the Christian to live in the manner of Jesus but also an event of communion who is constantly opening reality to become relational. Similarly, when christology is not confined to the male historical Jesus and to the preexistent One but includes the *eschaton*, the *whole* Christ comes into focus. In this image divinity and creation are shown to be reconciled, to coexist as one for eternity, and the triune symbol becomes a living symbol of profound hope.

However, a theology of the Trinity requires not only a truly lifegiving theology of the Holy Spirit and a theology of the Christ that includes the essential wisdom of these mysteries from both West and East. It also requires that they be held in mutual and creative tension with one another. Only *in relation* can these symbols become what they are and be fully effective in communicating Divine Mystery. Christology conditions pneumatology and vice-versa. Both are conditioned by eschatology, and both are essential for ecclesiology and sacramental theology. Trinitarian theology thus becomes the matrix of the whole theological system.

The purpose of applying this principle is not simply to achieve some intellectual satisfaction that comes from the depth and coherence of an ordered theological system. Rather, Zizioulas's work convincingly demonstrates that applying this principle has critical practical and pastoral consequences. He shows, for instance, that as long as the relationship between pneumatology and christology remains in imbalance or the links between the economy and the eschaton are out of kilter, attempts to heal the profound divisions between Christians will be continually frustrated.[11] Moreover, the structures of the Christian Churches will remain fossilized, and the fullness of the triune Mystery of God will not be able to be offered and received by God's people. The destructive centralism that is presently such a feature of Roman Catholicism, for example, will not be able to be remedied until a theology of the Holy Spirit which values the many gifts that constitute an event of communion is restored to its proper place and can bring balance to the present overemphasis on the unity of the one Christ.

This essential and synthesizing insight suggests that in the case of the triune symbol of God, relationality is both the medium and the message. That principle needs to be applied within the Churches if the Trinitarian symbol is to be able to function in a transforming and enduring way that is truly liberating for the people of God.

[11] See Chapter 4.

5. *God as Communion: A Call for the Church to Be* Koinōnia

If a symbol is to be able to exercise transforming power, it must be able to become a living symbol. A symbol exercises its primary power, not by being spoken of as an ideal or through doctrine recorded in theological manuals, but in life. For that reason the doxological theology and practice of the Eastern Church have much to offer to a contemporary reclaiming of the triune symbol. That theology holds that it is through relating to the three persons that the believer can best come to know the mystery of the one God as a dynamic communion of persons in relationship. For the Orthodox believer, coming to know God is understood to include becoming one with God. That process of divinization (*theōsis*) is not a body of catechetical knowledge to be learned but an event, a work of the Holy Spirit. It is a transforming process into which the Christian is invited to enter ever more deeply throughout a lifetime.

The ritual initiation of the sacraments of baptism, confirmation, and Eucharist provides a powerful symbolic enactment of how this process is begun. Baptism takes place in the name of each of the persons of the Trinity, and Christian life is depicted as a participation in the dying and rising of Christ. It is being born anew through water and through the power of the Holy Spirit. Confirmation gives emphasis to the Spirit ever at work to renew and to create events of communion within daily life. In the Eucharist, in and with and through the one Body of Christ, the believer becomes, through the power of the Spirit, one with God, the Source of all life to whom all creation is inexorably drawn. The believer is invited into relationship with each of the persons of the Trinity throughout this initiation. And it is in the eucharistic celebration that the fullness of the eschatological future meets and shapes the Christian's experience of incompletion in the historical present. The weekly rhythm of gathering for Eucharist acts like a heartbeat at the center of life. Engaging with the persons of the Trinity is thus intrinsically related to the believer's ongoing life in the world.

A recovery of this strand as part of the rehabilitation of the triune symbol has huge pastoral implications. It implies that if the symbol of the Trinity is to be retrieved, the potential of the liturgical and community life of the Churches will need to be harnessed in full. In the West, it signals that the emergence of basic ecclesial communities as an "event of communion" and a gift of the Spirit in our times needs to be connected with the restored rites of sacramental initiation and a vibrant liturgy. In the East, the liturgy needs to spill over much more explicitly into a transforming action in the world that builds community and connections with all creation. If this were to happen, the Church would truly become a medium for a primary experience of the living God. The believer would come to experience the Church as *koinōnia* and to "know" God as persons in communion.

For the symbol of the Trinity to be retrieved in these times, the Christian Churches locally and universally will need to be impelled by this call to divinization: to become as God is, namely, Difference in Communion. That offers a massive challenge to a Church which is still essentially patriarchal and which excludes the mutual participation of women and the non-ordained. Where the Church's identity, structure, and mission are experienced as relational, collaborative, respectful and celebrative of equality and difference, there God is already being received and known as "persons in communion." A restored theology of the triune God is not enough. It will not lead to a retrieval of this symbol. It must be put into practice. The Church must become *koinōnia*.[12]

6. *The Triune Symbol as Source of a Transforming Ethos and Ethic*

If the triune symbol is to be a living symbol of God, not only must the Church mirror the *koinonia* of Godself in its way of being Church but the triune symbol must also be brought into active engagement with the issues of the world and of our times. The work of both Zizioulas and Johnson provides examples of how this can be done.

Participation in the liturgy celebrated at the heart of the ecclesial community can initiate a person not only into an authentic relating to the three persons of the Trinity but also to the "other" in the community and in creation. Those relationships, in turn, shape behavior. When creation is celebrated as an expression of God's very self, the air, the earth, the rivers, the seas, and all living species are treated differently. When people become part of a living community in which relationships are built and valued and in which links between creation and humanity and between present and future are recognized and celebrated, a culture and an ethos have begun to be forged. Persons are brought into dynamic relationship with the three persons in God, a salvific encounter occurs, and the symbol's transforming power is released. In that way the symbol ceases to be an inert doctrine within a credal formula—it becomes a source of life.

A compelling vision of the triune God situated within a contemporary cosmology also provides a significant alternative to the hierarchical dualism of modernity. A vision of Holy Mystery such as the one

---

[12] See Elizabeth Johnson, *Friends of God and Prophets: A Feminist Theological Reading of the Communion of Saints* (New York: Crossroad, 1998).

offered by Elizabeth Johnson signals that women with men are in the image of God and that all creation is of immense value and communicates something of God's very being. Inclusive imagings of God that are faithful to biblical witness and tradition provide a holy space that is truly redemptive for all, a space where the poorest and those who are considered "different" can be at home. An authentic imaging of God as Communion invites each person into relationship and collaboration with her triune self who is mercy, and inexorably challenges the believer toward an ethic and action on behalf of all peoples who suffer injustice and on behalf of the Earth itself.

Such inclusive imaging places the Trinitarian symbol at the center of an ethos that effects transforming action. It both facilitates the participation of believers within God's life and within the human community and provides the basis for a truly Christian ethic and praxis. Reflection on experience within communities so formed in turn reveals that the reverse is also true. When such an ethic is lived out and people are empowered to transform human society according to God's image, persons *in so doing* are drawn into a living communion with God's very self. Engaging in praxis that promotes communion leads to relationship with, and knowledge of, the One who is Divine *Koinōnia*—Three-Personed God.

Conclusion

I have described six strands that I believe are essential for any constructive retrieval of the symbol of the triune God. As is evident, some of these strands need further work from theologians, and most need to be engaged by the full spectrum of God's people. Each is woven from many other strands; none of them exists alone. They are all intrinsically interrelated and together point to a new synthesis. Based on a re-reading of the tradition, they suggest inclusive names and alternative orderings for the divine persons, so that Christians are called beyond the set forms of the symbol to encounter Godself. They speak of the one Holy Trinity who needs to be named by many names, of a triune God who could be called Divine *Koinōnia:* Three-Personed God, God as Communion.

These strands give witness to a Trinitarian God who continues to be revealed within the doxology and praxis of the ecclesial community as well as within the lives and prayer of prophets and of all who are "friends of God." They suggest a God of persons-in-communion, whose imprint of interconnectedness and relation is clearly marked within the very fabric of the universe. They ensure the transcendence and "otherness" of God by stretching human imagination well beyond all safe boundaries of definition and into the realm of "not-knowing." Furthermore, they show that the triune symbol of God can become a profound symbol of hope for a world searching for meaning and direction. A weaving of these strands suggests a synthesis that gives witness to the Holy Trinity, who, while remaining totally "other," is also a personal God of compassion who relentlessly pursues those who search for meaning, freedom, and truth and who invites them to become partners in transforming communion *(theōsis)*.

This search leads me to conclude that the ancient symbol of the Trinity, held for so long at the center of Christian life and worship, is a symbol whose time has finally come. It is only in these times that humanity has been able to glimpse the full implications of the intrinsically relational nature of personhood and creation, the interconnectedness of all the entities of the universe, and the potential of difference in communion. It is only in these times that planet Earth has become "small enough," through global communication, for its peoples to be confronted with the urgency of the need for all the varied cultures and traditions to learn from one another and for women's voices to be heard equally with men's. Only in these times has it become apparent that if humanity is to have any future at all, women and men must heed the imperative to be in relation, in communion, with one another and with everything in the universe. I believe that those interlocking factors enable Christians today, in a way never before possible in our history, to "receive" more fully this Christian teaching that is new: that God is revealed as a three-personed God of Compassion whose very being is communion.

Select Bibliography

Books

Baillargeon, Gaëtan. *Perspectives Orthodoxes sur L'Eglise-Communion: L'oeuvre de Jean Zizioulas.* Montréal: L'Editions Paulines, 1989.

Best, Thomas F., and Gunther Gassman, eds. *On the Way to Fuller Koinonia: Official Report of the Fifth World Conference of Faith and Order.* Geneva: World Council of Churches Publications, 1994.

Boff, Leonardo. *Church, Charism and Power: Liberation Theology and the Institutional Church.* Trans. J. W. Dierckmeier. New York: Crossroad, 1985.

_____. *Trinity and Society.* Maryknoll, N.Y.: Orbis Books, 1988.

Borresen, Kari. *Subordination and Equivalence: The Nature and Role of Women in Augustine and Thomas Aquinas.* Washington: University Press of America, 1981.

_____, ed. *The Image of God: Gender Models in Judeo-Christian Tradition.* Minneapolis: Fortress Press, 1991.

Bracken, Joseph. *What Are They Saying About the Trinity?* New York: Paulist Press, 1979.

Brock, Rita N. *Journeys by Heart: A Christology of Erotic Power.* New York: Crossroad, 1988.

Bulgakov, Sergius. *Sophia, The Wisdom of God: An Outline of Sophiology.* Hudson, N.Y.: Lindisfarne Press, 1993.

Carr, Anne E. *Transforming Grace: Christian Tradition and Women's Experience.* San Francisco: Harper & Row, 1988.

Case-Winters, Anna. *God's Power: Traditional Understandings and Contemporary Challenges.* Louisville: Westminster/John Knox Press, 1990.

Chittister, Joan. *Job's Daughters: Women and Power.* New York: Paulist Press, 1990.

Chopp, Rebecca S. *The Power to Speak: Feminism, Language, God.* New York: Crossroad, 1991.

Chung, Hyun Kyung. *Struggle to be the Sun Again: Introducing Asian Women's Theology.* Maryknoll, N.Y.: Orbis Books, 1990.

Congar, Yves. *I Believe in the Holy Spirit.* 3 vols. Trans. David Smith. New York: Seabury Press, 1983.

Daly, Mary. *Beyond God the Father: Toward a Philosophy of Women's Liberation.* Boston: Beacon Press, 1973.

Davis, Stephen, Daniel Kendall, and Gerald Collins, eds. *The Trinity.* Oxford: Oxford University Press, 1999.

Dickey Young, Pamela. *Feminist Theology/Christian Theology: In Search of a Method.* Minneapolis: Fortress Press, 1990.

Duck, Ruth C. *Gender and the Name of God: The Trinitarian Baptismal Formula.* New York: The Pilgrim Press, 1991.

Edwards, Denis. *Jesus the Wisdom of God: An Ecological Theology.* New York: Orbis Books, 1995.

Farley, Margaret A. *Personal Commitments: Beginning, Keeping, Changing.* San Francisco: Harper & Row, 1986.

Gebara, Ivone. *Trinidade, Palavra sobre Coisas Velhas e Novas: Una Perspectiva Ecofeminista.* Sao Paulo: Paulinas, 1994.

Gilson, Etienne. *The Spirit of Medieval Philosophy.* New York: Scribner's, 1940.

Goldenburg, Naomi. *The Changing of Gods: Feminism and the End of Traditional Religions.* Boston: Beacon Press, 1979.

Graff, Ann O'Hara. *In the Embrace of God: Feminist Approaches to Theological Anthropology.* Maryknoll, N.Y.: Orbis Books, 1995.

Graham, Elaine. *Making the Difference: Gender, Personhood and Theology.* Minneapolis: Fortress Press, 1996.

Hampson, Daphne. *Theology and Feminism.* Oxford: Blackwell, 1990.

Harrison, Beverley Wildung. *Making the Connections: Essays in Feminist Social Ethics.* Boston: Beacon Press, 1985.

Hartshorne, Charles. *The Divine Relativity: A Social Conception of God.* New Haven: Yale University Press, 1948.

Heywood, Carter. *The Redemption of God: A Theology of Mutual Relation.* Washington: University Press of America, 1982.

Hill, William. *The Three-Personed God: The Trinity as a Mystery of Salvation.* Washington: Catholic University of America Press, 1982.

Hinsdale, Mary Ann, and Phyllis H. Kaminski, eds. *Women and Theology: The Annual Publication of the College Theology Society, 1994.* Maryknoll, N.Y.: Orbis Books, 1995.

Hopkins, Julie M. *Towards a Feminist Christology: Jesus of Nazareth, European Women and the Christological Crisis.* Grand Rapids, Mich.: Wm. B. Eerdmans, 1995.

Hunt, Mary E. *Fierce Tenderness: A Feminist Theology of Friendship.* New York: Crossroad, 1992.

Jantzen, Grace M. *Power, Gender and Christian Mysticism.* Cambridge: Cambridge University Press, 1995.

Jenson, Robert W. *The Triune Identity: God According to the Gospel.* Philadelphia: Fortress Press, 1982.

Johnson, Elizabeth A. *Consider Jesus: Waves of Renewal in Christology.* New York: Crossroad, 1990.

_____. *Friends of God and Prophets: A Feminist Theological Reading of the Communion of Saints.* New York: Continuum, 1998.

_____. *SHE WHO IS: The Mystery of God in Feminist Theological Discourse.* New York: Crossroad, 1992.

_____. *Women, Earth and Creator Spirit.* New York: Paulist Press, 1993.

Jungel, Eberhard. *God as the Mystery of the World.* Trans. Darrell Guder. Grand Rapids, Mich.: Wm. B. Eerdmans, 1983.

Kasper, Walter. *The God of Jesus Christ.* Trans. Matthew J. O'Connell. New York: Crossroad, 1991.

Kelly, Anthony. *The Trinity of Love.* Wilmington, Del.: Michael Glazier, 1989.

————. *An Expanding Theology: Faith in a World of Connections.* Newtown, Australia: E. J. Dwyer, 1993.

Kelly, J. N. D. *Early Christian Doctrines.* San Francisco: Harper & Row, 1978.

Kim, C. W. Maggie, Susan M. St. Ville, Susan M. Simonaitis, eds. *Transfigurations: Theology and the French Feminists.* Minneapolis: Fortress Press, 1993.

King, Ursula, ed. *Feminist Theology from the Third World: A Reader.* New York: Orbis Books, 1994.

LaCugna, Catherine Mowry. *God for Us: The Trinity and Christian Life.* New York: HarperSanFrancisco, 1991.

————, ed. *Freeing Theology: The Essentials of Theology in Feminist Perspective.* New York: HarperSanFrancisco, 1993.

Lash, Nicholas. *Believing Three Ways in One God.* London: SCM Press, 1992.

Mackey, James P. *The Christian Experience of God.* London: SCM Press, 1983.

May, Melanie A., ed. *Women and Church: The Challenge of Ecumenical Solidarity in an Age of Alienation.* New York: Eerdmans Publishing Co. and Friendship Press, 1991.

McFague, Sallie. *Models of God: Theology for an Ecological, NuclearAge.* London: SCM Press, 1987.

————. *The Body of God: An Ecological Theology.* Minneapolis: Fortress Press, 1993.

McGinn, B., J. Meyendorff, and J. Leclerq, eds. *Christian Spirituality: Origins to the Twelfth Century.* New York: Crossroad, 1986.

McPartlan, Paul. *The Eucharist Makes the Church: Henri de Lubac and John Zizioulas Dialogue.* Edinburgh: T&T Clark, 1993.

Moltmann, Jürgen. *The Crucified God: The Cross of Christ as the Foundation and Criticism of Christian Theology.* Trans. R. A. Wilson and John Bowden. New York: Harper & Row, 1973.

————. *History and the Triune God.* New York: Crossroad, 1992.

————. *The Trinity and the Kingdom of God.* New York: Harper & Row, 1981.

O'Donnell, John. *The Mystery of the Triune God.* London: Sheed & Ward, 1988.

Peacocke, A. R. *Creation and the World of Science.* The Bampton Lectures 1978. Oxford: Clarendon Press, 1979.

Rahner, Karl. *The Trinity.* Trans. Joseph Donceel. London: Burns & Oates, 1970.

Ramshaw, Gail. *God Beyond Gender: Feminist Christian God-Language.* Minneapolis: Fortress Press, 1995.

Reid, Duncan. *Energies of the Spirit: Trinitarian Models in Eastern Orthodox and Western Theology.* Atlanta: Scholars Press, 1997.

Ruether, Rosemary Radford. *Gaia and God: An Ecofeminist Theology of Earth Healing.* San Francisco: HarperCollins, 1992.

————. *New Woman, New Earth: Sexist Ideologies and Human Liberation.* New York: Seabury Press, 1975.

_____. *Sexism and God-Talk: Toward a Feminist Theology.* Boston: Beacon Press, 1983.

_____, ed. *Women Healing Earth: Third World Women on Ecology, Feminism, and Religion.* London: SCM Press, 1996.

Russell, Letty. *The Future of Partnership.* Philadelphia: Westminster Press, 1979.

Russell, Letty, and J. Shannon Clarkson, eds. *Dictionary of Feminist Theologies.* Louisville, Ky.: Westminster John Knox Press, 1996.

Saliers, Don E. *Worship as Theology: Foretaste of Glory Divine.* Nashville: Abingdon Press, 1994.

Schaff, Philip, and Henry Wace, eds. *A Select Library of Nicene and Post-Nicene Fathers of the Christian Church.* Volume 7: *S. Cyril of Jerusalem, S. Gregory Nazianzen.* Reprint 1978. Grand Rapids, Mich.: Wm. B. Eerdmans, 1893.

_____. *A Select Library of Nicene and Post-Nicene Fathers of the Christian Church.* Volume 8: *St. Basil: Letters and Select Works.* Reprint 1978. Grand Rapids, Mich.: Wm. B. Eerdmans, 1893.

Schillebeeckx, Edward. *Church: The Human Story of God.* New York: Crossroad, 1991.

Schneiders, Sandra. *Women and the Word: The Gender of God in the New Testament and the Spirituality of Women.* New York-Mahwah, N.J.: Paulist Press, 1986.

Schüssler Fiorenza, Elisabeth. *But She Said: Feminist Practices of Biblical Interpretation.* Boston: Beacon Press, 1992.

_____. *Jesus: Miriam's Child, Sophia's Prophet: Critical Issues in Feminist Theology.* New York: Continuum, 1994.

_____. *In Memory of Her: A Feminist Theological Reconstruction of Christian Origins.* New York: Crossroad, 1983.

_____, ed. *The Power of Naming: A Concilium Reader in Feminist Liberation Theology.* Maryknoll, N.Y.: Orbis Books, 1996.

Schüssler Fiorenza, Francis, and John P. Galvin, eds. *Systematic Theology: Roman Catholic Perspectives.* Volumes 1 and 2. Minneapolis: Fortress Press, 1991.

Studer, Basil. *Trinity and Incarnation: The Faith of the Early Church.* Collegeville, Minn.: The Liturgical Press, 1993.

Torrance, Alan J. *Persons in Communion: An Essay on Trinitarian Description and Human Participation.* Edinburgh: T&T Clark, 1996.

Torrance, Thomas F. *The Christian Doctrine of God, One Being Three Persons.* Edinburgh: T&T Clark, 1996.

Tracy, David. *The Analogical Imagination: Christian Theology and the Culture of Pluralism.* New York: Crossroad, 1991.

_____. *Blessed Rage for Order: The New Pluralism in Theology.* New York: Crossroad, 1975.

Volf, Miroslav. *After Our Likeness: The Church as the Image of the Trinity.* Grand Rapids-Cambridge: Wm. B. Eerdmans, 1998.

Wilson-Kastner, Patricia. *Faith, Feminism and the Christ.* Philadelphia: Fortress Press, 1983.

Zizioulas, John D. *Being As Communion: Studies in Personhood and the Church.* New York: St. Vladimir's Press, 1985.

_____. *L'Etre Ecclesial.* Geneva: Labor et Fides, 1981.

(Zizioulas) De Pergame, Jean. *L'Eucharistie, l'evêque et l'Eglise durant les trois premiers siècles.* Trans. Jean-Louis Parlierne. Paris: Theophanie, Desclee de Brouwer, 1994.

Articles

Allik, Tiina. "Human Finitude and the Concept of Women's Experience." *Modern Theology* 9, no. 1 (January 1993) 67–85.

Borresen, Kari Elisabeth. "Women's Studies of the Christian Tradition: New Perspectives." In *Religion and Gender.* Ed. Ursula King, 245–55. Oxford, U.K.: Blackwell, 1995.

Bynum, Caroline Walker. "Did the Twelfth Century Discover the Individual?" In *Jesus as Mother: Studies in Spirituality of the High Middle Ages.* Berkeley, Calif.: University of California Press, 1982.

Carr, Anne. "The New Vision of Feminist Theology." In *Freeing Theology: The Essentials of Theology in Feminist Perspective.* Ed. Catherine LaCugna, 5–29. San Francisco: HarperSanFrancisco, 1993.

Clark, Mary T. "An Inquiry into Personhood." *Review of Metaphysics* 46 (1992) 3–28.

Collins, Mary. "Naming God in Public Prayer." *Worship* 59 (1985) 291–304.

Cooke, Bernard. "Non-Patriarchal Salvation." *Horizons* 10, no. 1 (1983) 22–31.

Daggers, Jenny. "Luce Irigaray and 'Divine Women': A Resource for Postmodern Feminist Theology." *Feminist Theology* 14 (1997) 35–50.

Dean-Drummond, Celia. "Sophia: The Feminine Face of God as a Metaphor for an Ecotheology." *Feminist Theology* 16 (1997) 11–31.

De Vogel, Cornelia J. "The Concept of Personality in Greek and Christian Thought." In *Studies in the Philosophy and the History of Philosophy.* Vol. 2. Ed. John K. Ryan. Washington: The Catholic University Press, 1963.

Farley, Margaret. "Sexism." *New Catholic Encyclopedia* 17:604. New York: McGraw Hill, 1978.

_____. "New Patterns of Relationship: Beginnings of a Moral Revolution." *Theological Studies* 36 (1975) 627–46.

Florovsky, Georges. "Patristic Theology and the Ethos of the Orthodox Church." *Collected Works.* Vol. 4. Belmont: Nordland, 1975.

_____. "The Patristic Age and Eschatology." *Collected Works.* Vol. 4 Belmont: Nordland, 1975.

Halkes, Catharina. "The Rape of Mother Earth: Ecology and Patriarchy." In *Motherhood: Experience, Institution, Theology.* Concilium 206. Ed. Anne Carr and Elisabeth Schüssler Fiorenza, 91–100. Edinburgh: T&T Clark, 1989.

Halleux, André de. "Personalisme ou essentialisme trinitaire chez les pères cappadociens? Une mauvaise controverse. *Revue théologique Louvain* 17 (1986) 129–55, 265–92.

Hardman Moore, Susan. "Towards Koinonia in Faith, Life and Witness." *The Ecumenical Review* 47 (1995) 3–11.

Harrison, Beverley. "The Power of Anger in the Work of Love." In *Weaving the Visions: New Patterns in Feminist Spirituality.* Ed. Judith Plaskow and Carol Christ, 214–25. San Francisco: Harper & Row Publishers, 1989.

Johnson, Elizabeth A. "Between the Times: Religious Life and the Postmodern Experience of God." *Review for Religious* (January–February, 1994) 6–12.

_____. "Christology's Impact on the Doctrine of God." *Heythrop Journal* 26 (1985) 143–63.

_____. "Does God Play Dice? Divine Providence and Chance." *Theological Studies* 57 (1996) 3–18.

_____. "Discipleship: The Root Model of the Life Called 'Religious.'" *Review for Religious* 42 (1983) 864–72.

_____. "God Poured Out: Recovering the Holy Spirit." *Praying* 60 (May–June 1994) 4–8, 41.

_____. "Heaven and Earth Are Filled with Your Glory." In *Finding God in All Things.* Ed. Michael Himes and Stephen Pope, 84–101. New York: Crossroad, 1996.

_____. "Images of the Historical Jesus in Catholic Christology." *Living Light* 23 (1986) 47–66.

_____. "The Incomprehensibility of God and the Image of God Male and Female." *Theological Studies* 45 (1984) 441–65.

_____. "Jesus and Salvation." *CTSA Proceedings* 49 (1994) 1–18.

_____. "Jesus, the Wisdom of God: A Biblical Basis for a Non-Androcentric Christology." *Ephemerides Theologicae Lovanienses* 61, no. 4 (1985) 262–94.

_____. "Lutheran/RC Dialogue (USA) Achieves Statement on The One Mediator, The Saints and Mary." *Ecumenical Trends* 19, no. 7 (1990) 97–101.

_____. "The Maleness of Christ." In *The Special Nature of Women?* Ed. Anne Carr and Elisabeth Schüssler Fiorenza, 108–16. Philadelphia: Concilium/Trinity Press International, 1991.

_____. "Marian Devotion and the Western Church." In *Christian Spirituality: High Middle Ages and Reformation.* Ed. J. Raitt, B. McGinn, and J. Meyendorff. New York: Crossroad, 1987.

_____. "The Marian Tradition and the Reality of Women." *Horizons* 12, no. 1 (1985) 116–35.

_____. "Mary and Contemporary Christology: Rahner and Schillebeeckx." *Eglise et Théologie* 15 (1984) 155–82.

_____. "Mary and the Female Face of God." *Theological Studies* 50 (1989) 500–26.

_____. "Mary as Mediatrix." In *The One Mediator, the Saints and Mary.* Ed. H. Anderson, 311–26. Minneapolis: Augsburg Publishing, 1992.

_____. "May We Invoke the Saints?" *Theology Today* 44 (1987) 41–60.

_____. "The Ongoing Christology of Wolfhart Pannenberg." *Horizons* 9, no. 2 (1982) 237–50.

_____. "Redeeming the Name of Christ." In *Freeing Theology: The Essentials of Theology in Feminist Perspective.* Ed. Catherine Mowry LaCugna, 115–37. San Francisco: HarperSanFrancisco, 1993.

_____. "Resurrection and Reality in the Thought of Wolfhart Pannenberg." *Heythrop Journal* 24 (1983) 1–18.

_____. "Resurrection: Promise of the Future." *Sisters Today* 67, no. 6 (1995) 404–11.

_____. "Review Symposium: Author's Response." *Horizons* 20 (1993) 339–44.

_____. "The Right Way to Speak About God? Pannenberg on Analogy." *Theological Studies* 43 (1982) 673–92.

_____. "Saints and Mary." In *Systematic Theology: Roman Catholic Perspectives*. Vol. 11. Ed. Francis Schüssler Fiorenza and John P. Galvin, 143–77. Minneapolis: Fortress Press, 1991.

_____. "The Search for the Living God." *Grail* 10 (1994) 11–29.

_____. "The Symbolic Character of Theological Statements About Mary." *Journal of Ecumenical Studies* 22, no. 2 (Spring, 1985) 312–35.

_____. "A Theological Case for God-She." *Commonweal* 120 (January 29, 1993) 9–14.

_____. "Theology and the Heisenberg Uncertainty Principle." *Proceedings of the Forty-Seventh Annual Convention of the Catholic Theological Society of America* 47. Ed. Paul Crowley, 131. Santa Clara: Santa Clara University, 1992.

_____. "The Theological Relevance of the Historical Jesus: A Debate and a Thesis." *Thomist* 48 (1984) 1–43.

_____. "Trinity: To Let the Symbol Sing Again." *Theology Today* 34, no. 3 (1997) 299–311.

_____. "Turn to the Heavens and the Earth: Retrieval of the Cosmos in Theology." *CTSA Proceedings* 51 (1996) 1–14.

_____. "Wisdom Was Made Flesh and Pitched Her Tent Among Us." In *Reconstructing the Christ Symbol: Essays in Feminist Christology*. Ed. Maryanne Stevens, 95–117. New York- Mahwah, N.J.: Paulist Press, 1993.

Johnson, Elizabeth A., Susan A. Ross, Mary Catherine Hilkert. "Feminist Theology: A Review of Literature." *Theological Studies* 56 (1995) 327–52.

Kelly, Gerard. "On the Way to Fuller Koinonia: The Fifth World Conference on Faith and Order." *Pacifica* 8 (1995) 155–73.

Kiesling, Christopher. "On Relating to the Persons of the Trinity." *Theological Studies* 47 (1986) 599–616.

LaCugna, Catherine. "The Baptismal Formula, Feminist Objections, and Trinitarian Theology." *Journal of Ecumenical Studies* 26, no. 2 (1989) 235–50.

_____. "Reconceiving the Trinity as the Mystery of Salvation." *Scottish Journal of Theology* 38 (1985) 1–23.

_____. "The Relational God: Aquinas and Beyond." *Theological Studies* 46 (1985) 647–63.

_____. "The Trinitarian Mystery of God." In *Systematic Theology: Roman Catholic Perspectives*. Ed. Francis Schüssler Fiorenza and John P. Galvin, 152–90. Minneapolis: Fortress Press, 1981.

LaCugna, Catherine M., and Kilian McDonnell. "Returning from 'The Far Country': Theses for a Contemporary Trinitarian Theology." *Scottish Journal of Theology* 41 (1988) 191–215.

Liveris, Leonie B. "Feminist Ecclesiology: An Orthodox Perspective from Australia." In *Women's Visions: Theological Reflection, Celebration, Action*. Ed.

Ofelia Ortega, 152–63. Geneva: World Council of Churches Publications, 1995.

Loomer, Bernard. "Two Kinds of Power." *Criterion* 15, no. 1 (1976) 11–129.

Moore, Susan Hardman. "Towards Koinonia in Faith, Life and Witness." *The Ecumenical Review* 47 (1995) 3–11.

Mulder, Anne-Marie. "Thinking About the *Imago Dei:* Minimalizing or Maximalizing the Difference between the Sexes: A Critical Reading of Rosemary Radford Ruether's Anthropology Through the Lens of Luce Irigaray's Thought." *Feminist Theology* 14 (1997) 9–33.

Parsons, Susan F. "The Dilemma of Difference: A Feminist Theological Exploration." *Feminist Theology* 14 (1997) 51–72.

Pergamon, Metropolitan John (Zizioulas). "The Eucharist and the Kingdom of God." Trans. Elizabeth A. Theokritoff. *Sourozh* 58 (1994) 1–12; 59 (1995) 22–38; 60 (1995) 32–46.

————. "Come Holy Spirit, Sanctify Our Lives." *Sourozh* 44 (1991) 1–3.

————. "Communion and Otherness." *St. Vladimir's Theological Quarterly* 38, no. 4 (1994) 347–61.

————. "Ethics Versus Ethos: An Orthodox Approach to the Relation Between Ecology and Ethics." In *The Environment and Ethics: Presentations and Reports, Summer Session on Halki '95.* Ed. Deuteron Tarasios, 25–27. Militos Editions, 1997.

————. "Orthodoxy and Ecological Problems: A Theological Approach." In *The Environment and Religious Education: Presentations and Reports, Summer Session on Halki 1994.* Ed. Deuteron Tarasios, 26–30. Militos Editions, 1997.

————. "To einai tou Theou kai einai tou anthropou." *Synaxis* 37 (1991) 11–36.

Pergamos, Metropolitan John (Zizioulas). "Address to the 1988 Lambeth Conference." *Sourozh* 35 (1989) 29–35.

Rist, John. "Individuals and Persons." *Human Value: A Study in Ancient Philosophical Ethics.* Philosophia Antiqua 40. Leiden: Brill, (1982) 145–63.

Ruether, Rosemary Radford, "Dualism and the Nature of Evil in Feminist Theology." *Studies in Christian Ethics* 5, no. 1 (1992).

Stroumsa, Gedaliahu G. "*Caro salutis cardo:* Shaping the Person in Early Christian Thought." *History of Religions* 30 (1990) 25–50.

Tanner, Mary. "Cautious Affirmation and New Direction: A First Assessment of the Fifth World Conference on Faith and Order." *The Way* 34 (1994) 314–22.

Telepneff, Gregory, and Bishop Chrysostomos. "The Transformation of Hellenistic Thought on the Cosmos and Man in the Greek Fathers." *Patristic and Byzantine Review* 9, no. 2–3 (1990) 123–35.

Thunberg, Lars. "The Human Person as Image of God: Eastern Christianity." In *Christian Spirituality: Origins to the Twelfth Century.* Ed. B. McGinn, J. Meyendorff, and J. Leclerq, 291–312. New York: Crossroads, 1986.

Tracy, David. "Theological Method." In *Christian Theology: An Introduction to Its Traditions and Tasks.* Rev. ed. Eds. Peter Hodgson and Robert King, 35–60. Philadelphia: Fortress Press, 1985.

————. "The Hidden God: The Divine Other of Liberation." *Cross Currents* 46, no. 1 (1996) 5–16.

_____. "The Return of God in Contemporary Theology." *Concilium* 6 (1984) 37–46.

_____. "The Uneasy Alliance Reconceived: Catholic Theological Method, Modernity and Postmodernity." *Theological Studies* 56 (1989) 548–70.

Uhr, Marie Louise. "Jesus Christ, the Sophia of God: A Symbol of Our Salvation." *Women-Church* 19 (1996) 15–21.

Wainwright, Elaine M. "What's in a Name? The Word Which Binds/The Word Which Frees." In *Freedom and Entrapment: Women Thinking Theology.* Ed. Maryanne Confoy, Dorothy Lee, and Joan Nowotny, 100–20. North Blackburn, Victoria: Dove, 1995.

Ware, Kallistos. "The Human Person as an Icon of the Trinity." *Sobornost* 8, no. 2 (1986) 6–23.

Zizioulas, John D. "Christologie et Existence: La dialectique crée et incrée et le dogme de Chalcédoine." *Contacts* 36 (1984) 154–73.

_____. "The Church as Communion." *St. Vladimir's Theological Quarterly* 38 (1994) 3–16.

_____. "Conciliarity and the Way to Unity—An Orthodox Point of View." In *Churches in Conciliar Fellowship.* Geneva: Conference of European Churches, 1978.

_____. "The Contribution of Cappadocia to Christian Thought." In *Sinasos in Cappadocia.* Ed. Frosso Pimenides and Stelios Roïdes, 23–37. London: Agra Publications, 1985.

_____. "The Development of Conciliar Structures to the Time of the First Ecumenical Council." In John Anastasiou and others, *Councils and the Ecumenical Movement,* 34–51. World Council of Churches Studies 5. Geneva: World Council of Churches, 1968.

_____. "Déplacement de la perspective eschatologique." In *La Chrétienté en débat: histoire, formes et problèmes actuels.* Ed. G. Alberigo and others, 89–100. Paris: Cerf, 1984.

_____. "Discours du métropolite Jean de Pergame." *Istina* 33 (1988) 197–203.

_____. "The Doctrine of God the Trinity Today: Suggestions for an Ecumenical Study." In *The Forgotten Trinity.* Ed. Alasdair I. C. Heron, 19–32. London: BCC/CCBI, 1991.

_____. "The Doctrine of the Holy Trinity: The Significance of the Cappadocian Contribution." In *Trinitarian Theology Today: Essays on Divine Being and Act.* Ed. Christoph Schwöbel, 44–60. Edinburgh: T&T Clark, 1995.

_____. "The Early Christian Community." In *Christian Spirituality: Origins to the Twelfth Century.* Ed. Bernard McGinn, John Meyendorf, Jean Leclerq, 23–43. London: Routledge & Kegan Paul, 1986.

_____. "The Ecclesiological Presuppositions of the Holy Eucharistic." *Nicolaus* 10 (1982) 333–49.

_____. "Ecclesiological Issues Inherent in the Relations Between Eastern Chalcedonian and Oriental Non-Chalcedonian Churches." In *Does Chalcedon Divide or Unite? Towards a Convergence in Orthodox Christology.* Ed. Paulos Gregorios and William H. Lazareth, 138–56. Geneva: World Council of Churches, 1981.

_____. "The Ecumenical Dimensions of Orthodox Theological Education." In *Orthodox Theological Education for the Life and Witness of the Church.* Geneva: World Council of Churches, 1978.

_____. "Episkopé and Episkopos in the Early Church: A Brief Survey of the Evidence." In *Episcopé and Episcopate in Ecumenical Perspective,* 30–42. Faith and Order Paper 102. Geneva: World Council of Churches, 1980.

_____. "Eschatology and History." In *Cultures in Dialogue: Documents from a Symposium in Honour of Philip A. Potter.* Ed. T. Weiser, 30–39. Geneva, 1985.

_____. "L'Eucharistie, foyer de l'Eglise locale." Unpublished lecture to the Conference on "Les paroisses dans L'Eglise d'aujourd'hui," Louvaine-la Neuve, 14–16 September 1981, 1–15.

_____. "The Eucharistic Prayer and Life." *Emmanuel* 85 (1979) 181–96, 201–3.

_____. "Human Capacity and Human Incapacity: A Theological Exploration of Personhood." *Scottish Journal of Theology* 28 (1975) 401–48.

_____. "Implications ecclésiologiques de deux types de pneumatologie." In *Communio Sanctorum: Mélanges offerts à Jean-Jacques von Allmen,* 141–54. Geneva: Labor et Fides, 1981.

_____. "Informal Groups in the Church: An Orthodox Viewpoint." In *Informal Groups in the Church.* Ed. R. Metz. Trans. M. O'Connell, 275–98. Pittsburgh: Pickwick Press, 1975.

_____. "The Institution of Episcopal Conferences: An Orthodox Reflection." *The Jurist* 48 (1988) 376–83.

_____. "The Meaning of Ordination: A Comment." *Study Encounter* 4 (1968) 191–93.

_____. "The Mystery of the Church in the Orthodox Tradition." *One in Christ* 24, no. 4 (1988) 294–303.

_____. "On Being a Person. Towards an Ontology of Personhood." In *Persons, Divine and Human: King's College Essays in Theological Anthropology.* Ed. Christoph Schwöbel and Colin Gunton. Edinburgh: T&T Clark, 1991.

_____. "On the Concept of Authority." *The Ecumenical Review* 21 (1969) 160–66.

_____. "Ordination and Communion." *Study Encounter* 6 (1970) 187–92.

_____. "Ordination—A Sacrament? An Orthodox Reply." *Concilium* 4 (1972) 33–39.

_____. "Orthodox-Protestant Bilateral Conversations: Some Comments." In *The Orthodox Church and the Churches of the Reformation: A Survey of Orthodox-Protestant Dialogues,* 55–56. Faith and Order Paper 76. Geneva: World Council of Churches, 1975.

_____. "Ortodossia." In *Enciclopedia del Novecento* 5. Rome: Istituto della Enciclopedia Italiana, 1980.

_____. "The Pneumatological Dimension of the Church." *Communio* 1 (1974) 142–58.

_____. "Preserving God's Creation: Three Lectures on Theology and Ecology." *King's Theological Review* 12 (1989) 1–5; 41–45; 13 (1990) 1–5.

_____. "Reflections of an Orthodox." *The Ecumenical Review* 23 (1971) 30–34.

_____. "Some Reflections on Baptism, Confirmation and Eucharist." *Sorbonost* 5, no. 9 (1969) 644–52.

_____. "The Teaching of the 2nd Ecumenical Council on the Holy Spirit in Historical and Ecumenical Perspective." In *Credo in Spiritum Sanctum*. Ed. J. S. Martins, 1:29–34. Vatican City: Libreria Editrice Vaticana, 1983.

_____. "The Theological Problem of 'Reception.'" *One in Christ* 21 (1985) 187–93.

_____. "La vision eucharistique du monde et l'homme contemporain." *Contacts* 19 (1967) 83–92.

Index